VAN BUREN DISTRICT LIBRARY
DECATUR, MICHIGAN 49045

P9-DNC-006

DISCARDED

Guide and Reference to
the Amphibians of Eastern
and Central North America
(North of Mexico)

UNIVERSITY PRESS OF FLORIDA

Florida A&M University, Tallahassee
Florida Atlantic University, Boca Raton
Florida Gulf Coast University, Ft. Myers
Florida International University, Miami
Florida State University, Tallahassee
University of Central Florida, Orlando
University of Florida, Gainesville
University of North Florida, Jacksonville
University of South Florida, Tampa
University of West Florida, Pensacola

Guide and Reference to the

Amphibians

of Eastern and Central North America (North of Mexico)

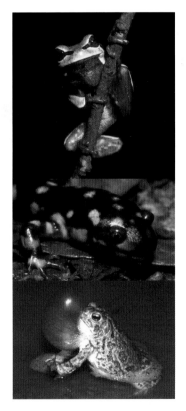

R. D. Bartlett and Patricia P. Bartlett

University Press of Florida

GAINESVILLE · TALLAHASSEE · TAMPA · BOCA RATON

PENSACOLA · ORLANDO · MIAMI · JACKSONVILLE · FT. MYERS

597.8097
Bar

Copyright 2006 by R. D. Bartlett and Patricia P. Bartlett
Printed in China on acid-free paper
All rights reserved

11 10 09 08 07 06   6 5 4 3 2 1

Library of Congress Cataloging-in-Publication Data
ISBN 0-8130-2950-3

The University Press of Florida is the scholarly publishing
agency for the State University System of Florida, comprising
Florida A&M University, Florida Atlantic University, Florida
Gulf Coast University, Florida International University, Florida
State University, University of Central Florida, University
of Florida, University of North Florida, University of South
Florida, and University of West Florida.

University Press of Florida
15 Northwest 15th Street
Gainesville, FL 32611–2079
http://www.upf.com

Contents

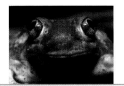

Species

Frogs, Toads, and Treefrogs

Family Bufonidae, family Bufonidae

(1) Eastern American Toad, *Bufo americanus americanus*
    (2) Dwarf American Toad, *Bufo americanus charlesmithi*
(3) Great Plains Toad, *Bufo cognatus*
(4) Eastern Green Toad, *Bufo debilis debilis*
    (5) Western Green Toad, *Bufo debilis insidior*
(6) Fowler's Toad, *Bufo fowleri*
(7) Canadian Toad, *Bufo hemiophrys*
(8) Houston Toad, *Bufo houstonensis*
(9) Cane Toad, *Bufo marinus* (Florida populations introduced)
(10) Gulf Coast Toad, *Bufo nebulifer* (= *Bufo valliceps*)
(11) Red-spotted Toad, *Bufo punctatus*
(12) Oak Toad, *Bufo quercicus*
(13) Texas Toad, *Bufo speciosus*
(14) Southern Toad, *Bufo terrestris*
(15) Rocky Mountain Toad, *Bufo woodhousii woodhousii*
    (16) Southwestern Woodhouse's Toad, *Bufo woodhousii australis*
    (17) East Texas Toad, *Bufo woodhousii velatus*

Family Hylidae, Cricket Frogs, Chorus Frogs, and Treefrogs

CRICKET FROGS

(18) Northern Cricket Frog, *Acris crepitans crepitans*
    (19) Blanchard's Cricket Frog, *Acris crepitans blanchardi*
    (20) Coastal Cricket Frog, *Acris crepitans paludicola*
(21) Southern Cricket Frog, *Acris gryllus gryllus*
    (22) Florida Cricket Frog, *Acris gryllus dorsalis*

TYPICAL TREEFROGS

(23) Pine Barrens Treefrog, *Hyla andersonii*
(24) Canyon Treefrog, *Hyla arenicolor*
(25) Western Bird-voiced Treefrog, *Hyla avivoca avivoca*
   (26) Eastern Bird-voiced Treefrog, *Hyla avivoca ogechiensis*
(27a) Cope's Gray Treefrog, *Hyla chrysoscelis*
   (27b) Gray Treefrog, *Hyla versicolor*
(28) Green Treefrog, *Hyla cinerea*
(29) Pine Woods Treefrog, *Hyla femoralis*
(30) Barking Treefrog, *Hyla gratiosa*
(31) Squirrel Treefrog, *Hyla squirella*
(32) Cuban Treefrog, *Osteopilus septentrionalis* (introduced)
(33) Australian Green Treefrog, *Pelodryas (Litoria) caerulea* (introduced)
(34) Mexican Treefrog, *Smilisca baudinii*

CHORUS FROGS

(35) Mountain Chorus Frog, *Pseudacris brachyphona*
(36) Brimley's Chorus Frog, *Pseudacris brimleyi*
(37) Spotted Chorus Frog, *Pseudacris clarkii*
(38) Northern Spring Peeper, *Pseudacris crucifer crucifer*
   (39) Southern Spring Peeper, *Pseudacris crucifer bartramiana*
(40) Upland Chorus Frog, *Pseudacris feriarum feriarum*
   (41) New Jersey Chorus Frog, *Pseudacris feriarum kalmi*
(42) Boreal Chorus Frog, *Pseudacris maculata*
(43) Southern Chorus Frog, *Pseudacris nigrita nigrita*
   (44) Florida Chorus Frog, *Pseudacris nigrita verrucosus*
(45) Little Grass Frog, *Pseudacris ocularis*
(46) Ornate Chorus Frog, *Pseudacris ornata*
(47) Strecker's Chorus Frog, *Pseudacris streckeri streckeri*
   (48) Illinois Chorus Frog, *Pseudacris streckeri illinoensis*
(49) Western Chorus Frog, *Pseudacris triseriata*

Family Leptodactylidae, Tropical Frogs

(50) Balcones Barking Frog, *Eleutherodactylus augusti latrans*
(51) Puerto Rican Coqui, *Eleutherodactylus coqui* (introduced)
(52) Rio Grande Chirping Frog, *Eleutherodactylus cystignathoides campi*
(53) Spotted Chirping Frog, *Eleutherodactylus guttilatus*

(54) Cliff Chirping Frog, *Eleutherodactylus marnockii*

(55) Greenhouse Frog, *Eleutherodactylus planirostris* (introduced)

(56) Mexican White-lipped Frog, *Leptodactylus fragilis*

Family Microhylidae, Narrow-Mouthed Toads and Sheep Frogs

(57) Eastern Narrow-mouthed Toad, *Gastrophryne carolinensis*

(58) Great Plains Narrow-mouthed Toad, *Gastrophryne olivacea*

(59) Sheep Frog, *Hypopachus variolosus*

Family Scaphiopodidae (formerly Pelobatidae), Spadefoots

(60) Couch's Spadefoot, *Scaphiopus couchii*

(61) Eastern Spadefoot, *Scaphiopus holbrookii*

(62) Hurter's Spadefoot, *Scaphiopus hurterii*

(63) Plains Spadefoot, *Spea bombifrons*

(64) New Mexico Spadefoot, *Spea multiplicata stagnalis*

Family Pipidae, Tongueless frogs

(65) African Clawed Frog, *Xenopus laevis* (introduced)

Family Ranidae, Typical Frogs

BULLFROG GROUP

BRONZE FROG, MINK FROG, AND RELATIVES

(66) Bullfrog, *Rana catesbeiana*

(67) Bronze Frog, *Rana clamitans clamitans*

   (68) Northern Green Frog, *Rana clamitans melanota*

(69) Pig Frog, *Rana grylio*

(70) River Frog, *Rana heckscheri*

(71) Florida Bog Frog, *Rana okaloosae*

(72) Mink Frog, *Rana septentrionalis*

(73) Carpenter Frog, *Rana virgatipes*

WOOD FROG

(74) Wood Frog, *Rana sylvatica*

Family Rhinophrynidae, Burrowing Toads

Salamanders and Newts

Family Ambystomatidae, Mole Salamanders

(96) Eastern Tiger Salamander, *Ambystoma tigrinum tigrinum*
  (97) Gray Tiger Salamander, *Ambystoma tigrinum diaboli*
  (98) Barred Tiger Salamander, *Ambystoma tigrinum mavortium*
  (99) Blotched Tiger Salamander, *Ambystoma tigrinum melanostictum*

Family Amphiumidae, Amphiumas

(100) Two-toed Amphiuma, *Amphiuma means*
(101) One-toed Amphiuma, *Amphiuma pholeter*
(102) Three-toed Amphiuma, *Amphiuma tridactylum*

Family Cryptobranchidae, Hellbenders

(103) Eastern Hellbender, *Cryptobranchus alleganiensis alleganiensis*
  (104) Ozark Hellbender, *Cryptobranchus alleganiensis bishopi*

Family Plethodontidae, Lungless Salamanders

SUBFAMILY DESMOGNATHINAE, DUSKY SALAMANDERS,

Seepage and Pygmy Salamanders
(105) Seepage Salamander, *Desmognathus aeneus*
(106) Pygmy Salamander, *Desmognathus wrighti*
Mountain Dusky Salamanders
(107) Apalachicola Dusky Salamander, *Desmognathus apalachicolae*
(108a) Allegheny Mountain Dusky Salamander, *Desmognathus ochrophaeus*
  (108b) Cumberland Dusky Salamander, *Desmognathus abditus*
  (108c) Carolina Mountain Dusky Salamander, *Desmognathus carolinensis*
  (108d) Imitator Salamander, *Desmognathus imitator*
  (108e) Ocoee Salamander, *Desmognathus ocoee*
  (108f) Blue Ridge Dusky Salamander, *Desmognathus orestes*
Dusky Salamanders
(109) Southern Dusky Salamander, *Desmognathus auriculatus*
(110a) Northern Dusky Salamander, *Desmognathus fuscus*
  (110b) Spotted Dusky Salamander, *Desmognathus conanti*
  (110c) Santeetlah Dusky Salamander, *Desmognathus santeetlah*
(111) Ouachita Dusky Salamander, *Desmognathus brimleyorum*
(112) Black Mountain Dusky Salamander, *Desmognathus welteri*
Shovel-nosed and Seal Salamander
(113) Shovel-nosed Salamander, *Desmognathus marmoratus*

(114) Seal Salamander, *Desmognathus monticola*

Black-bellied Salamanders

(115a) Common Black-bellied Salamander, *Desmognathus quadramaculatus*

    (115b) Dwarf Black-bellied Salamander, *Desmognathus folkertsi*

Red Hills Salamander

(116) Red Hills Salamander, *Phaeognathus hubrichti*

SUBFAMILY PLETHODONTINAE, ALL OTHER EASTERN
AND CENTRAL LUNGLESS SALAMANDERS

NONPAEDOMORPHIC BROOK SALAMANDERS

Two-lined Salamanders

(117a) Northern Two-lined Salamander, *Eurycea bislineata*

    (117b) Southern Two-lined Salamander, Eurycea cirrigera

    (117c) Blue Ridge Two-lined Salamander, *Eurycea wilderae*

(118) Junaluska Salamander, *Eurycea junaluska*

Long-tailed Salamanders

(119) Three-lined Salamander, *Eurycea guttolineata*

(120) Long-tailed Salamander, *Eurycea longicauda longicauda*

    (121) Dark-sided Salamander, *Eurycea longicauda melanopleura*

Cave Salamander

(122) Cave Salamander, *Eurycea lucifuga*

Four-toed Brook Salamanders

(123) Chamberlain's Dwarf Salamander, *Eurycea chamberlaini*

(124) Common Dwarf Salamander, *Eurycea quadridigitata*

OUTGROUPS

(125) Many-ribbed Salamander, *Eurycea multiplicata*

(126) Grotto Salamander, *Eurycea spelaeus*

(127) Oklahoma Salamander (Gray-bellied Salamander), *Eurycea tynerensis*

PAEDOMORPHIC BROOK SALAMANDERS

(128) Salado Salamander, *Eurycea chisholmensis*

(129) Cascade Caverns Salamander, *Eurycea latitans* complex

(130) San Marcos Salamander, *Eurycea nana*

(131) Georgetown Salamander, *Eurycea naufragia*

(132) Texas Salamander, *Eurycea neotenes*

(133) Fern Bank Salamander, *Eurycea pterophila*

(134) Texas Blind Salamander, *Eurycea rathbuni*

(135) Blanco Blind Salamander, *Eurycea robusta*
(136) Barton Springs Salamander, *Eurycea sosorum*
(137) Jollyville Plateau Salamander, *Eurycea tonkawae*
(138) Comal Blind Salamander, *Eurycea tridentifera*
(139) Valdina Farms Salamander, *Eurycea troglodytes* complex
(140) Austin Blind Salamander, *Eurycea waterlooensis*
(141) Georgia Blind Salamander, *Haideotriton wallacei*

RED AND SPRING SALAMANDERS GROUP

(142) Berry Cave Salamander, *Gyrinophilus gulolineatus*
(143) Pale Cave Salamander, *Gyrinophilus palleucus palleucus*
   (144) Big Mouth Cave Salamander, *Gyrinophilus palleucus necturoides*
(145) Northern Spring Salamander, *Gyrinophilus porphyriticus porphyriticus*
   (146) Blue Ridge Spring Salamander, *Gyrinophilus porphyriticus danielsi*
   (147) Carolina Spring Salamander, *Gyrinophilus porphyriticus dunni*
   (148) Kentucky Spring Salamander, *Gyrinophilus porphyriticus duryi*
(149) West Virginia Spring Salamander, *Gyrinophilus subterraneus*
(150) Eastern Mud Salamander, *Pseudotriton montanus montanus*
   (151) Midland Mud Salamander, *Pseudotriton montanus diasticus*
   (152) Gulf Coast Mud Salamander, *Pseudotriton montanus flavissimus*
   (153) Rusty Mud Salamander, *Pseudotriton montanus floridanus*
(154) Northern Red Salamander, *Pseudotriton ruber ruber*
   (155) Blue Ridge Red Salamander, *Pseudotriton ruber nitidus*
   (156) Black-chinned Red Salamander, *Pseudotriton ruber schencki*
   (157) Southern Red Salamander, *Pseudotriton ruber vioscai*

WOODLAND SALAMANDERS

Affiliations unknown
(158) Catahoula Salamander, *Plethodon ainsworthi*
Ouachita Mountain Salamanders
(159) Caddo Mountain Salamander, *Plethodon caddoensis*
(160) Fourche Mountain Salamander, *Plethodon fourchensis*
(161) Rich Mountain Salamander, *Plethodon ouachitae*
Red-Backed, Zigzag, and Big Levels Salamanders
(162) Eastern Red-backed Salamander, *Plethodon cinereus*
(163) Southern Red-backed Salamander, *Plethodon serratus*
(164) Big Levels Salamander, *Plethodon sherando*
(165) Ozark Salamander, *Plethodon angusticlavius*
(166a) Northern Zigzag Salamander, *Plethodon dorsalis*

(183a) Red-legged Salamander, *Plethodon shermani*
   (183b) Cheoah Bald Salamander, *Plethodon cheoah*

SPECIES WITHOUT ADDITIONAL (EASTERN) AFFILIATIONS

(184) Green Salamander, *Aneides aeneus*
(185) Four-toed Salamander, *Hemidactylium scutatum*
(186) Many-lined Salamander, *Stereochilus marginatus*

Family Proteidae, Mudpuppies and Waterdogs

(187) Black Warrior Waterdog, *Necturus alabamensis*
(188) Gulf Coast Waterdog, *Necturus beyeri*
(189) Neuse River Waterdog, *Necturus lewisi*
(190) Common Mudpuppy, *Necturus maculosus maculosus*
   (191) Red River Mudpuppy, *Necturus maculosus louisianensis*
(192) Dwarf Waterdog, *Necturus punctatus*
(193) Eastern Gulf Coast Waterdog, *Necturus* species cf *beyeri*

Family Salamandridae, Newts

(194) Texas Black-spotted Newt, *Notophthalmus meridionalis meridionalis*
(195) Striped Newt, *Notophthalmus perstriatus*
(196) Red-spotted Newt, *Notophthalmus viridescens viridescens*
   (197) Broken-striped Newt, *Notophthalmus viridescens dorsalis*
   (198) Central Newt, *Notophthalmus viridescens louisianensis*
   (199) Peninsula Newt, *Notophthalmus viridescens piaropicola*

Family Sirenidae, Sirens

(200) Narrow-striped Dwarf Siren, *Pseudobranchus axanthus axanthus*
   (201) Everglades Dwarf Siren, *Pseudobranchus axanthus belli*
(202) Broad-striped Dwarf Siren, *Pseudobranchus striatus striatus*
   (203) Gulf Hammock Dwarf Siren, *Pseudobranchus striatus lustricolus*
   (204) Slender Dwarf Siren, *Pseudobranchus striatus spheniscus*
(205) Eastern Lesser Siren, *Siren intermedia intermedia*
   (206) Western Lesser Siren, *Siren intermedia nettingi*
(207) Greater Siren, *Siren lacertina*
(208) Texas Siren, *Siren texana*

Preface

Except for a few common amphibians of back yards and residential areas, this "other half" of the herpetological (reptile and amphibian) clan are less well known to most folks than the reptiles. In eastern North America there are, roughly, 200 species of amphibians. The group comprises the frogs (anurans) and the very secretive salamanders (caudatans). The life histories of most members of this huge group are poorly known. But we do that the long-term continued existence of many of these interesting creatures is currently facing challenges. The populations of many species, especially those in montane habitats, are dwindling, and we simply don't know why. Conjecture abounds, but that is all there is at the moment—conjecture. Cold, hard facts defining the cause(s) of the problem simply are not to be had. We have not yet even truly ascertained whether the problem is human caused or a more or less naturally cyclic phenomenon. The amphibian disappearance is chronicled adroitly in *Tracking the Vanishing Frogs: An Ecological Mystery* by Kathryn Phillips—a book that we suggest you read. The problem, whatever it may be, does not seem as accentuated in eastern and central North America as in the west, Australia, and Latin America, yet there are causes for concern.

For example, in our area northern leopard frogs are reduced in numbers, but not yet critically so, and there does seem to be cyclic increases in some populations. Across many areas in the northern portions of their ranges, various chorus and cricket frogs have become rare or have disappeared. However, these same species remain common further south.

But resilient though it may seem, the South is not impervious to amphibian reductions. In the Gulf Coast states, Houston toads, dusky gopher frogs, and flatwoods salamanders are considered endangered. The Catahoula salamander may already be extinct. Southern dusky salamanders seem to have disappeared from vast portions of their range. We must be concerned.

On the plus side, a burgeoning interest in these creatures now exists. Research into population statistics, morphological abnormalities, and life histories is virtually always under way.

We can hope that before the call of the toad is silenced forever, causes and solutions for accentuated disappearances will be found and the problem will be rectified.

In these pages we cover the 239 recognized species and subspecies (taxa) of amphibians of eastern and central North America. Of these, only four are introduced species. Time and again you will see our comment that "very little is known about . . ." Rather than accepting this statement as a dead end, we hope you will be inspired by it to add to and share additional information about the day-to-day existence of one or more of these intriguing little creatures.

This book is intended solely as an identification guide. There are many other books, some periodicals, and a never-ending succession of websites that delve deeply into the systematics, biology, and captive care of amphibians. We have listed numerous titles under Additional Reading, in the back of the book. Should you not have a computer, your library has one that you may use free of charge. A wealth of additional information is readily at your fingertips. Please take the time to make use of all avenues of information.

Acknowledgments

Thanks are due many friends and colleagues for their comments and contributions.

We gratefully acknowledge Jeff Boundy, Jim Harding, Dennie Miller, Paul Moler, Dan Pearson, Tom Tyning, and Wayne VanDevender, who provided help and suggestions over and above the call of duty.

Collette Adams, Ray E. Ashton, Henry Bart, Chris Bednarski, Will Bird, Michael Brennan, Karin Burns, Carlos Camp, Dennis Cathcart, Paul Chippindale, Joseph T. Collins, Betty Crump, Scott Cushnir, Dave Davenport, C. Kenneth Dodd, William E. Duellman, Kevin Enge, William D. Flint, Billy Griswold, Mark Gumbert, Terry Hibbitts, Troy Hibbitts, Steven Johnson, F. Wayne King, Kenneth King, William (Bill) Love, David Manke, John MacGregor, Rob MacInnes, Theron Magers, Michael Manfredi, Barry Mansell, Carl May, Chris McQuade, Walter Meshaka, David Nelson, Matthew Niemiller, Sandra Oldershaw, Phil Peake, Andrew Price, Phil Ralides, Gus Rentfro, Henry Robison, Michael Smith, Eric Thiss, Rick Van Dyke, Jerry Walls, Maleta Walls, and Maria Camarrilla Wray either joined us, or allowed us to join them, in the field, provided specimens for us to photograph, or, in some cases, provided the photographs themselves. Thanks all.

A special note of thanks must be extended to Kenny Wray, who has not only contributed magnificent illustrations but has always "gone the extra mile" as we have crisscrossed North America in search of photogenic herpetofauna.

chapter 1

Introduction

The class Amphibia, a grouping of creatures that came into existence some 350 million years ago during the Devonian period, now contains three divergent groups of vertebrates: the frogs (including toads and treefrogs), the salamanders, and the caecilians. There are a total of about 5,500 species. Representatives of only the first two groups occur in eastern North America.

Though of diverse appearance, amphibians have many characteristics in common. They have moist skins and lack hair, feathers, or scales, they lack true claws, and by definition (but sometimes not in actuality) amphibians lead a "double life": most spend a larval state in the water and adulthood on land.

As they metamorphose from larva to adult, amphibians undergo dramatic body reorganization. They resorb their gills, grow lungs, develop eyelids, and grow legs. Their skin cells adapt to a largely nonaqueous environment. Their mouths are reshaped, intestines shorten, and other internal organs change during metamorphosis.

But the "double life" is not always apparent. Some amphibians are fully aquatic throughout their lives and others live a fully terrestrial existence. Reproduction modes vary as well; most amphibians reproduce by eggs, but a few give birth to living young. The eggs are laid in the water or in moisture-retaining terrestrial situations often very near water.

The larvae of frogs—all frogs, toads, and treefrogs—are called tadpoles or pollywogs. Tadpoles have internal gills (external when first hatched) and modified scraping mouthparts and lack eyelids.

Most tadpoles are herbivorous and have a very long intestine to enable processing and digestion of vegetable matter. As they begin metamorphosis (which can take a few weeks to more than a year, depending on the species) the tail is resorbed, providing energy for the creature as its gut shortens and changes to enable adult digestion of an animal-matter diet. Often many tadpoles metamorphose simultaneously, and there are times when hundred of tiny toadlets or froglets may be found hopping around the edge of the breeding pond. Newly metamorphosed frogs are often as difficult to identify as the tadpoles from which they transformed. However, within days identifying characteristics become more apparent.

Larval salamanders are called larvae rather than tadpoles. By and large the larvae have gills and undergo metamorphosis to become air-breathing adults.

Salamanders have many exceptions to this "double life." Many species lay their eggs in water and the larvae are aquatic, but some species lay their eggs on land. Of these, some place their eggs near the water so the hatching larvae can drop into water, or the larvae undergo direct development within the egg before hatching. The aquatic salamanders may lack functional legs at hatching (many pond-dwelling species) or their legs may be fully functional (stream dwellers).

Larval aquatic salamanders have three pairs of external gills until they metamorphose and develop lungs. Not all salamanders have lungs; one family, the Plethodontidae, are lungless, relying on their moist skin and mucous membranes for oxygen absorption.

Amphibians are, for the most part, secretive creatures of the darkness and some are quite specific in their habitat requirements. For example, some species occur only between certain elevations in mountain chains (a few only on a specific mountain), some species occur only in acidic bogs, others are dwellers in pockets of moisture in aridlands, and still others may require wetlands. An amphibian may be abundant in one part of its range yet rare in another. A few species are common and habitat generalists.

Because of varying and ever changing state laws, we have not attempted in most cases to advise readers of the legal status of an amphibian. However, we urge that before you seek a particular species you check both federal and state laws to determine the animal's legal status. A permit may be needed to collect or possess some amphibians.

The amphibians of eastern North America are of diverse appearance and size, but none come close to attaining the length of some reptiles. For example, when adult, a frog may be ⅝ inch in length (little grass frogs) or 8 inches long (bullfrog or giant toad). Salamanders vary from 2 inches (pygmy salamander) to 3½ feet (two-toed amphiuma). Most species are on the small end of that spectrum.

Amphibians are subject to many pressures, including habitat modifications (fragmentation and the filling of breeding ponds), death on roadways as the creatures try to access breeding ponds or new habitats, collection for the pet trade, herbicides, insecticides, and other pollutants in the environment, and pathogens, including what seem to be the newest, chytrid fungi. All said, many native reptiles are having a tough go of things.

Can diminishing amphibian populations be saved? Perhaps, but to reverse the lots of many of those most seriously imperiled will take Herculean research and dedication. First we must accurately identify amphibian species (some are impossible to differentiate in the field), understand their entire life history processes and, consequently, determine where in their life cycle they might be most vulnerable. The causes for the proliferation of pathogens such as chytrid fungi must be identified and their reversal effected. Habitats, and not just fragmented remnants of habitats, must be saved. Atmospheric deterioration must be faced head on and corrected.

Assuring that these creatures remain for us and our descendants to view and appreciate in the wild will take a concerted effort on the parts of all of us. Whether we are researchers or herpetoculturists, or merely have an interest in the creatures with which we share our world, it is time for us to join forces and promote the conservation of these interesting, beneficial, and highly specialized animals. We hope that our comments in this identification guide will help you to better understand and appreciate the lifestyles of our eastern and central amphibians.

How to Use This Book

Some amphibians are easily identifiable in the field. Because of the similarity of appearance, others are impossible to field identify. These latter can be separated from closely allied species only by laboratory analyses. Adding to the possibility of confusion is the fact that some amphibians have two or even more very different color phases, and some are capable of changing color and pattern from one minute to the next! Subspecies and even species may interbreed and produce young with a confusing suite of characteristics. Many amphibians are very dark when cold or quiet and very light when warm or active.

Subtle characteristics are often important identifying factors. Characters such as the number of toes on the hind feet and whether those feet are webbed, or whether the skin is warty or smooth, can be important and will be discussed in the individual species accounts. Other features such as whether the creature has a nasolabial groove or external gills may be useful. Because amphibians are comparatively small creatures, many identifying characteristics are not easily determined unless the creature is in hand.

We have opted to list the eastern amphibians alphabetically in family groups. We have elected to use the most conservative taxonomy but have made mention of molecularly defined species and changes that have been proposed. Time and usage will determine the taxonomy that will prevail.

We have numbered all species and subspecies in the table of contents. The numbers coincide with the numbers in both text and photographs. All except one species, the enigmatic Catahoula salamander, *Plethodon ainsworthi*, are depicted in photograph or illustration.

A Comment on Taxonomy

The common and scientific names used in this book are those suggested in *Scientific and Standard Common Names of Amphibians and Reptiles of North America North of Mexico, with Comments Regarding Confidence in our Understanding*, published by the Society for the Study of Amphibians and Reptiles (Crother, 2000). We have, however, occasionally felt it necessary to diverge, using older names for the sake of clarity.

Captive Care

Before we begin this section a couple of caveats are in order.

Because they absorb chemicals through their porous skin, amphibians may be killed immediately by topical insecticides, perfumes, hand lotions, or medications. Be certain to wash your hands carefully both before and after handling any amphibian.

The statements in this section must be considered nothing more than an overview—a starting point if you will. More detailed husbandry books are available (some are listed in Additional Reading) and should be sought if you intend to keep amphibians long-term.

Some amphibians are easily kept, requiring only a secure terrarium, food, water, and frequent cleaning to live quietly for many years. Other species (and an occasional individual of normally easily kept kinds) may prove to be very difficult captives.

Once captive, amphibians should never be released into the wild because there is a very real chance of introducing a pathogen contracted from you or from other captive amphibians into wild populations. If you decide to keep them, be ready for a long-term commitment. Some species can live more than a quarter century!

The terrarium should be designed with the particular amphibian that you intend to keep in mind. Research the needs of your potential pet carefully. The availability of fresh water or a moist substrate is of paramount importance. Amphibians do not drink, but absorb their water requirements from their surroundings through their skin. Although some amphibians are more tolerant of dryness than others, essentially, if these creatures dry (or if they absorb impurities from your hands or from unclean surroundings), they die.

Amphibians may be housed in simple fashion or in intricately designed and planted terraria. If you are diligent in your cleaning regimen (which you must be) either will work well. Because a spacious habitat is more forgiving of occasional husbandry lapses, we suggest that you provide terraria that are as large as possible.

A clear plastic container of shoebox size will give very basic housing for most salamanders and many of the smaller anurans. Several thicknesses of dampened, unbleached paper towels may be used for the substrate and a crumpled one (or three), also dampened, will provide a hiding area for the amphibians. Should you be housing large amphibian species, you'll need a bigger container.

Planted terraria can be both ideal homes for your amphibian(s) and visually pleasing.

Although there are now many types of cages made specifically for reptiles and amphibians available, we usually use covered aquaria. Choose one spacious enough for the creature(s) you wish to keep. Providing a tight cover is a necessity. Never place a glass terrarium or cage in full strength sunlight. Glass intensifies the heat; the elevated temperatures will quickly kill even the hardiest of amphibians.

In general, amphibians will need to be kept at room temperature (78°F) or cooler to remain comfortably active. Some, especially montane forms or those that inhabit cool streams, may need to be even cooler. Research the needs of your amphibians carefully and provide terrarium conditions that approximate natural conditions as closely as possible. Do not attempt to keep those species you cannot readily accommodate. Provide woodland, semiaquatic, or fully aquatic terraria as needed.

Most of the smaller amphibians, be they frogs or salamanders, aquatic or terrestrial, feed upon small invertebrates. Tiny caterpillars, worms, termites, some ants, and other nonnoxious "field plankton" form an excellent diet for most amphibians. Wintertime can make it difficult to obtain some foods no matter where you live.

Cannibalism is a trait that is not so endearing to an amphibian keeper but entirely natural for the creatures themselves. Big amphibians eat small amphibians. Keep yours singly or group them by size. Remember, too, that the skin secretions of some species can be lethal to others.

For any of a number of reasons, some amphibians can be a little difficult to keep. Narrow-mouthed toads, for example, seem to prefer a diet of ants and termites. Pine-barrens treefrogs have proven difficult for some keepers for reasons not yet understood. Hellbenders need cool running water. Many frogs have the disconcerting habit of leaping headlong into the terrarium sides when startled, soon injuring themselves.

First research the legalities of keeping a particular amphibian species, and then research its needs. If you cannot accommodate it easily, choose another kind lest a long-term commitment quickly turn burdensome.

Terraria or aquaria should be provided with hiding spots, suitable substrate, live plants (these help keep humidity high), and tight fitting doors and tops. Terrestrial species will often soak in a shallow dish of clean water. Other types may absorb their moisture requirements from a freshly sprayed plant or substrate. In all cases the water used must be free of chlorine and/or chloramine. The substrate for most species should be barely moist. We prefer to use a clean loam with no insecticides, pesticides, or Perlite or styro beads. Excessive substrate moisture for some species can be as detrimental as too little, causing some salamanders to autotomize (discard) their tail.

If you are keeping aquatic species, use a setup such as you would for goldfish, with room-temperature, clean, filtered, chemical-free water.

Habitats

To survive, amphibians need moisture. Some don't need much and they are very able to work hard to avail themselves of this life-giving necessity, wherever and however it may be found. Spadefoots, robust little toad look-alikes, for example, burrow deeply into the ground, following moisture lines. By doing this, they have been able to expand their habitats into desert regions, ecosystems that are often dry on top but with a moisture line some distance beneath the soil surface. Other amphibians are adapted to life deep in moisture-retaining fissures associated with cliff faces, outcroppings, road cuts, or even the earth itself. Here, shaded and away from breezes, they conserve body moisture, exposing themselves only on foggy, dewy, or rainy nights when moisture loss would be negligible. Many amphibians dwell in damp woodlands, seeking shelter beneath rocks or logs or retreating to burrows during daylight and at times of dryness. Others are creatures of riparian habitats, and some are fully aquatic, as unable to leave the water as a fish. But wherever they may be found, almost all amphibians are preferentially nocturnal, out and about at night. Then, they are most protected from predators, have a greater availability of prey, and suffer the least water-loss.

To find a particular species or subspecies of amphibian, you must first determine its period of activity, be within its range, and then be in its habitat. Some amphibians may be habitat generalists but many are not. Some occur only in streams, others prefer ponds or other quiet waters. Some are flatlanders, being denizens of low-elevation habitats. Others may be found only between specific elevations in the mountains. Most prefer freshwater habitats, but a few can tolerate brackish water situations. Trash piles or building rubble may be home to some species. Woodlands, pastures, old fields, or river edges are home to others.

Key to Amphibian Families

FROGS, TOADS, TREEFROGS (NOT INCLUDING TADPOLES)

1a. Comparatively short hind limbs 2
1b. Comparatively long hind limbs 6

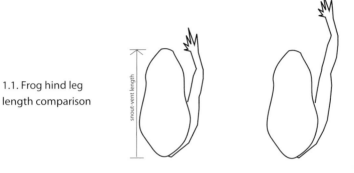

1.1. Frog hind leg length comparison

snout-vent length

2. Body warty, snout broad and bluntly rounded, pupils not vertically el-
    liptical, elongate parotoid gland . . . .**toads, family Bufonidae**
    Body not warty, snout broad 3

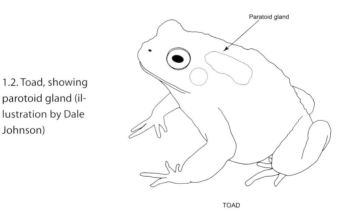

Paratoid gland

1.2. Toad, showing parotoid gland (il-lustration by Dale Johnson)

TOAD

3. Pupils vertically elliptical . . . .**spadefoots, family Scaphiopodidae**
    Body not warty, snout narrow 4

1.2a. Spadefoot toad hind foot, showing digging spade (*dark marking*)

4. Body skin smooth, nose pointed, eyes tiny, color blackish with strawberry highlights, size large. . . . . **Mexican burrowing toad, family Rhinophrynidae**
    Color otherwise. 5

5. Size small, fold of skin across rear of head. . . **narrow-mouthed toads, family Microhylidae**
    No skin fold on nape. 6

6. Webbed toes, body skin tuberculate or not, prominent eyes . . **typical frogs, family Ranidae**
    No webbing on toes, or very reduced. 7

7. Ventral disc present. . . . . **tropical frogs, family Leptodactylidae**
    Ventral disc absent 8

1.3. Ventral disc on a tropical frog (illustration by K. P. Wray III)

8. Reduced to full webbing, tiny to large toepads . . . . **chorus and cricket frogs, treefrogs, family Hylidae**

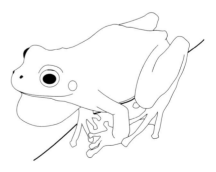

1.4. Treefrog (illustration by Dale Johnson)

Toes fully webbed, eyelids lacking, lateral line comprises short, vertically oriented ridges . . . . **aquatic clawed frog, family Pipidae**

1.5. Clawed Frog

SALAMANDERS (INCLUDING PAEDOMORPHIC SPECIES, WHICH PERMANENTLY RETAIN LARVAL CHARACTERISTICS, BUT NOT INCLUDING LARVAE OF SPECIES THAT NORMALLY METAMORPHOSE)

1. Body attenuate, eel-like. 2
   Body not attenuate and eel-like 3

2. No external gills, 4 tiny legs . . . . . . **amphiuma, family Amphiumidae**
   3 pairs of external gills, forelimbs only . . . . . . **sirens, family Sirenidae**

3. 3 pairs of external gills, no nasolabial groove, no costal grooves, 4 toes on every foot . . . . **mudpuppies/waterdogs, family Proteide**
   3 pairs of external gills, costal grooves, 4 or 5 toes on hind feet 4

4. Nasolabial grooves (4 or 5 toes on hind foot) **larval or paedomorphic lungless salamanders, family Plethodontidae**
   No nasolabial groove. 5

5. Costal grooves prominent . . . . **mole salamanders, family Ambystomatidae**
   Costal grooves indistinct or absent. 6

6. No costal grooves, no nasolabial groove, 5 toes on hind foot . . . **larval newt, family Salamandridae**
   Fleshy wrinkles along side, no external gills 7

7. Horizontally flattened, aquatic, single gill opening **hellbender, family Cryptobranchidae**
    Costal grooves, no external gills 8

8. Nasolabial groove . . . . **adult lungless salamanders, family Plethodontidae**
    No nasolabial groove. 9

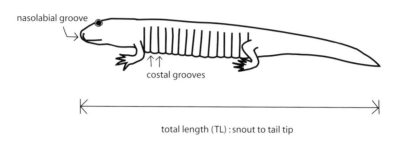

total length (TL) : snout to tail tip

1.6. Identifying characteristics for salamanders: total length, costal grooves, and nasolabial groove

9. Costal grooves   **adult mole salamanders, family Ambystomatidae**
    Costal grooves indistinct or absent. . . . . **adult newts, family Salamandridae**

chapter 2

Frogs, Toads, and Treefrogs

The frogs, toads, and treefrogs (the anurans or tailless amphibians) are well represented in eastern North America. They are, unquestionably, the most readily recognized of the various amphibians, if not to particular species, at least to group.

The anurans of eastern North America are contained in seven families:

- toads, family Bufonidae, with 13 species
- spadefoots, family Pelobatidae, with 5 species
- narrow-mouthed toads, family Microhylidae, with 3 species
- Mexican burrowing toad, family Rhinophrynidae, with 1 species
- treefrogs, family Hylidae, with 25 species
- true frogs, family Ranidae, with 15 species
- tongueless frogs, family Pipidae, with 1 species, and
- tropical frogs, family Leptodactylidae, with 7 species.

The frogs, toads, and treefrogs of eastern North America, indeed, of the world, have many similarities. Their skin (even those that live in desert habitats) must always be on the moist side. Except for the introduced African clawed frog, the frogs, toads, and treefrogs of eastern North America all have eyelids. All anurans have muscular hind legs for hopping or leaping.

Male anurans of all species in eastern North America produce territoriality-breeding calls. Some vocalizations, such as the bass booms of the bullfrog, can be heard for long distances. Others, like the tinkling calls of the greenhouse frog, are audible for only a few feet. In many cases the calls are so distinctive that it is possible to identify the particular species calling. However, there are some frogs, such as the many species of leopard frogs, that have calls so similar that it may be possible to identify the caller only to a group of species.

Treefrogs of many species voice "rain calls" that are different in timbre and structure than the breeding calls. These frogs may often be heard calling from trees prior to or during spring and summer storms.

High-quality CDs and tapes of the calls of frogs, toads, and treefrogs are available (see Additional Reading).

A Green Toad Interlude

Bzzzzzzzzzzzzzzzzz! Bzzzzzzzzzzzzzzzzz! Bzzzzzzzzzzzzzzzzz! The nasal buzzes came wafting on gentle breezes across the modified prairie—really now a pasture—but somewhere among the cud-chewing cattle was a pond and in that pond were a fair number of the prettiest toad species of the eastern and central states—eastern green toads. The toads of the United States have among their rank only three forms that are consistently of striking color. These are the two races of *Bufo debilis* and the Sonoran green toad, *Bufo retiformis*, of the Southwest. They are anurans that I never tire of seeing and photographing.

In the distance I (RDB) could see the lights from a ranch house, so I stopped to ask permission to find and photograph the little prairie gems we were hearing.

Permission was granted and I was soon wending my way among grazing range cattle. I was hoping against hope there were no belligerent bulls in their number.

As I neared the pond, the calls sorted themselves into two very different buzzes—those of the green toads that had initially caught my attention, and a somewhat softer and more penetrating buzz—the calls of Great Plains narrow-mouthed toads, *Gastrophryne olivacea*.

I was thinking of a two-for-one night. First I'd try for pictures of the green toads, but I'd be sure to save enough film for a few photos of the narrow-mouths.

The pond was now only twenty feet away and I slowed my pace a bit to try to pinpoint the position of the nearest green toad. Another step and—the ground crumpled beneath my weight and I found myself in a chest deep hole! I wondered, as I considered the throbbing pain in my knees, how the cattle had managed to avoid this pitfall? Apparently much of the bank had been undercut by flowing waters, now long receded, and probably long forgotten. After contemplating the livestock question unsuccessfully, I began to wonder how to extricate myself from this pit.

Suffice it to say that although it took some doing, I was successful but decided as I dragged myself from the hole that there would be no photos that night, no matter how plentiful, pretty, or cooperative those toads.

I'd hope for another opportunity at a more user-friendly locale later in the trip.

The anurans typically have a complex development cycle. Most breed in the water and lay eggs that hatch into aquatic tadpoles (larvae) that metamorphose into small adults. Of the anurans of eastern North America, it is only the six species of tropical frogs of the genus *Eleutherodactylus* that have no free-swimming tadpole stage. These six frogs deposit their small egg clutches in moist terrestrial spots, and the development of each baby occurs entirely within its egg capsule.

2.1. Toad (illustration by K. P. Wray III)

Like most amphibians, the frogs, toads, and treefrogs of the East are most easily found after nightfall with a flashlight. It is then that most emerge from their daytime lairs to hunt for insects and worms or to vocalize at breeding ponds. It is also after nightfall, especially on warm, misty evenings during the passage of a low-pressure system or during darkness of the new moon, that anurans can be most easily approached. Conversely, they can be very difficult to approach on brilliantly moonlit nights.

In the north, temperature, barometric pressure, rains, and photoperiod—the hours of daylight versus darkness—dictate the arrival of anurans at breeding ponds. The arrival is progressive, with males arriving first and females responding to their calls. The more cold-tolerant species such as wood frogs and spring peepers arrive as the pond ice begins to break up. They may often chorus from ponds still edged with winter's ice. At the other end of the spectrum are the warmth-loving green frogs and bullfrogs. Those males don't begin to call until the nights have truly warmed.

In the southeast a dozen or more species may appear at the ponds in response to the passage of a single rainy springtime frontal system. In the drought-prone Midwest and desert areas, anurans quickly gather at newly flooded depressions and replenished watercourses during the spring, summer, or early autumn. They often begin breeding while the waterholes are still filling. To compensate for the rapid evaporation of many ephemeral puddles, the anurans dependent on them develop quickly. Some, such as spadefoots, may go from egg to metamorph in only two weeks. Those that breed in permanent waters, like bullfrogs, may take two or more years to attain metamorphosis.

Those frogs that are predominantly aquatic (clawed frogs, bullfrogs, and pig frogs) usually remain at their breeding ponds throughout the year. Other species (spring peepers and leopard frogs) disperse widely once breeding activities are over.

There is surprisingly little concrete information about the activities of even common anurans once they have left the breeding ponds.

Toads, family Bufonidae

This is a large and diverse family with members on most of the world's continents. The bufonids include not only the very familiar terrestrial "hop-toads" of North America (and elsewhere), but arboreal, live-bearing species from Africa and brook-dwelling species in the Neotropics as well. One of the most widely occurring is the cane toad, which has been introduced into many areas of both the Old and New World in an effort to control crop-destroying insects.

Because they are more resistant to desiccation than many other anurans, the toads are creatures of varied habitats. Although many species are found in moist woodlands and meadows, others are associated with dry grasslands and deserts. They may utilize both permanent and ephemeral water sources as breeding sites. Where standing surface water is a luxury, some toads readily breed in shallow backyard fish and lily ponds. The calls produced by chorusing males vary from harsh rattles (Great Plains toad) though slowly pulsed low-pitched trills (cane toad) to the musical trill of the American toad. The most unusual and untoadlike call is the shrill chicklike peeping of the tiny oak toad. Calls are usually heard from dusk to midnight, but on overcast or rainy days toads often call during the hours of daylight. The vocal sac of most species is large and rounded. A few species have huge, elongate vocal sacs that have been likened in shape to a sausage. Males in breeding condition have a gray to yellowish gray throat. The throat of nonbreeding males is lighter; the throat of the female is off-white to cream. Tadpoles are black and often move together in schools.

Except for rather minor differences in external appearance and a somewhat greater discrepancy of size, the toads of eastern North America are all quite similar. Most toads have a rather dry-appearing warty skin and, except while breeding, often inhabit relatively dry habitats. There are thirteen species in eastern North America. They range in size from the 7 inches of the cane toad to the 1¼ inches of the oak toad. Females are larger than the males.

Toads are primarily crepuscular and nocturnal, but may be active on overcast, rainy days.

Toads avoid predation in part by producing toxins in their skin. The toxins vary in potency by species. The toxins of some seem to be merely distasteful

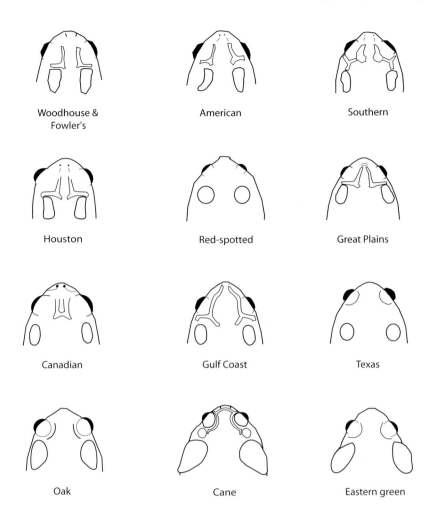

2.2. Toad heads (illustration by Patricia Bartlett)

while others may be lethal to predators (including domestic dogs). The parotoid glands produce the greatest amount of these toxins. If threatened by a predator, toads bow their head and try to butt the aggressor. This may simply be an attempt to intimidate, but it seems more likely that the effort is a concerted attempt to bring the parotoid glands, and the toxin they secrete, into contact with the aggressor.

While most species of toads lay their eggs in long strings, the red-spotted toad and the oak toad lay their complement of eggs singly or in very short strings. The number laid may be from only 100 by small species to more than

10,000 by the Brobdignagian cane toad. Amplexus (the breeding embrace) is axillary, females being clasped just behind their forelimbs. New metamorphs are virtually impossible to identify to species.

1. Eastern American Toad

Bufo americanus americanus

Abundance/Range: This toad ranges from Labrador to Manitoba then southward to northern Georgia, northeastern Louisiana and eastern Kansas. Although this is still a commonly seen species, it is reduced in numbers in some areas.

Habitat: The eastern American toad may be seen from woodlands and meadows to backyards. Like most other toads of eastern and central North America, it breeds in shallow water. Breeding waters may be ephemeral or permanent, small or large, in open woodland or clearings.

Size: The adult body length is 2¼–4¼ inches.

Identifying features: The color of the back and sides may be red, gray, or

1. American Toad

brown. Dark dorsal spots are usually light-edged and contain only one or two large warts. A white vertebral stripe is present. The parotoid glands are large and elongate. They may be separated from the postorbital ridge or connected by a short spur. Large tibial warts are present. The venter is off-white to cream and usually spotted with dark pigment anteriorly.

Voice: The call of the eastern American toad is a sustained and frequently repeated musical trill.

Similar species: Spadefoots have vertically elliptical pupils. Woodhouse's and Fowler's toads have the parotoid gland directly in contact with the postorbital ridge. The southern toad has very prominent cranial ridges and its interorbital ridges are knobbed posteriorly. The interorbital ridges of the Canadian toad are thickened and form a hump (boss) between the eyes.

Comments: In the northeast this species often hybridizes with the Fowler's toad, producing individuals that are difficult to identify. Hybrid males have intermediate voices.

Additional subspecies

2. The Dwarf American Toad, *Bufo americanus charlesmithi*, ranges from eastern Oklahoma and adjacent Kansas and Texas to western Tennessee, western Kentucky, and southern Indiana. The adult size of this race is 1¾–2½ inches. This toad tends to have a uniform dorsal and lateral color that is often red but may be grayish or brown. Few dark dorsal spots are present. A vertebral stripe may or may not be present. The venter is off-white to cream and usually unspotted or only sparsely so. The call is somewhat higher in pitch than that of the eastern American toad.

2. Dwarf American Toad

3. Great Plains Toad

Bufo cognatus

Abundance/Range: This common toad ranges south-ward through the Plains states from southern Manitoba to central Mexico. Check the range map for details.

Habitat: This toad is a denizen of grasslands and aridlands, deserts and plains. It may wander some distance from standing water but may be abundant near irrigated fields.

Size: The record size is 4½ inches.

Identifying features: Most Great Plains toads have a strongly defined pattern, but occasional examples may be almost unicolored. The ground color is tan, olive, brown, or gray. The back and sides are usually patterned with large, light-edged, paired, dark green markings. A well-defined light vertebral stripe is typically present. The belly is white to off-white and bears no dark spots. The vocal sac, when fully distended, is huge and elongate, extending upward over the tip of the snout. When deflated the sac folds back under a lappet of throat skin. This toad has a blunt, rounded snout. The interorbital crests converge in a V anteriorly and usually touch at the tip of the snout. Juvenile Great Plains toads are patterned much like the adults but often have numerous tiny red tubercles on the back and sides.

Voice: This is one of the loudest and most disharmonious of toads. The call is

3. Great Plains Toad

a long, slowly pulsed, metallic trill that can be heard clearly for a distance of more than half a mile.

Similar species: Poorly marked examples may be confused with the Texas toad, but the latter lacks strongly defined cranial crests and one of the two digging spades on each foot is sickle shaped.

4. Eastern Green Toad

Bufo debilis debilis

eastern green toad
western green toad

Abundance/Range: This is a common toad. It is found from central Texas and adjacent Oklahoma to northeastern Mexico.

Habitat: To protect itself from the desiccating sun, this desert and grassland toad hides under all manner of surface debris. It is often seen some distance from standing water but can be particularly common near ditches, ephemeral ponds, and stock watering tanks.

Size: This is a small, flattened toad. Two inches is the largest recorded length.

Identifying features: The back and sides of this toad may be pale green, pea green, or bright green. The dorsum bears many tiny black spots. The belly is white, yellowish, or the palest olive. Sparse dark dots may be present. Breeding males have black throats while those of nonbreeding males are gray. Females have white throats. The cranial crests are low or absent; the parotoid glands are large and diverge posteriorly down the shoulders.

4. Eastern Green Toad

Voice: This toad produces buzzing whistles. This is the only toad species of the East to have such a call.

Similar species: Couch's spadefoots may be green, but they have vertically elliptical pupils. See also the western green toad (5).

5. Western Green Toad

Additional subspecies

5. The Western Green Toad, *Bufo debilis insidior*, is common from West Texas, extreme western Oklahoma, and western Kansas westward to southeastern Arizona. This subspecies is paler than its eastern relative and has many of the black dots interconnected by thin black lines. This race of the green toad is well adapted to aridland conditions.

6. Fowler's Toad

Bufo fowleri

Abundance/Range: Depending on where in its range you look, Fowler's toad may vary in abundance from common (much of the range) to rare (Florida). The range of this toad extends from central New England westward to southeastern Iowa, southward to eastern Louisiana and eastward to the western Florida panhandle.

Habitat: Fowler's toad utilizes a wide range of habitats, but west of the Atlantic coastal plain it is often most common in well-drained sandy areas. In the deep southeast it is restricted to bottomland habitats. In the interior of the nation it is often associated with quiet standing waters.

Size: The average size of this toad is 2½–3¼ inches, with a record of 3½ inches.

6. Fowler's Toad

Identifying features: Because all markings are precisely outlined, this toad appears neat and tidy. The back and upper sides are usually of some shade of gray. Three or more warts are contained in each of the dark dorsal and dorsolateral spots. The dark spots are narrowly edged in very light gray. The interorbital crests do not bear any large knobs and the parotoid glands touch the postorbital crests. There is usually only a single large, dark spot on the chest. The belly is light. There are no enlarged tubercles on the tibia.

Voice: Male Fowler's toads voice their unmusical "waaaaaaah" while sitting a few inches from the waterline.

Similar species: American toads usually have only one or two tubercles in each dark spot and large tubercles on each tibia, and the postorbital ridges do not contact the parotoid gland. Southern toads are often red in color and, if dark spots are present, each spot may contain only one large wart. Southern toads have a large knob on the rear of each interorbital ridge. Woodhouse's toads have small, often poorly defined dark spots, but can be confusingly similar.

The eastern spadefoot has vertically elliptical pupils. Hybrids between Fowler's and the American toad or Fowler's and the southern toad can be difficult to identify.

Comments: Like other toads, in urban areas the Fowler's toad may often be seen at night beneath porch lights and streetlights foraging for insects.

7. Canadian Toad

Bufo hemiophrys

Abundance/Range: This is a relatively common toad species. It ranges further northward than any other eastern toad and is of predominantly Canadian distribution. It ranges southward from extreme south central Northwest Territories throughout eastern Alberta, most of Saskatchewan, and southwestern Manitoba to northern Montana, eastern North and South Dakota, and western Minnesota.

Habitat: A typical toad in its use of a multitude of habitats, the Canadian toad in southern portions of its range may be found in suburban backyards, in city parks, or amid pond- and lakeside vegetation. It seems more restricted to water-edge habitats in the North. It swims readily.

Size: 2–3¼ inches.

Identifying features: Over the more northerly part of its range, this is the only toad found. This is a dark toad. The ground color is usually a dark grayish brown and the dorsal and lateral markings are dark brownish black. The paired dark dorsal blotches contain 1–5 tubercles. A light vertebral stripe and a light dorsolateral stripe on each side are usually very evident. The light dorsolateral stripes are paralleled below by an irregular dark stripe. The belly, which is white anteriorly and (often) yellowish posteriorly bears small dark spots. The parotoid

7. Canadian Toad

gland is not strongly evident. The Canadian toad has well-developed interorbital crests, but the postorbital crests are less well developed. The interorbital crests thicken as the toad ages, converging and elevating centrally to form a boss. With advancing age the boss and the cranial crests may smoothly integrate, showing only a narrow central depression posteriorly.

Voice: Male Canadian toads produce a soft musical trill of moderately high pitch that does not have great carrying power. They may vocalize either from the bank or while sitting in shallow water.

Similar species: The Great Plains toad has postorbital ridges and its interorbital crests converge anteriorly to form a V. Woodhouse's toad usually does not have strongly contrasting body blotches and has postorbital ridges that contact the parotoid glands. The eastern American toad lacks a boss between the eyes and has prominent postorbital ridges. The eastern American toad and the Canadian toad occasionally hybridize in western Minnesota. The resulting offspring can be difficult to identify.

Comments: Because of low nighttime temperature constraints, the Canadian toad may be diurnal in the North, but is also active on warm nights. It is more nocturnal at the southern extremes of its range.

8. Houston Toad

Bufo houstonensis

Abundance: This toad is now found only in the proximity of a few small ponds in central eastern Texas. It is a federally endangered species.

Habitat: The Houston toad occurs in areas of sandy pine and mixed woodlands. It breeds in shallow, temporary to semipermanent grassy ponds and marshes, including those on golf courses. A number of the ponds in which the species now breeds are in protected parklands.

Size: The record size for this species is only 3¼ inches.

Identifying features: This prominently tubercled, brown, gray, or reddish toad looks very much like its closest relative, the widespread American toad. Dorsal tubercles may be reddish and may or may not be encircled with black. Larger dark spots, if present, are poorly defined. A light vertebral line, extending from snout to vent, is usually present. Both the interorbital and postorbital crests are well developed. At their outermost end, each ridge usually bears a posterior projecting spur that touches the large parotoid glands. The belly is light but bears numerous dark spots.

Voice: Although somewhat higher in pitch than those of the American toad, the vocalizations of the Houston toad are an otherwise similar trill.

8. Houston Toad, chorusing

Similar species: The Texas toad has no vertebral stripe or well-developed cranial crests. The red-spotted toad is flattened and has rounded parotoid glands. Woodhouse's toad has the parotoid gland in contact with the postorbital ridge. The Gulf Coast toad has a deep rounded valley between the eyes, triangular parotoid glands, and the interorbital ridges extend well posterior to the postorbital ridges. Spadefoots have vertically elliptical pupils.

9. Cane (Giant) Toad (introduced)

Bufo marinus

Abundance: The cane toad, primarily a native of tropical America, ranges northward naturally to the Lower Rio Grande Valley of Texas. Introduced populations are now established in Dade, Broward, Lee, Pinellas, Monroe, and Palm Beach counties, Florida. It is thought that the Texas populations are diminishing.
Habitat: This is both a city and a country toad. It breeds in canals, flooded ditches, shallow pools, and backyard lily ponds and fishponds. Many succumb to the occasional freezes that pass through southern Florida and the Lower Rio Grande Valley of Texas.

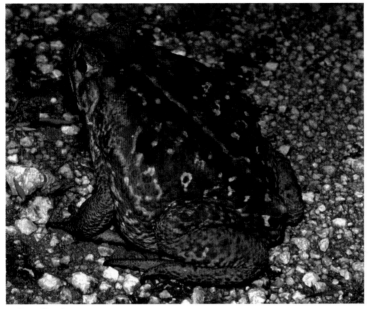

9. Cane Toad

Size: In the United States this toad seldom exceeds 7 inches in length.

Identifying features: This, the largest species of toad in the United States, is brown to reddish brown on the back. The sides are lighter. It usually has poorly defined darker and lighter markings. Except during the breeding season when males develop tiny spines on their warts, this is a rather smooth skinned toad. The parotoid glands are immense and extend far down onto the shoulders. The cranial crests are prominent but not knobbed.

Voice: Males voice a low-pitched, slowly pulsed rattling trill. The largest males have the deepest voices. Males have a comparatively small vocal sac and call while sitting on the shore or in shallow water.

Similar species: The immense downward angling parotoid glands should readily identify this toad.

Comments: Cane toads readily eat smaller frogs and toads. The toxins produced in the parotoid glands are formidably virulent and have been implicated in deaths of pets. Wash your hands thoroughly if you handle this toad. In Florida the cane toad eats inanimate foods and can be seen in yards eating dog or cat food from a pet's food dish. Those of Texas seem less prone to do so. At the southern extreme of their range in the United States these toads get very large. Perhaps in response to cool winter temperatures that result in lessened food availability, adults in central Florida are now seldom more than 4½ inches in length.

10. Gulf Coast Toad

Bufo nebulifer (formerly *Bufo valliceps*)

Abundance: This common toad ranges westward along the Gulf Coast from southwestern Mississippi throughout much of southeastern Texas and southward into Mexico. There are isolated populations in central Mississippi, on the Louisiana-Arkansas border, and in the Big Bend region of Texas.

Habitat: The Gulf Coast toad utilizes habitats as varied as backyards, city parks, seashore dunes, and open woodlands. This toad is not as well adapted to drought and dry regions as some species. Look for it near standing water.

Size: The Gulf Coast toad occasionally attains a robust 5 inches in length.

Identifying features: The back and upper sides are some shade of brown. There is a broad light vertebral stripe. The head is often lighter than the back. A broad light lateral stripe with irregular edges extends from the head to the groin. The lateral stripe is bordered beneath by a narrow dark stripe. The vocal sac is huge, extending from the chest to the lip. The interorbital ridges are well defined, in the shape of angled parentheses, and extend well posterior to the postorbital ridges. The parotoid glands are roughly triangular but may occasionally be nearly round. A rearward-directed spur connects each postorbital ridge to each parotoid gland. The crown, between the interorbital ridges, is concave.

10. Gulf Coast Toad

The cream-colored belly is usually copiously spotted with dark pigment. These slightly flattened toads often sit with their elbows flexed.

Voice: The call is a loud, low-pitched trill.

Similar species: The shape of the cranial ridges and the depressed crown will provide positive identification of this toad.

11. Red-spotted Toad

Bufo punctatus

Abundance/Range: This is an abundant western toad that enters our area of coverage in the western two thirds of Texas, western Oklahoma, and extreme southwestern Kansas.

Habitat: A species of the rocky aridlands, the red-spotted toad is typically found in the proximity of desert water-holes and streams, as well as near irrigated fields and stock watering tanks.

Size: The adult length of this flattened toad is 2¼ inches. The record length is 3 inches.

Identifying features: The color on the back and sides of this angular toad may be olive, tan, gray, brown, or reddish brown. When of the lighter ground colors, there may be irregular, but well defined, darker spots. A profusion of tiny red

11. Red-spotted Toad

spots is present on all color phases. The parotoid glands are round. There is no light vertebral line. If present at all, the cranial crests are poorly developed. The white belly is sparsely peppered with tiny black spots.

Voice: The male may sit at water's edge or a few feet back from the waterline while producing his melodious trills.

Similar species: This is the only eastern or central toad having the combination of round parotoid glands and no cranial crests.

12. Oak Toad

Bufo quercicus

Abundance/Range: The oak toad is less common than in the past, but where its habitat remains intact it may still be found in numbers. It is a species of the Atlantic and Gulf coastal plains from southeastern Virginia through Florida and westward to eastern Louisiana.

Habitat: This toad prefers sandy pine-oak scrublands where it breeds in shallow ephemeral ponds and ditches.

Size: The record size for this elfin toad is 1¼ inch. It is the smallest species in North America.

12. Oak Toad, chorusing

Identifying features: The dorsal color is some shade of gray, at times so dark that the paired black spots that are always present may be difficult to see. Tiny red or yellowish warts are usually present and the prominent vertebral stripe may be white, yellow, or orange. The belly is white. The parotoid gland is large and elongate. The cranial crests are not strongly defined. The vocal sac is enormous and sausage shaped.

Voice: Oak toads are so well camouflaged that they may be almost impossible to see even when the loud, shrill peeps (with no rising inflection at the end) are emanating almost at your feet. Calling males typically conceal themselves amid emergent grasses or along grassy, overgrown banks.

Similar species: Except for very young individuals, all other toads are much larger than the oak toad. Juveniles of other toad species do not usually have the prominent light vertebral line or well-developed parotoid glands.

13. Texas Toad

Bufo speciosus

Abundance/Range: This common toad is restricted largely to Texas, but is found also in adjacent Oklahoma, southern New Mexico, and northern Mexico.

Habitat: This is a toad of sandy, yielding soils. It may be found in prairie grasslands, open woodlands, or backyards. It is often found in the vicinity of ephemeral ponds and stock watering tanks.

13. Texas Toad

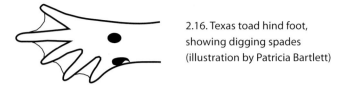

2.16. Texas toad hind foot,
showing digging spades
(illustration by Patricia Bartlett)

Size: This robust toad is adult at 3 inches in length. The record length is 3½ inches.

Identifying features: This very nondescript toad may be easier to identify by negative quantities than by positive. The Texas toad lacks well- developed cranial crests. It has neither a light vertebral stripe nor a strongly contrasting dorsal pattern. The back and sides are olive gray to brown. If present, the dorsal spots are usually greenish. The parotoid glands are oval. The belly is white to off-white and lacks dark spots. Although all toads have two digging tubercles on each hind foot, those of the Texas toad are free-edged and sharp, and the innermost tubercle is crescent shaped.

Voice: The calls of the Texas toad are short, high-pitched, unmusical trills. The sausage-shaped vocal sac curves upward beyond the tip of the snout.

Similar species: Other sympatric toads have well-developed cranial crests and light vertebral stripes. The red-spotted is flattened, and has round parotoid glands. Giant toads are restricted to the Lower Rio Grande Valley and have very large parotoid glands that extend downward onto the sides. Spadefoots have vertically elliptical pupils.

14. Southern Toad

Bufo terrestris

Abundance/Range: This is the common hop-toad of the southeastern United States. It is found in coastal plain habitats southward from Virginia through Florida and westward to eastern Louisiana.

Habitat: The southern toad is a habitat generalist, found from isolated open woodlands to suburban backyards.

Size: Although they are usually smaller, southern toads may attain a length of 4½ inches.

Identifying features: This dark toad usually has a weak pattern. Its back and upper sides can be gray, brown, or red. Dark dorsal spots may or may not be present. If present, each spot often contains one or two (sometimes more) reddish to white warts. A weak lateral stripe is present. The venter is light but

14. Southern Toad

usually variably pigmented with black spots or flecks. The parotoid glands are kidney shaped. Cranial crests are prominent. Each of the two interorbital crests has a prominent knob on the posterior end.

Voice: The rapidly pulsed call of the southern toad is shrill and uncomfortably penetrating. Males call while sitting in exposed areas of the shoreline (occasionally in short grasses) or in very shallow water.

Similar species: No other eastern toad has such pronounced knobs on the interorbital crests.

15. Rocky Mountain Toad

Bufo woodhousii woodhousii

Abundance/Range: This big toad ranges widely through the plains, prairie, and Rocky Mountain states. The principal range of this toad is from Texas to the Dakotas and Montana. It occurs also in Arizona and Utah with relict populations even further west.

Habitat: The Rocky Mountain toad remains common throughout much of its range. It occurs in both rural and urban settings, usually fairly near water-holding prairie potholes, irrigation canals, or backyard ponds.

Rocky Mountain
southwestern Woodhouse's
east Texas

15. Rocky Mountain Toad

Size: The record size for this toad is 5 inches. Most individuals are an inch or so smaller.

Identifying features: The Rocky Mountain toad is gray to gray brown with variably light edged but often obscure, paired, dark dorsal markings. From one to several brown or vaguely reddish tubercles are contained in each dark spot. The interorbital crests are well developed but lack knobs and do not converge on the snout. Parotoid glands are oval to elongate and usually touch the postorbital ridge. The venter is light with few if any dark markings. A white vertebral stripe runs from nose to rump.

Voice: The call is a loud, nasal, waaaah.

Similar species: Use range to eliminate the southwestern Woodhouse's toad and the East Texas toad. The Great Plains toad is strongly marked, has a very different call, and the prominent cranial ridges form a V on the snout. The Texas toad lacks both well-developed cranial crests and a white vertebral line. Spadefoots have vertically elliptical pupils.

16. Southwestern Woodhouse's Toad

Additional subspecies

16. The Southwestern Woodhouse's Toad, *Bufo woodhousii australis*, is a locally abundant aridland toad. Its range parallels the Rio Grande and its tributaries (on both sides of the U.S.-Mexico border) from Big Bend westward to central New Mexico. In New Mexico there is a wide swath of intergradation with the Rocky Mountain toad. Look for this toad in sandy, moist habitats such as irrigated areas, or near surface water of some sort.

The southwestern Woodhouse's toad is very similar in appearance to the Rocky Mountain toad, but the white vertebral stripe usually begins on the shoulders rather than on the head.

17. East Texas Toad

17. The East Texas Toad, *Bufo woodhousii velatus*, is of problematic taxonomic status. But no matter its roots, it is the most variable member of this complex both in color and pattern. It is found from eastern Texas northward and eastward to eastern Oklahoma, western Missouri, and Louisiana west of the Mississippi River.

Dorsally and laterally the East Texas toad may vary from gray to reddish brown. If spots are present on the back or sides they are sparse and inconspicuous. A light vertebral stripe may be visible. Lateral stripes may be present. Warts may be many or few. The belly is lighter than the dorsum, but is usually rather heavily pigmented anteriorly with dark flecks or spots. The maximum length of this toad is 3¼ inches and its calls are variable. They may range from short abrupt trills to a single lengthy "waaahh."

chapter 3

Treefrogs

Cricket Frogs, Treefrogs, and Chorus Frogs, family Hylidae

Across the world, frogs of many families have become adapted to arboreal life. Among these are the so-called true treefrogs, the frogs of the family Hylidae, which is well represented in North America.

The hylids of eastern and central North America (north of Mexico) can be broken roughly into three groups, cricket frogs, typical treefrogs, and chorus frogs. The cricket frogs and most of the chorus frogs are essentially terrestrial. Typical treefrogs, on the other hand, are arboreal acrobats often heard calling from the canopy at the advent of summer storms.

Cricket Frogs, genus *Acris*

Although not difficult to identify as cricket frogs, the several species and subspecies all tend to look alike. As a group, cricket frogs have tiny, largely nonfunctional toepads, a dark triangular or V-shaped mark between the eyes, and striping on the hidden surface of the thighs. Subtle characters, such as the presence or absence of anal papillae (tiny tubercles around the vent) and the appearance of the thigh stripe, are important in differentiating species and subspecies. Males have a dark throat and a single large, rounded, subgular vocal sac.

3.1. Bird-voiced Treefrog (illustration by K. P. Wray III)

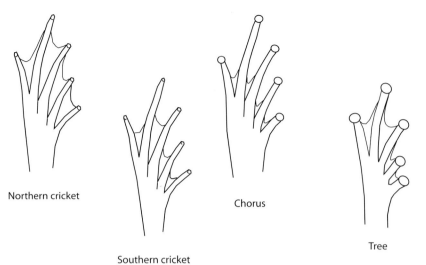

Northern cricket

Chorus

Tree

Southern cricket

3.2. Hylid frog feet (illustration by Patricia Bartlett)

Cricket frogs may call sporadically during cool weather, but they are actually hot weather breeders.

Cricket frogs are alert and adept at evading capture. They make long, erratic leaps that carry them rapidly from danger. When they are sitting quietly atop mats of vegetation, their colors and patterns afford a remarkable camouflage.

Eggs are laid in small clumps and attached to submerged plants. A normal complement is 100–200 eggs.

18. Northern Cricket Frog

Acris crepitans crepitans

Abundance/Range: This frog can be quite common in suitable boggy habitats. It ranges from extreme southeastern New York to eastern Texas.

Habitat: The northern cricket frog is associated with permanent water sources and especially favors sunny shallows that are matted with sphagnum and emergent vegetation.

northern cricket frog
Blanchard's cricket frog
coastal cricket frog

18. Northern Cricket Frog

Size: This tiny, agile frog is fully adult at 1–1¼ inches.

Identifying features: This is a tiny frog with a tubercular skin. It is variably colored in hues that conceal it and can be almost impossible to see when motionless. The dorsal ground color may be brown, tan, charcoal, green, or various combinations of any of these colors. The brightest color is usually longitudinally oriented in the center of the back and acts as a disruptive camouflaging marking. The markings may be yellow, green, russet, or brown. The single broad thigh stripe has an uneven edge. The hind leg is comparatively short. If the leg is *gently* extended and drawn forward (adpressed), the heel usually does not extend beyond the snout. A dark triangle is present between the eyes. The webbing of the toes is extensive, reaching the tips of all except the longest toe, which has one phalange with no webbing.

Voice: The series of clicks starts slowly then accelerates. The sound produced by a large chorus is harsh and discordant.

Similar species: If the two species of cricket frogs are compared, the northern cricket frog is the shorter-nosed and shorter-legged of the two. At least one phalange (3 on the longest toe) is free of webbing on each of the 3 longest toes of the southern cricket frog. It also has an even-edged thigh-stripe. Chorus frogs have very reduced webbing on all toes and treefrogs have discernible toepads.

19. Blanchard's Cricket Frog

Additional subspecies

19. The population statistics of Blanchard's Cricket Frog, *Acris crepitans blanchardi*, are problematic. Although it remains an abundant frog over much of its southern range, it is now absent or rare in many northern areas where once common. It ranges southward through the central states from Wisconsin to Texas.

It has a rougher skin than the northern cricket frog, is somewhat more pallid in coloration, and has a somewhat heavier body. The ground color can be buff, brown, tan, or pale green. Refer to range maps for help in identifying this subspecies.

20. Coastal Cricket Frog

20. The Coastal Cricket Frog, *Acris crepitans paludicola*, is a poorly differentiated race of the northern cricket frog that is restricted to the coastal marshes of extreme eastern Texas and southwestern Louisiana. Its dorsal skin is smoother than either of the other subspecies, but this is subjective and difficult to determine in the field. The dorsal ground color is pinkish and the pattern poorly defined. This frog also lacks a well-defined thigh stripe. Males have a yellowish throat.

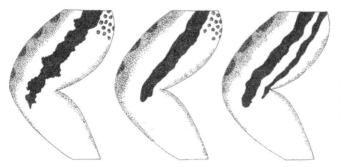

3.6. Cricket frog leg markings (illustration by K. P. Wray III)

21. Southern Cricket Frog

Acris gryllus gryllus

Abundance/Range: This is a remarkably abundant frog. It ranges southward from southeastern Virginia to eastern Louisiana.

Habitat: Look for this frog in the shallows and at the edges of grassy or mossy ponds, lakes, bogs, marshes, and open sphagnaceous swamps.

Size: This frog is fully adult at ¾–1 inch in length.

Identifying features: The southern cricket frog is a long-legged rendition of the northern cricket frog. It, too, is very variable in ground and pattern color. The back and upper sides may be tan, brown, russet, or green. The pattern is often (but not always) orange. Dark diagonal bars are often visible on the thighs and flanks. There is a single, rather even-edged thigh stripe, and anal papillae are present. The legs are long: if carefully extended forward along the body, the heel extends beyond the tip of the snout. The webs stop far short of the tips of the three longest toes.

Voice: The clicking vocalizations are quite metallic in tone and are produced in a series of 1–7 or 8 rapidly repeated notes.

21. Southern Cricket Frog, amplexing

Similar species: See accounts 18–20 for descriptions of the northern cricket frogs and account 22 for the Florida cricket frog. Chorus frogs have very reduced webbing on the toes.

Comments: The common name of Coastal Plain cricket frog has been proposed for this species. Because of the similarity of this name to "coastal cricket frog," the common name for *Acris crepitans paludicola*, we have elected to retain usage of southern cricket frog for *Acris gryllus gryllus*.

Additional subspecies

22. Florida Cricket Frog, *Acris gryllus dorsalis*, replaces the southern cricket frog over most of Florida. The two are very similar, but the Florida race has two stripes on the posterior of the thigh and lacks anal papillae.

22. Florida Cricket Frog

Typical Treefrogs, genera *Hyla*, *Osteopilus*, *Pelodryas*, and *Smilisca*

Hyla is a large genus that is abundantly represented in the Americas, and representatives also occur in Europe and Asia. *Osteopilus* is a genus of three West Indian treefrogs. One is now established in the United States where it is restricted to Florida. *Osteopilus* have the cranial skin co-ossified (attached) to the underlying bone. They are referred to collectively as bone-headed treefrogs. *Pelodryas* is a genus of three Australopapuan treefrogs. One species, a pet trade animal, has been found on numerous occasions in Florida. Of the six species of the Mexican and Central America genus *Smilisca*, only the Mexican treefrog ranges northward to the lower Rio Grande Valley of Texas.

Although they vary in size, color, toe webbing, habitat preference, breeding season, and much else, the various treefrogs of eastern and central North America are easily identified. The ability to change color may allow the same frog to be brown or gray and heavily patterned one moment and green or unpatterned only a short time later. When cold, treefrogs are often the darkest.

Treefrogs are easily approached on overcast or, especially, rainy nights, when they are calling at their breeding sites. Except when they are vocalizing, the presence of these frogs may be unsuspected. The treefrogs of the genera *Hyla* and *Pelodryas* have a single, prominent (when inflated) subgular vocal sac. Although those of the genera *Osteopilus* and *Smilisca* have a single vocal sac, it is divided and inflates to each side of the medial line, thus appearing double. Amplexus (the breeding embrace) is axillary (behind the front leg). Breeding males of some species have well developed nuptial (grasping) pads on the thumbs.

Although adept at climbing, many species of treefrogs remain near the ground and may hide under any manner of cover available. Others are persistently arboreal and found high in the trees.

Warm weather storms often induce "rain songs," vocalizations that are quite different from the calls given at breeding ponds. Breeding activities are stimulated by spring and summer rains, especially when in conjunction with a substantial lowering of barometric pressure. If standing water is available, even a short thunderstorm may induce breeding. Differing by species, eggs (which may number from several hundred to more than 1,000) are laid in clumps or deposited singly and may either float or submerge and attach to subsurface vegetation.

Treefrogs may hybridize and produce offspring that are difficult to identify. Some of the known combinations are green treefrog–barking treefrog, pine woods treefrog–Cope's gray treefrog, and Pine Barrens–pine woods treefrogs.

23. Pine Barrens Treefrog

Hyla andersonii

Abundance/Range: This treefrog is present in small, disjunct colonies in western Florida, adjacent Alabama, north central South Carolina, southeastern North Carolina, and the Pine Barrens of southern New Jersey. It is a protected species.
Habitat: The Pine Barrens treefrog is found in acidic pitcher plant and sphagnum moss bogs and hillside seeps.

North America's Most Beautiful Treefrog

There are some anurans that are so pretty that they are inscribed indelibly in one's mind. The Pine Barrens treefrog, *Hyla andersonii*, is such an anuran. I (RDB) first met this green, orange, and plum-colored frog in the mid-1950s in an acidic pitcher-plant bog in the New Jersey Pine Barrens. When I first saw a calling male, I thought (without actually having seen all species in the United States) that this must be the most beautiful member of that family in North America. Now that I've actually seen all other species in the region, I'll say that my first impression was absolutely right.

That first male was quonking loudly from a head-high perch in a cat-briar entangled thicket. Gordy Johnston and I had stopped at the bog as the first stop on a trip that was to take us to coastal South Carolina.

It was my first truly long-distance herping adventure, and the finding of that Pine Barrens treefrog (and some carpenter frogs, *Rana virgatipes*) were, to me, the most memorable anuran sightings of the trip.

A few years later I moved to Florida, and I thought then that I had left the Pine Barrens treefrog far behind me. In those years it was not known to occur any further south than North Carolina.

But it ultimately turned out that *Hyla andersonii* actually ranges in small patches of precise habitat all the way south to the western panhandle of Florida and adjacent Alabama.

A few years ago I decided to try to reacquaint myself with the species in the wild. While returning to Florida from a herp-photography trip to California, I crossed the border into the Sunshine State and veered a bit northward to Pine Barrens treefrog habitat. Green treefrogs and Cope's gray treefrogs, *Hyla cinerea* and *H. chrysoscelis* respectively, honked and trilled from newly freshened flooded roadside ponds. Choruses of two species of cricket frogs, *Acris* species, clicked stridently as I drove, but I heard no calling treefrogs. I continued.

I slowed as I neared one dip in the road to see whether water was present. It was. And the muggy night seemed perfect for Pine Barrens treefrogs to be chorusing, but all was quiet. Then suddenly, as I was about to drive on, I heard a few honking notes—green treefrogs? I pulled from the road, stopped, turned the car off, and sat in the sultry summer darkness. Silence. Two cars sped by and suddenly the vocalizations, not honks but quonks, began again. No green treefrogs, these, but the species I had hoped to find—the Pine Barrens treefrog!

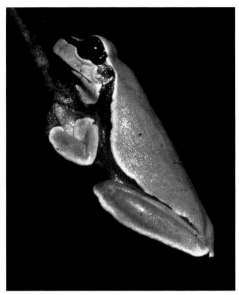

23. Pine Barrens Treefrog

Size: Pine Barrens treefrogs are adult at 1¼–1¾ inches.

Identifying features: This species is, arguably, the most beautiful of the eastern North American treefrogs. It is certainly one of the least frequently seen. Normally Pine Barrens treefrogs are jade to leaf green dorsally. When cold or otherwise stressed, the frogs may be dull olive green. A broad purplish to cinnamon stripe extends rearward from the nostril, through the eye and tympanum, to the groin. A pencil-thin darker line borders the stripe dorsally. The hands and feet are purplish. Golden to orange spots and reticulation are present on the groin and the underside and rear of the thighs. The belly is white.

Voice: The call notes of this frog are an oft-repeated, high-pitched "quank."

Similar species: There are no similar species in the New Jersey range of this frog. Elsewhere the green and the squirrel treefrogs may be sympatric. The green treefrog is slenderer and usually has a metallic white lateral stripe. The squirrel treefrog may be brown or green and never has a purplish lateral stripe.

24. Canyon Treefrog

Hyla arenicolor

Abundance/Range: This common aridland treefrog is easily overlooked. In our area of coverage, this treefrog occurs in a range disjunct from the more westerly main range in the Big Bend region of Texas.

Habitat: Canyon treefrogs are restricted in distribution to montane areas where at least some water is permanently available. It may be found hunkered down on streamside boulders, rock faces, and even concrete bridge foundations.

Size: This robust treefrog attains a length of 1¼–2½ inches.

Identifying features: The changeable but always pallid coloration of this treefrog blends remarkably well with the boulders of the region. At night the canyon treefrog may be quite strongly patterned dorsally with darker lichenate markings or variable spots against a buff, gray, or olive ground color. During

24. Canyon Treefrog. Photo by Scott Cushnir

the daytime, and especially when the frog is sitting in the sun, it is often simply a pasty white to tan and devoid of markings. The dorsal skin is rough. A dark-bordered light spot is nearly always discernible beneath the eye. The concealed surfaces of the hind legs are yellowish to orange. Males have a dark throat skin; that of the females is light.

Voice: The call is a rapidly repeated echoing trill.
Similar species: None in this treefrog's West Texas range.

25. Western Bird-voiced Treefrog

Hyla avivoca avivoca

Abundance/Range: This is a fairly common treefrog. During drought it can be difficult to find. It occurs from western Florida and southwestern Georgia westward to central and northern Louisiana and extreme southern Illinois. There are numerous disjunct populations.

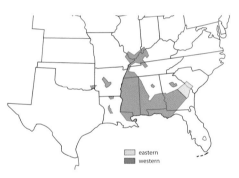

eastern
western

Habitat: The bird-voiced treefrog is a resident of the tree-canopied southern swamps. It is arboreal.
Size: This treefrog occasionally attains a length of 1¾ inches in length but is usually a little smaller.
Identifying features: The western bird-voiced treefrog is pale or pea green to gray or charcoal on its back and sides. It may change quickly from green to gray. A large, dark, central figure with rough edges is usually visible on the back. Dark bars are present on all limbs and there is a dark interorbital marking. The groin and concealed surfaces of the hind legs are green. Small white spots are present on the rear of each thigh. A dark-edged, light (white to yellowish green) spot, usually wider than high, is beneath each eye. Males have a dark throat.
Voice: The calls of this frog are flutelike ululations that meld with the hootings of barred owls to typify the great southern swamplands.

25. Western Bird-voiced Treefrog, chorusing

Similar species: The gray treefrogs are larger and more robust and have a wartier skin, with orange in the groin and on the hind legs.

Additional subspecies

26. The Eastern Bird-voiced Treefrog, *Hyla avivoca ogechiensis*, is poorly differentiated from the western race. It has a pale green to yellowish wash under the hind legs and ranges eastward from central Georgia to southern South Carolina.

26. Eastern Bird-voiced Treefrog

27a. Cope's Gray Treefrog

Hyla chrysoscelis

27b. Gray Treefrog

Hyla versicolor

Cope's treefrog, composite map

Abundance/Range: Because of the ease with which these treefrogs are confused, the range shown is a composite for both species. As a composite, it is greater than the range of any other eastern central species of typical treefrog. Together, these treefrogs range southward from New Brunswick and Manitoba to Florida and Texas. They are common to abundant in many areas, but local and uncommon in others.

Habitat: The gray treefrogs are denizens of wet hardwood or mixed woodland habitats.

Size: Both species attain 2¼ inches in length.

Identifying features: These two treefrogs are identical in external appearance and capable of undergoing great color changes. The same frog may be pea green at one moment and dark gray a few minutes later. A large and intricate black-edged figure that is darker than the ground color is usually prominently visible on the back. All limbs are barred. A light spot is present beneath each eye. The groin and undersurface of the hind legs are orange yellow to bright orange. The rear of the thighs is orange reticulated with black. Males have a dark throat.

Voice: The calls of these two frogs are trills. That of Cope's gray treefrog, *Hyla chrysoscelis*, is a high-pitched, rapid staccato somewhat similar to the

27a. Cope's Gray Treefrog

27b. Gray Treefrog

call of a red-bellied woodpecker. That of the gray treefrog, *Hyla versicolor*, is pulsed more slowly and quite musical. The chosen calling station is usually a limb or tree trunk a foot or more above the water. Chorusing gray treefrogs may be heard from late March to June or July.

Similar species: The somewhat smaller bird-voiced treefrog has a smoother skin and a greenish wash beneath the hind limbs.

Comments: Although the two gray treefrogs are identical in all external aspects, they differ in chromosome number and in voice. *Hyla chrysoscelis* is a diploid species while *Hyla versicolor* is tetraploid. Chorusing males can be field identified by comparing the trill rate of the calls of the two. At identical temperatures the call of *Hyla versicolor* has a slower trill rate, hence a much more melodious call.

28. Green Treefrog

Hyla cinerea

Abundance/Range: This is a common to abundant treefrog. It is found from the Delmarva Peninsula, comprising lower Delaware and the Eastern Shore counties of Maryland and Virginia, southward through the Florida Keys, westward to eastern Texas and northward to southern Illinois.

Habitat: This species prefers the environs of grassland and pasture pools but may also be found in open mixed woodlands. It readily finds and colonizes backyard fish and lily ponds. By day green treefrogs may occasionally be encountered resting, eyes tightly closed, on emergent or pond side vegetation. At night they forage and chorus in diverse habitats, from emergent vegetation to halos cast by porch lamps.

Size: The green treefrog is adult at a slender 1¾–2¼ inches.

Identifying features: When active

28. Green Treefrog, chorusing

this frog is usually a brilliant green on the back as well as the upper sides. Resting frogs may be green, but just as apt to be olive or brown. A broad, dark-edged enamel-white stripe extends from the snout to the groin and separates the green dorsum from the white venter. On some specimens the line may be foreshortened or entirely lacking. A white femoral and heel stripe is often present. Small, but well-defined, gold or orange dorsal spots may be present. The throat of male green treefrogs is green on the sides and yellowish green to yellowish white centrally.

Voice: The "quonks" of the green treefrog are loud and carry for some distance. The frogs often call while sitting on the leaves of emergent vegetation but may also call from limbs or while floating.

Similar species: The squirrel treefrog is smaller. If it has a white lateral stripe, the stripe lacks black edging. Pine Barrens treefrogs have a plum-colored stripe bordered dorsally with a narrow dark line.

Comments: Hybrids between green treefrogs and barking treefrogs are well documented. The appearance of such hybrids may be similar to a parent or intermediate.

29. Pine Woods Treefrog

Hyla femoralis

Abundance/Range: This is a common southeastern anuran. It ranges eastward from eastern Louisiana to and through mainland Florida, then northward to southeastern Virginia.

Habitat: This appropriately named treefrog is almost always found in the proximity of pine woods habitats. Rarely, it may be found near cypress heads.

Size: This slender treefrog attains an adult length of 1¼–1¾ inches.

Identifying features: The pine woods treefrog lacks prominent field marks. The back and sides may be tan, gray, greenish, or a dark reddish brown. A large dark dorsal blotch of irregular shape is usually visible. A thin dark lateral stripe is usually visible. This line begins at the nostril, passes through the eye, then curves downward posterior to the tympanum and continues to the groin may. A dark blotch is usually visible between the eyes. There are light (often yellowish, sometimes greenish) irregular oval spots on the dark concealed surface of the thigh. Males have a dark throat.

Voice: This treefrog may have the most easily identifiable voice of any eastern frog. The call is a rapidly repeated series of harsh dot-dash notes often likened to the sounds produced by Morse code transmissions. Males may call while sitting on open muddy shores but often call from a height of 1–5 feet while clinging to pine trunks.

Similar species: The oval yellowish, greenish, or whitish thigh spots are diagnostic but nearly impossible to see unless the treefrog is in hand.

29. Pine Woods Treefrog

Comments: This species occasionally hybridizes with both the Pine Barrens and gray treefrogs, producing progeny with an array of intermediate characteristics.

30. Barking Treefrog

Hyla gratiosa

Abundance/Range: This is a common treefrog, and seems especially so in the southeastern part of its range. The principal range extends southward from eastern North Carolina through all but southernmost Florida, then extends westward to eastern Louisiana. Disjunct populations occur on the Delmarva Peninsula, in southeastern Virginia, and in western Kentucky and adjacent Tennessee.

Habitat: This is a frog of pinelands and mixed woodlands. It breeds in shallow ephemeral ponds, both in open woodlands and in pastures. It spends a good deal of time in the tree canopy. A congregation of several dozen have been found in North Florida in the winter, burrowed almost a foot deep next to a rotting pine stump.

Size: This is the largest native treefrog of the eastern seaboard. A record size of 2¾ inches has been confirmed.

Identifying features: Not only can this treefrog change its color, it can change its pattern as well, and it can do both rapidly. The same frog can change its color from yellowish green to brown or a number of intermediate hues. It may also be devoid of a pattern at one moment and then bear a profusion of solid rounded spots (often yellow or brown) or light-edged dark ocelli only minutes later.

30. Barking Treefrog, chorusing

Males have a greenish or yellow throat. The upper lip is white and an irregular white lateral line may be present anteriorly. The skin is strongly granular.

Voice: The rain call, often voiced from high in a tree at the advent of a storm, is a barking note. The call given at the breeding pond is a hollow sounding "dooonk."

Similar species: There are no other treefrogs of the southeast with granular dorsal skin and a profusion of ocelli.

31. Squirrel Treefrog

Hyla squirella

Abundance: This is an abundant frog throughout most of its range. It is found from southeastern Virginia, throughout Florida, then westward to southern Texas. There are several disjunct populations to the north and west of the main range. The squirrel treefrog is essentially a coastal plain species.

Habitat: This is a habitat generalist, colonizing habitats as diverse as open woodlands, pastures, and the environs of backyard lilyponds.

Size: This treefrog is fully grown at 1–1½ inches in length.

Identifying features: This small treefrog can be green, brown, spotted, or plain dorsally and on the upper sides. It usually has a light upper lip and may have a vaguely defined light lateral line. A darker interorbital marking (a blotch, spots, or triangle) may be present. This species is often best identified by ruling out more easily identified species.

Voice: The common name is derived from the rain call, often voiced from trees, which sounds much like a scolding gray squirrel. The breeding call is a continuously repeated quack.

Similar species: Other small treefrogs have spots on the rear of the thigh, yellow in the groin, or a dark-bordered white lateral line. Cricket and chorus frogs have only tiny toepads.

31. Squirrel Treefrog, chorusing

32. Cuban Treefrog (introduced)

Osteopilus septentrionalis

Abundance/Range: This is a very common treefrog in southern mainland Florida and the Keys and is expanding its range northward. It may now be found as far north as Hillsborough County on Florida's Gulf Coast and Indian River County on the east coast. Isolated populations occur in Pinellas, Sarasota, and Brevard counties, possibly in others. It is a West Indian species.

Habitat: This is a frog of tropical hammocks and urban gardens. It is also found along drainage canals and in citrus groves and other disturbed habitats. It hides among plants and beneath ground surface debris by day and in very dry weather. It is active year-round.

Size: This is the largest treefrog of the southeast. Males are adult at 1½–2¾ inches. Females regularly exceed 3 inches and may occasionally attain a heavy-bodied 5¼ inches in length.

32. Cuban Treefrog

32. Cuban Treefrog

Identifying features: This is a big, robust, tan to gray (rarely army green or bluish green) treefrog. Some individuals may have darker dorsal patterns. The skin is warty. The toepads are immense. Yellow is often present in the axil of each foreleg. The venter is white or off-white.

Voice: Male Cuban treefrogs produce a cacophony of snores and squeaks. Rain calls may be voiced from the tops of citrus trees during rainstorms. The rain call is shorter and less varied than the breeding vocalizations.

Similar species: None. The Cuban treefrog lacks the white suborbital spot borne by smaller tan to gray treefrogs. No other treefrog in Florida has the proportionately immense toepads of the Cuban.

Comments: This cold-sensitive alien species expands its range somewhat when Florida's winters are mild, but loses much gained ground during the periodic freezes. Males seem normally to live only one or two years, but females may survive more than a decade. This treefrog produces particularly noxious skin secretions.

33. Australian Green Treefrog (introduced)

Pelodryas (Litoria) caerulea

Abundance: This large pet trade treefrog has been occasionally found in South Florida. Although a few small choruses have been heard, it is not yet known whether it is established in the state or whether those individuals found are releasees.

Habitat: In Florida this treefrog is most often found near weed-choked canals and ephemeral ponds in Lee, Collier, Broward, and Dade counties.

Size: An occasional large female may attain 5 inches in length. Males are about half that length.

Identifying features: This is a smooth-skinned jade green, bluish green, forest green, or, occasionally, brown treefrog. Some individuals may bear scattered small white dorsal spots. The upper sides are the same color as the back.

The lower sides and the belly are white. The supraorbital and supratympanal ridges of this stocky treefrog may be obscure or greatly developed.

Voice: The vocalizations are a series of hoarse croaks.

Similar species: None. There are no other giant green treefrogs, ei-

33. Australian Green Treefrog

ther native or introduced, in Florida. The typical jade green coloration should differentiate juveniles of this species from the bright green native species.

34. Mexican Treefrog

Smilisca baudinii

Abundance/Range: This Latin American treefrog is an uncommon resident of Cameron County, Texas.

Habitat: Although it may be found in the vicinity of pools and resacas, this species seems most common near drainage ditches and backyard fishponds. It colonizes areas as diverse as thornscrub, palm thickets, and banana groves.

Size: An adult size of 3¾ inches in length is occasionally attained.

Identifying features: Mexican treefrogs are often quite light in color on hot days. At that time the dorsal pattern may be only weakly visible. At night the color and pattern are darker. The ground color of the back and sides may be brown or green. There may be a dark line along the canthus (the upper angle of the snout) that extends rearward to the axis of the arm. A light spot is present below each eye. The lower

34. Mexican Treefrog

34. Mexican Treefrog, showing bilateral vocal sacs inflated

sides are lighter than the back and may, or may not, show a reticulate pattern. The belly is light (at times with a greenish tinge posteriorly) and unmarked. Males have a dark throat while the throat of the female is light. The toepads are prominently developed.

Voice: The usual callnotes are a series of loud, harsh, "kecks." Chuckling sounds are also occasionally produced.

Similar species: Within the Mexican treefrog's limited Texas range, there are no frogs of similar appearance.

Chorus Frogs, genus *Pseudacris*

This group of hylid frogs is represented in eastern North America by eleven species. All are of small to moderate size with even the largest species, the rather chunky Strecker's chorus frog, attaining a length of only 1½ inches. Many of the smaller species are confusingly similar in appearance. Rely on range maps to help with identification.

The toepads of chorus frogs are relatively tiny and the hindfeet are scarcely webbed. Most often these frogs are encountered in terrestrial situations. However, the spring peeper readily climbs. During their winter to spring breeding season chorus frogs utilize shallow, often ephemeral, pools to vocalize and breed. They may then be heard by day, especially when overcast, or night. In fact, collectively, chorus frogs are much more frequently heard than seen, for all are well-camouflaged, secretive frogs that can be difficult to locate, even when abundant and vocalizing seemingly right at your feet.

Most chorus frogs produce ratcheting trills (a few species peep) that slow noticeably in pulse rate when temperatures cool. When the trill rate is the slowest, the calls sound much like the rapid stroking of the teeth of a pocket comb by a fingernail. During the height of the breeding season these frogs vocalize almost around the clock with the greatest amount of activity in the late afternoon and early evening. Eggs number up to several hundred per clutch and adhere to subsurface vegetation in pools.

The characteristic dark dorsal markings of these frogs are very variable in contrast, and often difficult to discern at night. The rounded, subgular vocal sac of the male is dark; the throat of the female is pale gray.

35. Mountain Chorus Frog

Pseudacris brachyphona

Abundance/Range: This common but secretive frog ranges southward from southwestern Pennsylvania to northern Alabama with a hiatus through southern Tennessee.

Habitat: This is very much an upland species, especially in the south. It is found in wooded regions, on hillsides and mountain slopes. During the summer months it may be found far distant from standing water. It breeds in all manner of standing water, from flooded tire ruts in dirt roads to shallow ephemeral and semipermanent pools and seepage puddles.

Size: This species is adult at 1–1½ inches in length.

Identifying features: Although warm tan to brown or gray seem to be the most common ground colors, some of these frogs are so pale that they appear pasty white. Darker dorsal patterns may be apparent. If present, the dorsal markings may be in the form of an H, reverse parentheses that may or may not touch, or two rough-edged but almost straight dorsal stripes. A dark interorbital marking is usually visible. A dark ear-stripe usually stops just above the insertion of the arm but may continue to the groin. The legs are banded. The ventral surfaces are palest gray to white and usually unmarked.

Voice: The voice of this frog is a rapid, somewhat discordant, high-pitched trill.

Similar species: Other species of chorus frogs have a pattern of 3 brown, black, or green stripes (except for the spotted chorus frog, which may have 2 stripes). Newly metamorphosed leopard frogs have dorsolateral folds.

35. Mountain Chorus Frog

36. Brimley's Chorus Frog

Pseudacris brimleyi

Abundance: This relatively common frog ranges southward from southeastern Virginia to northeastern Georgia. It is a coastal plain species.

Habitat: Brimley's chorus frog calls from lowland puddles, swamp and marsh edges, flooded drainage ditches, and other moist habitats.

Size: Brimley's chorus frogs are adult at 1¼ inches in length.

Identifying features: This elfin frog is prominently striped. There are three darker brown stripes on the light brown dorsum as well as a narrow, even-edged, black lateral stripe on each side. As with all chorus frogs, the dorsal pattern may vary in intensity, but the lateral stripes are always evident. There is a stripe, rather than a triangle, between the eyes. The venter is gray and bears a peppering of tiny black spots on the chest and along the sides.

Voice: The voice of this frog is a rapid, high-pitched, ratcheting trill.

Similar species: Most small species of chorus frogs are superficially similar. However, the precisely outlined black lateral stripes found on this species are diagnostic.

36. Brimley's Chorus Frog

37. Spotted Chorus Frog

Pseudacris clarkii

Abundance/Range: This very abundant frog forms immense breeding congresses. It ranges southward from central Kansas through Texas to extreme northeastern Mexico.

Habitat: This is a frog of the open prairie and grasslands. It is most common near the edges of shallow semipermanent to permanent ponds, irrigation canals, and cattle tanks.

Size: The spotted chorus frog is adult at a slender ¾–1¼ inches in length.

Identifying features: The back, upper sides, and limbs of this minuscule frog are light olive tan to greenish gray. The dorsal markings, be they spots, stripes, or a combination, are green and narrowly edged with darker pigment. All limbs bear either spots or bands of green. A lateral line, usually darker in color than the dorsal markings, begins near the tip of the snout and extends to the groin. A dark-edged green triangle or V, point posteriormost, is usually present between the eyes. The belly is pale gray to white.

Voice: The voice of this frog is a rapid, high-pitched trill. The pulse-rate of the trill is fastest at high temperatures, when the calls may be likened to hoarse quacks.

Similar species: This is the only chorus frog of the central states having a pattern of green. Newly metamorphosed leopard frogs have dorsolateral folds.

37. Spotted Chorus Frog

38. Northern Spring Peeper

Pseudacris crucifer crucifer

Abundance/Range: This abundant frog ranges southward from southern Canada to the Gulf Coast of the United States.

Habitat: Hardwood and mixed woodlands and woodland ponds, swamps, and marshes are preferred habitat of the peeper. As with many chorus frogs, the breeding biology of peepers is rather well understood but little is known about their life away from

the breeding ponds. This is the most arboreal of the chorus frogs.

Size: The spring peeper is adult at between ¾–1¼ inches in length.

Identifying features: The specific name of crucifer is derived from the dark X (a crucifix) on the peeper's back. The back and upper sides have a ground color of tan (often with a pinkish overcast) to olive brown. A dark stripe follows the canthus from nosetip to eye. A short ridge is present from the rear of each eye to about midway on the side. The belly is usually largely or fully white. Males have a yellowish to grayish chin. Tiny toepads are visible.

Voice: Although not known by appearance to many except ardent naturalists,

38. Northern Spring Peeper

the whistled calls of this frog are one of the most recognized of anuran songs. The peeping calls have a rising inflection and are produced in series. When approached by another male, a calling peeper may produce a short territorial trill. Once choruses are in full swing, peepers may call (albeit sparingly) even when temperatures dip into the high 30s.

Similar species: Pine woods treefrogs and brown-colored squirrel treefrogs may be confused with peepers. However, the treefrogs have prominent toetip discs and lack an X on their back. Illinois chorus frogs are bulkier and have irregular dorsal markings as well as a call more reminiscent of a metallic "ping" than the slurred "peep" of the peeper.

Comments: This abundant anuran is a true harbinger of spring in the North and a winter chorister in the South. The peeper currently rests uneasily in the genus *Pseudacris*. The generic name of *Parapseudacris* has been suggested for this frog but has not been widely accepted.

Additional subspecies

39. The Southern Spring Peeper, *Pseudacris crucifer bartramiana*, is found in the northern two-fifths of the Florida peninsula and the eastern half of the panhandle. It supposedly differs from the northern spring peeper primarily in having a strongly spotted belly, but the peepers of Louisiana, now considered the northern race, also have spotted bellies.

39. Southern Spring Peeper, chorusing. Photo by Scott Cushnir

40. Upland Chorus Frog

Pseudacris feriarum feriarum

Abundance/Range: This is one of the more common chorus frogs of the eastern and south central United States. It ranges northward from the northwestern Florida panhandle and eastern Texas to south central Oklahoma and eastern Pennsylvania.

upland
New Jersey

Habitat: In the north this is a species of upland habitats, but in the south it becomes a lowland frog. It occurs in hardwood and mixed woodlands where it breeds in temporarily flooded grassy depressions as well as at the edges of swamps and marshes.

Size: This chorus frog attains a length of 1½ inches.

40. Upland Chorus Frog

Identifying features: The back and sides of this frog are tan or brown (rarely gray). The variably dark vertebral and dorsolateral stripes are narrow and may be replaced by a series of linear spots. The vertebral stripe often extends forward between the eyes and may have a projection outward to each eyelid; this may be replaced by a dark, rearward pointing triangle. The lateral stripes are best defined and usually dark brown, but may be black in some populations. The venter is light but may bear dark pepper spots anteriorly.

Voice: This is another of the chorus frogs with a rapidly pulsed, "combtooth" voice. It begins breeding activities in December in the south and after winter temperatures moderate somewhat in the north.

Similar species: Spring peepers have a dark X on the back. Cricket frogs have fully webbed rear feet and stripes on the rear surface of the thighs. Southern chorus frogs are gray with black markings. Differentiating the very similar western chorus frog can be problematic. The western chorus frog is usually more prominently marked, with the stripes not usually broken into spots, and has slightly shorter limbs. The western and the upland chorus frogs often hybridize. Use range to help with identification.

41. New Jersey Chorus Frog. Photo by James Harding

Additional subspecies

41. The New Jersey Chorus Frog, *Pseudacris feriarum kalmi*, is a poorly differentiated subspecies. It is found only in extreme southeastern New York, eastern and southern New Jersey, and the Delmarva Peninsula. It is a somewhat stockier frog and the dorsal markings are more often stripes than spots.

42. Boreal Chorus Frog

Pseudacris maculata

Abundance/Range: This abundant chorus frog is found primarily in western North America, but reaches our area in Ontario, the Dakotas, Minnesota, and Nebraska.

Habitat: This is a frog of muskegs (tundra potholes), mountain meadows, prairie potholes, and high plains habitats.

Size: This slender chorus frog attains a length of about 1½ inches.

Identifying features: This chorus frog may have a ground color of gray, tan, or medium brown. The dark vertebral stripe may be broken and irregularly edged, but the dorsolateral stripes are quite prominent and usually not broken into spots. The lateral stripes are narrow but well defined. This species usually has a poorly defined stripe or spots between the eyes. The venter is light.

Voice: This is another of the several species of chorus frogs with a "combtooth" voice. The pulse rate of the trills is variable (faster when warm) but rapid. Males are usually well concealed amid emergent grasses when calling.

Similar species: Spring peepers have a dark X on the back. Cricket frogs have fully webbed rear feet and stripes on the rear surface of the thighs. Differentiating the western chorus frog can be difficult but it has much longer hind legs. The boreal and the western chorus frogs hybridize in some areas.

Comments: The boreal, the western, the upland and the New Jersey chorus frogs were all once considered subspecies of the same species.

42. Boreal Chorus Frog

43. Southern Chorus Frog

Pseudacris nigrita nigrita

southern
Florida

Abundance/Range: This is a common coastal plain frog found from central eastern North Carolina to northern Florida and southeastern Mississippi.

Habitat: This frog may be heard calling from flooded, grassy fields, roadside ditches, and other ephemeral sites in and along pine and mixed woodlands.

Size: The southern chorus frog is adult at a slender 1–1¼ inches in length.

Identifying features: The back and upper sides are light to very dark gray adorned with 3 black stripes. These may be broken into a series of irregular spots. There is also a broad and irregular black (sometimes with purplish overtones) stripe on each side that begins on the snout and continues to the groin. All four legs are barred, the rear legs prominently so. A white line extends the length of the upper lip. The belly is light.

Voice: The voice of this frog is best described as the noise made when a fingernail is drawn over the teeth of a pocket comb.

Similar species: Brimley's chorus frog is brownish with precise brown stripes dorsally and black lateral stripes. The upland chorus frog has brown lateral stripes. Cricket frogs have very extensive webbing on their hind feet and distinct stripes on the rear of the thigh. Squirrel treefrogs and pine woods treefrogs lack a lineate dorsal pattern and have webbed feet.

43. Southern Chorus Frog

Additional subspecies

44. The Florida Chorus Frog, *Pseud-acris nigrita verrucosus*, replaces the southern chorus frog over the southern four-fifths of the Florida peninsula. The two subspecies are very similar, but the Florida chorus frog is usually spotted dorsally rather than striped. However, the spots may occasionally coalesce into very uneven stripes. The dark lateral markings are in the form of stripes. The white upper lip of the Florida chorus frog is heavily spotted with black.

44. Florida Chorus Frog

45. Little Grass Frog

Pseudacris ocularis

Abundance/Range: This chorus frog is very abundant but difficult to observe. It ranges southward from the vicinity of the Great Dismal Swamp in southeastern Virginia, down the coastal plain, through the state of Florida except for the western panhandle and Keys.

Habitat: This hylid utilizes the heavily vegetated environs of grassy ponds, bayheads, swamps, marshes, and roadside ditches as habitat.

Size: This, the smallest frog in North America, is fully adult at ½–⅝ inch in length.

Identifying features: The ground color of the back and sides of this elfin frog vary from yellowish tan and rusty red to olive. A pair of dark dorsolateral stripes is usually visible and occasionally a dark vertebral stripe is present anteriorly. A thin dark lateral

45. Little Grass Frog, chorusing

stripe begins at the tip of the snout and, after broadening on the sides, continues to the groin. A dark interorbital triangle is usually visible. Little grass frogs are often most brightly colored during periods of daytime activity. The belly has a yellowish overwash.

Voice: The tinkling, cricketlike calls of this frog may be heard throughout much of the year.

Similar species: The large size alone will differentiate adults of all other frog species.

46. Ornate Chorus Frog

Pseudacris ornata

Abundance: This frog is now uncommon in many areas and seems to be diminishing in numbers throughout its range. It is found along the coastal plain and southern piedmont from central eastern North Carolina to northern Florida and extreme eastern Louisiana.

Habitat: This is a frog of pine and mixed woodlands. It breeds in shallow fish-free ponds, seasonally flooded meadows, and roadside ditches.

Size: Adult ornate chorus frogs may near 1½ inches in length.

Identifying features: This is the most variably and intensely colored of the chorus frogs. The back and upper sides may be similarly or very differently colored. Both may be olive brown, russet, or dark green. Or the back may be green and the upper sides be brown. Contrastingly colored (but not black), usually paired dorsolateral stripes may be well defined or obscure. A dark triangle is often present between the eyes. A weak vertebral stripe may be visible anteriorly. Prominent light-edged deep mahogany (almost black) markings are present on the sides and in the groin. A prominent dark stripe extends from the tip of the snout through each eye, encompasses the tympanum, and terminates above the forelimb. The belly is yellowish white, brightest posteriorly.

Voice: The metallic, abruptly ended peeps are voiced in series and are

46. Ornate Chorus Frog, gray morph, chorusing

unlike the calls of any other frog of the eastern seaboard.

Similar species: Treefrogs have fully webbed hind feet. Spring peepers have an X on the back and lack black lateral markings.

46. Ornate Chorus Frog, green morph

47. Strecker's Chorus Frog

Pseudacris streckeri streckeri

Strecker's
Illinois

Abundance: This chorus frog is locally distributed but fairly common. It ranges northward from coastal and central Texas to extreme southcentral Kansas.

Habitat: Once away from the breeding puddles, this frog burrows persistently. It prefers grasslands, prairies, and open woodlands having sandy or other yielding soils. It breeds in grassy, rain-filled roadside ditches and other temporary waters.

Size: This is the largest and most robust of the chorus frogs. It attains a length of 1⅝ inches.

Identifying features: The back and sides are tan to pale green. Darker dorsal markings are gray or green and may have a black edging. The lateral markings begin on the snout as a line, often encompass the tympanum, and continue as one or more spots onto

47. Strecker's Chorus Frog

each side. Except for the yellow groin, the belly is white and unpatterned. All limbs are banded.

Similar species: Toads have spiny-tipped body tubercles and parotoid (shoulder) glands.

Additional subspecies

48. The Illinois Chorus Frog, *Pseudacris streckeri illinoensis*, a geographic isolate, is found in three disjunct populations. Two of these are in Illinois and one in southeastern Missouri and adjacent Arkansas. This is a pale-colored race of Strecker's chorus frog that lacks yellow in the groin. Use range as the identifying factor.

48. Illinois Chorus Frog

49. Western Chorus Frog

Pseudacris triseriata

Abundance/Range: This once common chorus frog is found from southern Quebec southwestward to southwestern Oklahoma. It is becoming increasingly rare in the north. A disjunct population occurs in the central parts of New Mexico and Arizona.

49. Western Chorus Frog. Photo by James Harding

Habitat: An upland species throughout most of its vast range, it also occurs in relatively low riparian situations. It breeds throughout its range in marshes, swamps, and temporarily flooded areas.

Size: This species attains a length of 1½ inches.

Identifying features: The ground color of this frog may be gray but is more often tan to brown. The dark brown vertebral and dorsolateral stripes are broad and usually unbroken. The dorsolateral stripes may be more prominent than the vertebral stripe. The lateral stripes are black and usually well defined. A dark interorbital triangle is often visible. The venter is off-white to white but may bear dark pepper spots anteriorly.

Voice: The ratcheting trills of this chorus frog are common springtime sounds. The pulse rate of the trills is quite rapid. Males are usually well concealed amidst emergent grasses while calling.

Similar species: Spring peepers have a dark X on the back. Cricket frogs have fully webbed rear feet and stripes on the rear surface of the thighs. The upland chorus frog has weak dorsal markings that are often broken into spots. The boreal chorus frog has very short hind legs.

chapter 4

Tropical Frogs

Leptodactylid Frogs, family Leptodactylidae

The family Leptodactylidae is an immense aggregation of very diverse frogs. It is primarily of Latin American and West Indian distribution. There are seven species in eastern North America, five of them native and restricted to Texas. The remaining two were introduced to Florida from the West Indies. One, the greenhouse frog, is now also known from southern Louisiana.

Four of the seven species are tiny. Adults are hardly more than an inch in length. Two species attain a length of about 2 inches, and one grows to a 3 inches. All are secretive and even when active on rainy nights seldom stray far from cover.

Six of the seven species do not require water for breeding. The eggs are laid in moist terrestrial sites, and full (direct) development takes place within the egg capsule. The seventh species, the white-lipped frog, builds a frothy foam nest and does require standing water for breeding. All of these species have subgular vocal sacs but, except for the barking frog and the coqui, weak voices.

When startled, several of these frogs run rather than hop.

The webbing between the toes of these seven frogs is vestigial or lacking.

The Balcones barking frog was placed in the genus *Hylactophryne* before being moved to *Eleutherodactylus* and the three chirping frogs are in the genus *Syrrhophus*.

50. Balcones Barking Frog

Eleutherodactylus augusti latrans

Abundance/Range: Look for this frog in moist canyons and other rocky habitats in a crescent from the Edwards Plateau to the Big Bend of Texas, then northward to southern New Mexico. It also occurs in northern Coahuila, Mexico. This frog does not appear to be present anywhere in great densities.

Habitat: This frog hides in rock crevices and fissures, caves, mines, boulder fields, and even gypsum flats. In Texas, this frog is associated with creosote bush and mesquite on the western flats. In the eastern canyons it is associated with bigtooth maples and oaks.

Size: At an adult length of up to 3¾ inches, this is by far the largest of the leptodactylid frogs in the United States.

Identifying features: The ground color may vary from light to dark olive or some shade of brown. A variable darker pattern may be present. The limbs are barred. The belly is light in color. A fold of skin parallels the back of the head and continues rearward on each side as a dorsolateral fold. A U-shaped ventral (belly) disc is also present. The eyes are large. The fingers and toes are long and unwebbed. Toepads are present. Males have a large rounded subgular vocal sac. Juveniles are dark but encircled at midbody by a broad, irregular, greenish white to chalk-white band. They have white (or white banded) forelimbs and a white supralabial spot.

Voice: The barking calls of this frog may be heard echoing on summer nights from escarpments and canyons. Strangely, when heard up close the call sounds entirely different—like a rolling rrrrRRRRRRRRRrr rather than a bark.

Similar species: None. The dorsolateral and intertympanic folds and the ventral disc will identify this unusual frog. Color will identify juveniles.

Comments: Barking frogs easily climb nearly vertical rockfaces, and are among the most agile of frogs. They may peer from horizontal rock fissures, but will

50. Balcones Barking Frog

quickly sidle backwards as far as possible and inflate their body to prevent removal if disturbed.

51. Puerto Rican Coqui (introduced)

Eleutherodactylus coqui

Abundance/Range: This tiny Puerto Rican frog is an uncommon species in Florida, where it is known in and around a few greenhouses and nurseries in southern Dade County.

Habitat: In Florida this little frog is found in exotic bromeliads and amid other moisture-retaining ornamental plants. It may be heard calling from ground level to several feet high in trees.

Size: Coquis in Florida attain an adult length of about 2¼ inches.

Identifying features: The coqui is a robust frog. Dorsally the coqui is of some shade of brown. The sides are lighter. It may have a variable darker pattern of spots or dorsolateral stripes, but often does not. Many specimens have a dark W discernible on the nape, and a broad, light bar between the eyes. The belly is off-white to very light tan usually with at least some dark pigmentation. This species has large digital discs.

Voice: This frog derives its name from its two-syllabled call of "co-*qui*."

Similar species: The greenhouse frog is a rusty brown color and smaller, more slender, and rather prominently marbled or striped. When brown, the squirrel treefrog is similar to the coqui in appearance, but slenderer and without a lineate dorsal pattern.

Comments: This frog is very cold sensitive. It is possible that, rather than being actually established in Florida, the populations are continually replenished by frogs brought from Puerto Rico in shipments of ornamental plants.

51. Puerto Rican Coqui

52. Rio Grande Chirping Frog

Eleutherodactylus cystignathoides campi

Abundance/Range: This is a common but very secretive frog that occurs naturally in the Lower Rio Grande Valley of Texas and in northeastern Mexico. It is now also found in disjunct introduced colonies in Houston and San Antonio, Texas, and Baton Rouge and Shreveport, Louisiana.

Habitat: The Rio Grande chirping frog seeks cover not only beneath fallen natural vegetation, but also in trash piles, dumps, gardens, greenhouses, and nurseries, at times in great abundance. In urban areas this frog seeks seclusion beneath boards, mulch, fallen leaves, or stepping stones. It occasionally climbs.

Size: This minuscule frog is adult at about ¾–1 inch in length.

Identifying features: This is a very plain-colored frog with few unique characteristics. It is quite flattened and has a fairly wide head and tiny toepads. Fingers and toes both lack webbing. The back and sides may be tan, light brown, gray, or olive. Indistinct darker markings may be present. The limbs usually bear dark crossbars but, again, these may be indistinct. A dark mask is often present. The lower sides are somewhat lighter than the back and the belly is translucent. These are agile, fast frogs.

Voice: These frogs produce a varied series of cricketlike chirps and trills.

Similar species: Although the other chirping frogs of Texas are of quite similar appearance, range will identify them. The spotted chorus frog is gray with green markings.

52. Rio Grande Chirping Frog

53. Spotted Chirping Frog

Eleutherodactylus guttilatus

Abundance/Range: This is the most secretive of the chirp-ing frogs of Texas. Its actual population statistics are un-known. In the United States it is restricted to the Big Bend region of Texas and also occurs in Mexico.

Habitat: This frog is associated with rocky areas, including road cuts, fissured cliff faces, outcrops, canyons, escarpments, rocky hillsides, caves, and mine shafts. It is quick to retreat into the safety of crevices when ap-proached.

Size: The adult length of this species is 1⅝ inches.

Identifying features: The back and upper sides of adult spotted chirping frogs are tan, brown, olive green, or yellowish, with variable dark mottling. The lower sides are light (sometimes with a vague pinkish flush) and lack dark markings. The belly is yellowish. Juveniles are much darker than adults, a combination of charcoal and brown with white flecks. The limbs are prominently barred. The toes are unwebbed and tiny toepads are present. The frog is noticeably flattened in profile.

Voice: The notes produced by these nocturnal frogs are more insectlike than froglike. The chirps and whistles are heard from late winter until autumn. The notes are of very short duration, but are frequently repeated.

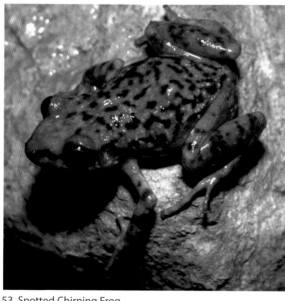

Similar species: No other chirping frogs are found within the range of this spe-cies. Refer to range maps. The canyon treefrog is a pasty white and largely un-marked during the day, but patterned with large, often rounded, dark spots at night. It has webbed toes.

53. Spotted Chirping Frog

54. Cliff Chirping Frog

Eleutherodactylus marnockii

Abundance/Range: This common chirping frog is found in south central Texas from the eastern Edwards Plateau to the eastern Trans-Pecos region.

Habitat: This is another of the frogs that has expanded its habitats from canyons and cliff faces to suburban backyards and city parks. It is most abundant where there is surface debris such as boards or bricks, or in fissured escarpments, canyon faces, and road cuts.

Size: At an adult length of 1½ inches, this is the largest of the three species of chirping frogs in the United States.

Identifying features: Dorsally and on the upper sides this chirping frog is pale gray to olive tan. Small, darker markings are present. The lower sides are only slightly paler than the back, but usually lack dark markings. The venter is purplish or brownish, often darkest in the groin area. The limbs are prominently barred. The toes are unwebbed. Tiny toepads are present. The frog is flattened in profile.

Voice: The chirps, trills, and whistles are of short duration, but frequently repeated. The calls of this species sound much like those of a cricket and have little carrying power. Males occasionally call on rainy days, but are most often heard at night as they call from road cuts and yard debris.

Similar species: Use range as the identification criterion. The ranges of the other two species of chirping frogs do not overlap with the range of the cliff chirping frog. The spotted chorus frog has a narrow head, pointed nose, and green dorsal markings.

54. Cliff Chirping Frog

55. Greenhouse Frog (introduced)

Eleutherodactylus planirostris

Abundance/Range: This West Indian frog is a firmly established species in Florida. It has slowly extended its range northward and is now found throughout the state. It has recently been found in southern Louisiana. This frog is regularly transported via ornamental plants to Georgia and the other Gulf states.

Habitat: The greenhouse frog is often more common in watered yards and gardens than in natural settings. However, it is also found in woodlands, scrub, and hammocks. It hides beneath boards, mulch, fallen leaves, or stepping stones and is adept at gaining quick access to the smallest of crevices and cracks.

Size: This slender frog is adult at about 1 inch in length.

Identifying features: The ground color of this frog is a mixture of browns. Both back and sides are dark and bear either mottling or dorsolateral stripes of orange. A narrow orange stripe connects the eyelids. The toes are unwebbed. The venter is usually an off-white but may be gray. The skin is warty.

Voice: Greenhouse frogs produce a series of chirps and trills that sound more like an insect than a frog. Males call from plants on rainy days or at night and are particularly vocal during the passage of summer storm systems that drop barometric pressure.

Similar species: Squirrel treefrogs may be brown but lack the rusty highlights that characterize the greenhouse frog and have webbed toes. Chorus frogs and cricket frogs are associated with marshes and other wetlands. Coquis (present only near Florida City, Florida) are usually lighter and have a broad light bar between the eyes.

Comments: Although very adversely impacted by winter cold fronts, the greenhouse frog is a firmly established alien species in Florida. Its continued presence may be more tenuous in Louisiana.

55. Greenhouse Frog

56. Mexican White-lipped Frog

Leptodactylus fragilis

Abundance/Range: In the United States this Latin American species is known only in the Lower Rio Grande Valley of Texas.
Habitat: This small frog may be found along drainage and irrigation ditches, in muddy areas near ephemeral ponds, and in temporarily flooded fields. In Texas this frog seems most common in degraded, occasionally flooded pasture-rangelands. It burrows beneath grass clumps or into the root system of other plants where it remains during periods of drought.
Size: The white-lipped frog attains a length of up to 2 inches.
Identifying features: This frog often has a reddish back and gray sides that bear tiny black mottlings. The lower sides and belly are white. A white stripe is very evident on the upper lip. Dorsolateral folds are present and a row of elongate tubercles extends from each tympanum, along the side, to the groin. The legs may be barred or blotched. A horseshoe-shaped ventral disc is present. The toes are devoid of webs.
Voice: The call is a low-pitched whistle with a rising inflection. Calling males usually dig small body pits beneath clods of mud or grass, hummocks, or surface debris but occasionally call from open sites.
Similar species: None. No typical (ranid) frogs have a ventral disc and all have webbed toes.

56. Mexican White-lipped Frog

chapter 5

Narrow-mouthed Toads

Narrow-mouthed Toads and Sheep Frogs, family Microhylidae

Although this is a large and diverse family elsewhere in the world, only three microhylids occur in the United States. All are of very similar external appearance, with a robust build (oval when viewed from above), pointed head, and short legs. A fold of skin crosses the back of the head just posterior to the eyes.

Termites and ants are the major food items of these frogs. These nocturnal frogs are so secretive that they may be present in large numbers but their existence not suspected. Narrow-mouths run or make short erratic hops rather than graceful leaps. Breeding males have a dark throat; the throat of the female is light. The vocal sac is rounded and subgular. Narrow-mouths often call while hunkered down amid grasses. When so positioned they are difficult to see even when calling. Occasionally they may call while floating or while sitting exposed on a bank.

The floating eggs are deposited in small clusters. A female may lay more than 800 eggs. All breed in temporary puddles or ditches and breeding activities are usually instigated by heavy rains. The breeding grasp is axillary. Sticky skin secretions assist amplexing males in retaining their breeding position.

Narrow-mouths are accomplished burrowers and seldom seen on the surface of the ground. They prefer sandy soils and may persist even in urban settings.

57. Eastern Narrow-mouthed Toad

Gastrophryne carolinensis

Abundance/Range: This common anuran is found over much of the southeastern United States.

Habitat: Eastern narrow-mouthed toads
inhabit many diverse areas with sandy
soils. They are common near the environs
of temporary and permanent water holes.
They may be found beneath all manner of moisture-retaining surface debris.

Size: This frog is adult at 1–1¼ inches in length.

Identifying features: The back and upper sides are variable and may change col-
or. Shades of gray and brown are the most common colors. The upper sides are

often more brightly col-
ored than the back. Dark
mottling may be present.
The lower sides and ven-
ter are usually gray with
darker mottling.

Voice: The call of the
male is a penetrating, nasal, sheeplike bleat.

Similar species: The Great
Plains narrow-mouth is
usually olive to gray and
lacks a dorsal pattern. It
has a light venter.

57. Eastern Narrow-mouthed Toad

58. Great Plains Narrow-mouthed Toad

Gastrophryne olivacea

Abundance/Range: This is an abundant toad. It is found
through most of Texas northward to southeasternmost
Nebraska and western Missouri.

Habitat: This tiny toad is well adapted to arid and semi-
arid habitats. It utilizes all types of surface debris, burrows
(including active tarantula burrows), and ground fissures
as hiding areas. It is inactive during droughts.

Size: This toad is adult at 1–1½ inches in length.
Identifying features: The back and sides of this toad are tan to olive gray. Scattered black spots (occasionally arranged as indistinct lines) may be present dorsally. The lower sides and belly are lighter than the back and lack dark markings.

58. Great Plains Narrow-mouthed Toad

Voice: The call of the male is a two-part, high-pitched, penetrating, buzzing bleat.
Similar species: The eastern narrow-mouthed toad is often some shade of brown dorsally and has profuse dark markings on its belly. The sheep frog has a thin (usually) orange middorsal and white midventral line. The much larger Mexican burrowing frog is darker (nearly black) dorsally and has strawberry highlights.

59. Sheep Frog

Hypopachus variolosus

Abundance/Range: Although common in Mexico, in South Texas this frog is locally distributed and uncommon.
Habitat: Sheep frogs occur in habitats as diverse as mesquite scrublands and irrigated agricultural areas. They burrow persistently but during rains may occasionally merely seek daytime shelter beneath boards, rocks, or mats of fallen palm fronds.
Size: The adult size of this frog is 1½ inches.
Identifying features: Although more variable in Mexico, in Texas sheep frogs are usually olive brown dorsally and on the upper sides. The middorsal area may be the most richly colored and may be outlined by a thin black line. A black lateral stripe usually separates the color of the dorsum from the lighter lower sides. A thread-thin orange vertebral line is usually present. The belly is mottled

dark and light gray and there is a light midventral line. An orange overwash may suffuse the upper arms and thighs. The hind limbs may be barred with black.

Voice: The call of the male is a loud, penetrating, nasal, sheeplike bleat.

Similar species: None; no other narrow-mouthed toad in our area has the threadlike middorsal and midventral lines.

59. Sheep Frog

chapter 6

Spadefoots

Spadefoots, family Scaphiopodidae

This frog family is represented in the United States by only seven species, including five found in eastern and central North America.

These nocturnal burrowing anurans are often called "spadefoot toads." Indeed, these creatures are toadlike, but they are frogs, rather than toads, because they have only one (rather than two) digging spades on the heel, indistinct parotoid glands, and vertically (rather than horizontally) elliptical pupils. The skin secretions of spadefoots smell vaguely like garlic and are not only distasteful but may also cause a burning sensation after the frog is handled. The secretions may help in retarding desiccation. It has been found that it is low frequency vibrations made by thunder and falling raindrops rather than (or perhaps in conjunction with) actual increase in soil moisture that arouse spadefoots, en masse, from aestivation.

The white subgular vocal sac is large but somewhat flattened. If floating, a calling male holds the center of his back bowed downward and his head and throat lifted almost clear of the water.

The breeding embrace of these toads is inguinal—that is, amplexing males grasp the females around the waist instead of just posterior to the forelimbs. Spadefoots, explosive breeders all, breed in ephemeral pools. Breeding activities are stimulated by heavy rain. Breeding may occur annually or only every several years. A female's several hundred (sometimes to more than 1,000) eggs are laid in a clump that attaches to submerged sticks or the substrate. Tadpole development is rapid; metamorphosis, if hastened by drying pools, can occur in a matter of only two to three weeks. If the pools are more stable, metamorphosis may take six weeks or more.

Spadefoot tadpoles eat some vegetation but seem primarily carnivorous. When crowded by deteriorating pond conditions, they are quite cannibalistic. Some leave drying ponds almost before resorption of the tail begins.

North American spadefoots are contained in two genera, *Scaphiopus* and *Spea*.

60. Couch's Spadefoot

Scaphiopus couchii

Abundance/Range: This is an abundant spadefoot species. It occurs over much of the American southwest and its range extends far southward into Mexico.

Habitat: This aridland spadefoot occurs in sandy grasslands, mesquite scrublands, and in desert areas that seem entirely inhospitable to an amphibian. It also persists in suburban and agricultural areas. This anuran burrows deeply.

Size: Although most adults are 2–2¾ inches long, the record size is 3½ inches.

Identifying features: The color of this, our largest spadefoot, may be buff, brownish, or olive green, with broad reticulations of yellowish green, lime, or bright olive. Some, males especially, may be yellow and brown. The lower sides do not bear contrasting markings and the belly is white. The parotoid glands are round but indistinct. There is no boss (hump) between the eyes. The single elongate digging spade on each heel is crescentic.

Voice: This anuran voices loud bleats while sitting at the edge or in the shallows of a newly flooded depression or while floating.

Similar species: Toads have horizontal pupils, prominent parotoid glands, and two tubercles rather than a single spade on each heel. Plains and New Mexico spadefoots have a short, often wedge-shaped spade. Hurter's and Plains spadefoots have a prominent hump (boss) between the eyes.

60. Couch's Spadefoots

61. Eastern Spadefoot

Scaphiopus holbrookii

Abundance/Range: Eastern spadefoots are abundant in some parts of their range and rare in others. They range southward from Massachusetts through most of Florida and westward to eastern Louisiana. This is the only spadefoot of the eastern seaboard and eastern Gulf Coast.

Habitat: This is an anuran of open sandy areas that is dependent on the formation of temporary pools for breeding. It persists in many urban areas and may be encountered as well in grasslands (including pastures), agricultural areas, and woodland edges.

Size: Although an occasional individual may attain a 3–inch length, most are mature at 1¾–2½ inches.

Identifying features: This anuran is a complex combination of brown and yellow (or cream) markings and shadings on its back and upper sides. The most consistent markings are a light interorbital bar and a cream or yellow lyre-shaped marking on the back. Most examples have scattered tiny red tubercles on the dorsum. The lower sides are lighter than the dorsum and may bear dark spots. The venter is white. The round parotoid glands are quite indistinct. A single sharp spade is present on each heel.

Voice: Eastern spadefoots call most often during rainstorms while floating or sitting in the shallows of a newly formed or still forming pond. Individual calls

61. Eastern Spadefoot

have been likened to moaning burps. The noise produced by a large distant chorus is a roar.

Similar species: Toads have horizontal pupils, prominent parotoid glands, and two, rather than one, digging spades on each heel.

62. Hurter's Spadefoot

Scaphiopus hurterii

Abundance/Range: Hurter's spadefoot is secretive and of localized occurrence, but can be common where soil conditions are right. It ranges southward from northeastern Oklahoma and southwestern Arkansas to northwestern Louisiana and most of the eastern one-third of the state of Texas.

Habitat: This is a spadefoot of sandy open woodlands, scrublands, and grasslands.

Size: The record size for this toad is 3¼ inches. Most examples are considerably smaller.

Identifying features: The back and upper sides of this anuran may vary from brownish to khaki green. A lighter lyre-shaped figure may be visible on the back. Sparse reddish tubercles may be present. The lower sides and forelimbs are often greenish yellow. The belly is white. The round parotoid glands are usually rather distinct. There is a prominent boss (hump) at the rear center of the head. A single sharp crescentic spade is present on each heel. This is the only spadefoot bearing both a crescentic digging spade and a prominent boss on the head.

Voice: Males produce moaning croaks while floating.

Similar species: Toads have horizontal pupils, prominent and usually elongate parotoid glands, and two tubercles rather than a single spade on each heel.

62. Hurter's Spadefoot

63. Plains Spadefoot

Spea bombifrons

Abundance/Range: This common spadefoot is widely distributed in the American and Canadian Plains states and is found from southern Manitoba and Alberta south to Texas and Chihuahua, Mexico.

Habitat: This is an aridland spadefoot. It favors the sandy, yielding soils of grasslands, plains, prairies, and agricultural areas, where it burrows deeply. It emerges periodically from its burrow to forage but is capable of undergoing rather extended fasts.

Size: This species attains a length of 2–2¾ inches in length.

Identifying features: The back and upper sides are of some shade of (often sand) gray patterned with variable darker markings that may be in the form of four lines. The dorsum may be adorned with sparse dark-edged, cream, yellow, or red tubercles. The lower sides and belly are white but the male's throat may be outlined with gray. Visible parotoid glands are absent. There is an interorbital boss. A single wedge-shaped to nearly round digging spade is present on each heel.

Voice: At the advent of a storm Plains spadefoots may produce moaning calls while still in their burrows. The harsh bleats of calling males are made while the frog is floating in the shallows.

Similar species: Toads have horizontal pupils, prominent parotoid glands, and two tubercles rather than a single spade on each heel. Both the New Mexican and the Couch's spadefoots lack the prominent boss between the eyes.

63. Plains Spadefoot

64. New Mexico Spadefoot

Spea multiplicata stagnalis

Abundance/Range: This primarily western spadefoot enters the range of our guide only in west Texas and Oklahoma where it is locally common.

Habitat: Like other western spadefoots, this species inhabits arid-lands, grasslands, and even alkali flats. It is seldom seen, awaiting substantial desert rains before emerging to breed and forage.

Size: Large examples occasionally attain 2½ inches in length.

Identifying features: This rather nondescript spadefoot is brownish to olive brown or gray on its back and sides. There are often greenish, brownish, or darker gray dorsal markings. These may form a linear pattern dorsolaterally. Red-tipped tubercles may be present. The lower sides and belly are white and unmarked. The male's throat is dark. Visible parotoid glands are absent. There is no convex boss between the eyes. The digging spade is wedge shaped to nearly round.

Voice: The call of the New Mexico spadefoot is a rapid trill that lasts a second or more. Males may call from the edges of their pools or while afloat.

Similar species: Toads have horizontal pupils, prominent parotoid glands, and two tubercles rather than a single spade on each heel. Couch's spadefoot has an elongate spade. The Plains spadefoot has a prominent boss between the eyes.

64. New Mexico Spadefoot

chapter 7

Tongueless Frogs

Tongueless Frogs, family Pipidae

This group of frogs is native to the Neotropics (Suriname toads) and Africa (clawed frogs). All are thoroughly aquatic. Two of the African species have long been available in the American pet marketplace as aquarium animals. One, the African clawed frog, has become established in North America. Although quite "cute" as a baby and interesting at all stages of its life, this frog grows large enough to consume fish, their eggs, and many aquatic invertebrates. It is a very slimy frog and difficult to hold. Before its stint as an aquarium animal, this frog was used in human pregnancy tests.

The breeding embrace (amplexus) is inguinal (pelvic). Breeding clawed frogs swim in vertical circles or half circles. Eggs are released and fertilized near the top of the circle. They adhere to plants and pond-bottom accumulations. The full complement numbers several hundred. The tadpoles are nektonic, hovering diagonally in the water with the head oriented downward. They have a barbel on each side of the mouth and look somewhat like a strange little catfish. The tail constantly undulates.

65. African Clawed Frog (introduced)

Xenopus laevis

Abundance/Range: This frog is established in some regions but its population statistics are unknown. It is now seen with some regularity in southern Texas and has been found in Florida, but is not known to be breeding there.

Habitat: A strictly aquatic species, this frog is most often seen in ponds and ditches near tropical fish farms and in other quiet waters.

Size: This strange looking frog is adult at 3½–5½ inches long.

Identifying features: This frog is unmistakable. It is somewhat flattened, has a narrow head with dorsally oriented, lidless eyes, and very powerful hind limbs.

The hind feet are large and fully webbed. Three toes on each hind foot are tipped with a black "claw." The primary color is olive and slate, prominently mottled or not, and albino and leucistic (white with black eyes) examples are well known. The skin is very smooth and slimy, but a series of distinct short ridges (a lateral line system) is present along each side.

Voice: Although seldom heard, a clicking trill is produced underwater.

Similar species: None.

Comments: Because it has no tongue, the clawed frog (there are actually many species, but only this one is known to be established in the United States) stuffs food into its mouth with its hands. It swims with its arms directed forward, and reacts immediately (apparently through exceptional tactile senses) to any small animals it touches.

65. African Clawed Frog

chapter 8

Typical Frogs

Typical Frogs, family Ranidae

The ranids are the typical, long-legged, far-jumping frogs that are usually associated with damp meadows, lakes, ponds, rivers, ditches, and other moist or wet habitats. All species in eastern North America have extensive webbing between the toes and web-free fingers. No North American ranids have toepads.

Breeding is often initiated by rains, but may occur spontaneously in dry weather if all other conditions (relative humidity, barometric pressure, photoperiod, and temperature) are suitable. Although many species are warm-weather breeders, others may breed during the short days and long nights of winter, while water temperatures are still cold or whenever sufficient rain falls to fill waterholes.

Adult frogs of the bullfrog–green frog complex can be sexed in the field. The tympani (exposed eardrums) of adult males of the bull, mink, bog, bronze, green, and pig frogs are conspicuously larger than the eyes. The tympani of adult females of these species are about the size of the eyes.

Adult males of some species (bullfrog complex) have yellow throats.

The arms and thumb-bases of most reproductively active male ranids are enlarged and horny keratinous excrescenses may be present.

Vocal sac morphology varies in ranids. It is bilateral and internal (causing the vocalizing male to look as if it has mumps) on some species, bilateral and external (like waterwings) on others, and largely subgular on still others. Male frogs may call from waterside positions, while sitting on floating debris or mats of vegetation, or while floating amid emergent plants. Male frogs (and the females of some species) stake out and defend a home territory. Some species are relatively communal but others are solitary.

The skin is usually relatively smooth, but may bear tubercles or glandular ridges. The presence or lack of dorsolateral ridges, their shape, and the amount of webbing on the hind feet may help with species identifications.

Eggs vary in number by species and the size of the female frog. Some clutches are produced as floating rafts that contain from a few thousand to about 20,000 floating eggs. Others are clumped amid submerged vegetation and contain only a few hundred eggs. The eggs hatch in several days. The tadpoles of most species

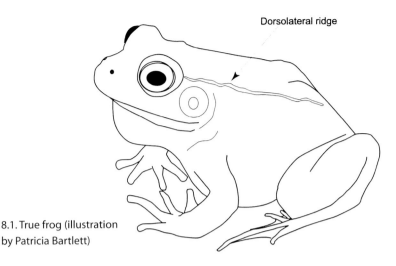

Dorsolateral ridge

8.1. True frog (illustration by Patricia Bartlett)

metamorphose in just a few weeks, while others (such as those of the river frogs and the bullfrogs) may take up to two years before transformation occurs.

Some frogs of this family are active both day and night but most are primarily nocturnal.

Bullfrog group

Bullfrog, Bronze Frog, Mink Frog, and relatives

These are the predominantly aquatic, fat, brown to green frogs. Three North American species are among the largest of the world's frogs and the remainder of those in our area are small. The larger species are voracious predators and eat not only insects and worms, but smaller vertebrates as well.

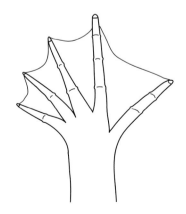

8.2. Hind foot of river frog, carpenter frog, and bullfrog (illustration by Patricia Bartlett)

Hunting the Bog Frog

In 1986 Dick and I went to the panhandle—Panhandular Florida, as I called it—to find the bog frog, *Rana okaloosae*. The species had recently been discovered and described by our friend Paul Moler and we both wanted to see the creature *in situ* and take photos of it.

The only hitch was that we'd be on Eglin Air Force Base property, not something one did without permission (especially at night), even twenty years ago. So we stopped by the base, made our request for nighttime access, and soon had a permit in hand.

As evening fell we found ourselves driving along dirt roads looking for slow-moving boggy streams. The twilight deepened into the dark softness of a moonless night and the tans and greens of landscape muted into gray and black. About half an hour after sundown, we paused next to a roadside bog to listen. The sounds of our engine had barely died away when we heard bronze frogs, *Rana clamitans clamitans*, plunking and decided to check the bog more closely.

A well-worn path led us from the road through a thicket of brambles to the water's edge. Bronze frogs called from all around us, but from somewhere near the back edge of the water we could hear the weak rapping call of an unfamiliar frog—because of its unfamiliarity, it could be only one kind, the Florida bog frog! We waded in, through water about eighteen inches deep, around hummocks studded with swamp maples that were draped with tendrils of cat briar, past cypress draped with long curls of Spanish moss.

As my eyes adjusted to the foreshortened depth of field in my flashlight beam, tiny beadlets of dew on the vats of purple pitcher plants winked back at me. These carnivorous plants were growing in profusion atop the floating sphagnum of the bog. The bog at night was a kaleidoscope of colors, bright greens of aquatic plants mingled with duller greens and browns of sphagnum and grays of tree trunks. As the surface of the bog moved with my footsteps, the plants seemed to nod and bow. Looking down into the water I saw layers of sphagnum, each layer further from the surface becoming less distinct. The ripples and our lights had silenced the anurans near us, but from distant corners of the bog, frog voices continued to be heard.

We checked each of the frogs, until finally, lying in the water near one of the pitcher plants, floated a bog frog; it was silenced but did not appear frightened by our presence. Dick moved slowly toward the frog, focused on it with the mini light atop his strobe, and took photos for several minutes. During that time, the frog never moved and was still silent and in place when we moved. It wasn't until we were in the car, windows rolled down and ready to leave, that the bog chorus again resumed.

66. Bullfrog

Rana catesbeiana

Abundance/Range: This common frog ranges southward from Nova Scotia and northern Michigan to eastern Texas and southern Florida. Metamorphs and juveniles are seen more frequently than the adults. It has been introduced into many areas where it was once unknown; once brought in, it tends to stay and reproduce.

Habitat: This aquatic frog inhabits all manner of quiet or slowly moving waters. Immature bullfrogs may be abundant in weedy shallows, but adults often choose deeper water among lilies and floating plants.

Size: This frog is adult at 5–8 inches in body length.

Identifying features: This is the largest frog of North America. The back, sides, and limbs are greenish brown to almost black. Darker mottling or spots may

66. Bullfrog

be present on the back, sides, and forelimbs. The hind legs are barred. The belly and throat are lighter. A variable amount of dark spotting is present on the belly. Adult males have yellow throats. The vocal sac is internal. A ridge of skin extends back from the rear of the eye to the rear of the exposed eardrum (tympanum). There are no dorsolateral ridges. The snout is not sharply pointed. At least half of the last joint of the longest toe is devoid of webbing.

Voice: The loud two- or three-syllabled "brrr-ummmmm" or "jug-o-rum" territorial calls of male bullfrogs may be heard throughout the warm months of the year.

Similar species: Pig frogs have a sharper nose than bullfrogs and webbing to the tip of all toes. River frogs have patterned lips and a heavily pigmented, dark throat. Bronze and green frogs have dorsolateral ridges and are smaller.

Comments: Although sought for food, the pet trade, and biological studies, this frog continues to expand its range.

67. Bronze Frog

Rana clamitans clamitans

bronze
northern green

Abundance/Range: This is a common frog. It ranges northward from north central Florida and eastern Texas to extreme southern Illinois and southeastern North Carolina.

Habitat: This frog inhabits quiet or slowly moving, shallow waters. It can be particularly common in swamps. The bronze frog often sits or floats concealed by vegetation.

Size: Adults have a head–body length of about 3 inches.

Identifying features: The back, limbs, and upper sides of this frog are bronzy to brownish. The lips and lower sides are light and usually heavily patterned with dark pigment. The snout may be brown or green. A light stripe may be visible beneath the eye. The hind leg is barred. The throat and belly are off-white (males have a yellow throat) with a variable amount of dark stippling. The lower lip may be spotted with white. A dorsolateral narrow ridge extends from each eye to the groin with a short fork paralleling the rear edge of each tympanum. There are bilateral internal vocal pouches.

67. Bronze Frog

Voice: This frog produces two distinctly different calls. One is a sharp "yelp" as it plunges to the safety of the water when startled from the bank. The second, the male's call-note, sounds like a loose banjo string being plucked.

Similar species: River, pig, carpenter, bog, and bullfrogs lack dorsolateral ridges. Mink frogs may have dorsolateral ridges but are usually strongly patterned dorsally. Leopard and pickerel frogs have a sharper nose and are usually spotted.

Additional subspecies

68. The Northern Green Frog, *Rana clamitans melanota*, ranges southward from Nova Scotia and extreme southeastern Manitoba to eastern Oklahoma and western South Carolina. This frog is of variable color, but usually much greener than the bronze frog. The green frog has green lips, dark banded hind limbs, and prominent dorsolateral ridges. Where the range of this species overlaps with the

68. Northern Green Frog. Photo by James Harding

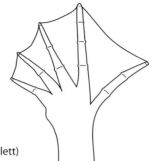

8.6. Hind foot of pig frog
(illustration by Patricia Bartlett)

range of the mink frog, hybridizing occurs. This results in specimens that are difficult to identify, with variable color and pattern and variably developed dorsolateral ridges.

69. Pig Frog

Rana grylio

Abundance/Range: This is a common frog of the Atlantic and Gulf coastal plains. It ranges southward from central eastern South Carolina, through Florida, then westward to extreme southeastern Texas.

Habitat: This very aquatic frog was once called the southern bullfrog. It is a resident of canals, lakes, ponds, swamps, marshes, ditches, and slowly flowing waters. It may be most common amid lilies or floating vegetation.

Size: At 5–6½ inches in length, females are much the larger sex. Males are usually about 4 inches long.

Identifying features: The dark-spotted back and sides of this frog may vary from brownish green to a rather bright green. The belly is light anteriorly but heavily vermiculated with dark pigment posteriorly. Females have a light throat. The throat of the adult male is yellow. Juvenile pig frogs have 4 tan stripes on their dark, spotted body and look superficially like carpenter frogs. The webbing of the hind foot extends to the tips of all toes. Pig frogs lack dorsolateral ridges but a narrow ridge extends from the eye around the rear of the tympanum. This frog has a sharply pointed snout and a single, laterally expanded internal vocal sac.

Voice: These frogs may yelp when startled, but the typical vocalization is one or more piglike grunts.

Similar species: The bullfrog has a blunter snout and the webbing does not extend to the tip of the longest toe. Adult carpenter frogs have less extensive webbing on the hind feet. Bronze frogs have dorsolateral ridges. Florida bog frogs (found only on Florida's western panhandle) are very small and have very reduced webbing on the hind feet. River frogs have dark and light spots on the lips.

69. Pig Frog

70. River Frog

Rana heckscheri

Abundance/Range: This frog is relatively common in suitable habitat. Although they are not as common as some of the other big frogs with which they share habitat, river frogs are not rare. They occur from central Florida to southeastern Mississippi and central North Carolina.

Habitat: The river frog may be in areas of heavily vegetated still waters such as ponds and swamps, as well as along rivers. It often sits on the shore overlooking the water.

Size: Most adults are fully grown at 4–5½ inches; an occasional adult will attain 6¼ inches.

Identifying features: The gray to brownish green (never bright green) back and sides of this large frog bear darker markings. Light and dark spots are present on the lips and often on the tympanum. Dark bars are present on the hind legs. The belly is gray with light markings. The throat may be darker than the belly. Males often have a yellow(ish) suffusion on the throat. There are no dorsolateral ridges. The skin secretions are particularly noxious and of an unpleasant odor.

70. River Frog

About half of the last phalanx of the longest toe extends beyond the webbing. The vocal sac is single and internal.

Voice: The call of this species is a deep roaring snore without great carrying power. Grunting calls may also be given.

Similar species: Other similar appearing frogs, both large and small, are often decidedly green and lack strongly spotted upper lips.

Comments: Unlike most other frogs that struggle to escape, when captured the river frog goes entirely limp. The tadpoles of this frog may congregate in vast numbers.

71. Florida Bog Frog

Rana okaloosae

Abundance/Range: This uncommon frog is protected by the state of Florida. It is found only in Walton, Santa Rosa, and Okaloosa counties, in Florida's western panhandle.

Habitat: The bog frog occurs only in slowly moving waters of acidic seeps and stream backwaters.

Size: This frog is adult at about 1¾ inches in length.

Identifying features: The unspotted back and upper sides of the Florida bog frog vary from brown to yellowish green. The dorsolateral ridges are often lighter in color and extend from the back of each eye to just posterior to the sacral

71. Florida Bog Frog

hump. Females have a light throat. Males have a yellowish throat. The light venter bears dark markings (vermiculations). There may be light spots on the green jaw. The tympanum lacks a raised center. At least two phalanges of each of the four shortest toes and three phalanges of the longest toe extend beyond the webbing. The vocal sac is single and internal.

Voice: The call, given while males float in shallow water or sprawl atop floating vegetation, is a series of low-pitched single clucks with little carrying power.

Similar species: The bronze frog may be larger and has more extensive webbing on the hind feet. The center of the male bronze frog's tympanum is elevated. Both the bull and the pig frog may be much larger and neither has dorsolateral ridges.

72. Mink Frog

Rana septentrionalis

Abundance/Range: Although local, this boreal frog can be of common occurrence in suitable habitats. It ranges from Labrador to southeastern Manitoba and southward to central Minnesota and northern New England.

Habitat: This frog may be found in heavily vegetated waters such as pools, ponds, potholes, and marshy lakes and oxbows. It often floats among water lilies and emergent grasses.

Size: This small frog is adult at 2¾ inches in length.

Identifying features: This is a green frog with a busy pattern of either discrete

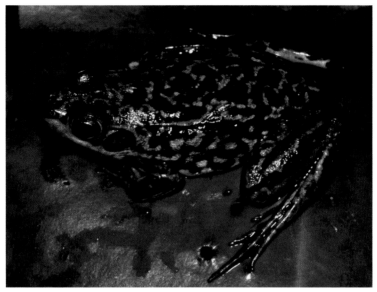

72. Mink Frog

dark spots or reticulations. The upper lip is green. The lower sides are yellowish and heavily spotted. The belly is not prominently marked. The hind limbs are spotted, not banded. The hind foot bears extensive webbing, the webs reaching the tip of the innermost toe. Dorsolateral ridges are variable, being prominent, partial, or absent. A very distinct musky odor is produced when the frog is disturbed. The bilateral vocal pouches are internal. Both body and throat swell noticeably when the frog choruses. Males (and some females) may have a yellowish throat.

Voice: The mink frog voices a rather rapidly repeated single hammering note. In the early summer, when breeding activities are in full swing, the din from a large chorus can be heard for a half-mile or more.

Similar species: Adult bullfrogs are much larger, often have a dark pattern on their posterior belly, and lack dorsolateral ridges. The green frog has prominent dorsolateral ridges but lacks the distinctive body odor of a disturbed mink frog.

Comments: Mink frogs are active both day and night. They often sit in the sun atop of, or float between, lilypads. They may occasionally sit on the bank very near the water. Their hammering calls are characteristic sounds of northern water holes.

73. Carpenter Frog

Rana virgatipes

Abundance/Range: The range of this small frog is discontinuous. It occurs in the Pine Barrens of New Jersey, on the Delmarva Peninsula in eastern inland Virginia, and then along the coastal plain from southeastern Virginia to the Okefenokee drainage of extreme northeastern Florida. It is relatively common in some areas and seemingly rare in others.

Habitat: Because its favored habitat is acidic bogs where sphagnum moss and pitcher plants abound, this frog is also called the sphagnum frog.

Size: The carpenter frog may attain an adult size of 2½ inches.

Identifying features: Four tan stripes are usually visible against the dark-spotted olive brown back and sides. There are two dorsolateral and two lateral stripes. The ground color is white below the lateral stripes and on the belly. The lower sides and belly are strongly reticulated with black. The white throat bears few dark markings. There are no dorsolateral ridges. The last half of the longest toe is devoid of webbing. Males have large, external, bilateral vocal sacs. When deflated these appear as dark folds at the angle of the jaws.

Voice: The series of two-syllabled hammering notes is loud at first but diminishes in volume toward the end.

Similar species: Bronze and green frogs have dorsolateral ridges. Bullfrogs lack dorsolateral striping. Immature pig frogs may have dorsolateral striping but the webbing of the hind foot extends to the tip of the longest toe.

Comments: Carpenter frogs often call from atop floating vegetation or from open water while stabilizing themselves on grass or a twig.

73. Carpenter Frog

WOOD FROG GROUP

This group is represented by a single small, primarily terrestrial species in our area.

74. Wood Frog

Rana sylvatica

Abundance/Range: This cold-tolerant frog ranges southward from northern Quebec to Northern Georgia and in the west from northern Alaska to northern Idaho.

Habitat: This is one of the more terrestrial of the typical frogs. Both sexes gather at the breeding ponds soon after ice-out. Their stay at the ponds is relatively abbreviated, the frogs lingering for only a week or two. They then become denizens of the woodlands, some remaining near seeps and pond edge, but others moving far from water.

Size: Wood frogs are adult at about 2¼ inches in length but occasionally attain 3¼ inches.

74. Wood Frog

Identifying features: This is a very pretty, alert, and agile frog. The ground color may be tan, buff, olive brown, or deep brown—even pinkish brown occasionally. This frog is capable of undergoing considerable color changes. A dark mask, beginning as a thin stripe on the snout, passing through the eye, and encompassing the tympanum, is present. Occasionally a wood frog from the more northerly populations has a thin light vertebral line. Dorsolateral ridges are present. The belly and throat may be immaculate white or bear some anterior dark spotting.

Voice: The calls are reminiscent of a duck's quacks, but are somewhat more musical.

Similar species: None in eastern North America.

Comments: This is a frog of humid, mixed, or coniferous woodlands, and is agile and alert. Its earthen colors allow it to blend well with the substrate of damp leaves and spruce needles in its woodland home.

GOPHER FROG GROUP

GOPHER AND CRAWFISH FROGS

The gopher and crawfish frogs are a grouping of two frog species (five subspecies) of similar appearing frogs. Collectively, these frogs are rather stocky, comparatively bigheaded and short-legged. Color changes rapidly, with darker colors predominating when conditions are wet and cold. The ground color may be so dark as to overwhelm the normally visible spots. They produce loud snoring calls and have huge bilateral vocal sacs. When not distended these sacs can be seen as folds of skin posterior to the angle of the jaw. Calls are usually produced while the male frog is floating in the water. Up to 6,000 eggs may be laid in a clutch.

The frogs of this group are associated with sand ridge and pine flatland habitats, and take their name from their habit of seeking shelter in the burrows of the gopher tortoises or crawfish. All are difficult to differentiate. Use range as a tool.

All seem to be diminishing in numbers and many populations have been extirpated.

It has recently been suggested that the federally endangered dusky gopher frog is a full species, rather than a race of *Rana capito*. You may see this frog referred to simply as *Rana sevosa* in future accounts.

75. Southern Crawfish Frog

Rana areolata areolata

Abundance/Range: The current population statistics of the southern crawfish frog are not known. It seems to have been extirpated from many areas and is thought to be uncommon. However, because it is so secretive, its numbers are difficult to assess. This frog ranges southward from southwestern Arkansas to southeastern Oklahoma, eastern Texas, and northwestern Louisiana.

Habitat: This is one of the most secretive of the true frogs. An inhabitant of pine flatwoods, prairies, meadows, and similar habitats, crawfish frogs are persistently nocturnal except when they are at the breeding ponds. They utilize abandoned crawfish burrows as well as those of small mammals. Shallow, often ephemeral, ponds heavily overgrown with emergent grasses are usually chosen for the breeding site.

Size: The southern crawfish frog can reach a snout–vent length of 3½ inches.

Identifying features: The southern crawfish frog bears a profusion of light-bordered, oval dark spots against a ground color of tan to dark gray. The spots are smallest and most irregular on the lower sides. A gray, tan, or brown dorso-

75. Southern Crawfish Frog

lateral ridge extends from each eye to a point posterior to the sacral hump. The dorsal skin is rather smooth. Some yellow *may* be present at the insertion of the forearms and in the groin. The white venter usually lacks dark markings.

Voice: Floating males produce a loud, roaring snore. This frog may also call loudly while totally submerged.

Similar species: Leopard frogs are slender, have a much sharper snout, and ground color of green, tan, or brown (or combinations of all). Pickerel frogs usually have squared dorsal spots and are bright yellow in the groin.

Comments: Following their breeding activities, southern crawfish frogs may disperse widely into areas of longleaf pine. They emerge from their burrows to forage on suitable nights. It is a wary frog that will dart into its hole at the slightest disturbance.

Additional subspecies

76. The Northern Crawfish Frog, *Rana areolata circulosa*, differs only subtly from its southern relative. It attains a somewhat larger size (to 4¼ inches), is of heavier build, and has more prominent dorsolateral ridges and a rougher dorsal skin. This subspecies occurs, in a range that is curiously serpentine, from Oklahoma to south central Iowa, western Indiana, and Arkansas. Use range as an identification tool.

76. Northern Crawfish Frog

77. Carolina Gopher Frog

Rana capito capito

Carolina
Florida
x? dusky

Abundance/Range: This frog, which is of spotty distribution and nowhere common, ranges southward from northeastern North Carolina to eastern Georgia.

Habitat: Unlike most frogs the Carolina gopher frog apparently seeks water only for breeding and then disperses into nearby turkey oak–pine woodlands. Because the gopher tortoise, the keystone species with which the gopher frogs are usually associated, is not found over much of the range of the Carolina gopher frogs, the frog utilizes other microhabitats. Stump holes, unused holes of small mammals (such as armadillos), and crawfish burrows are typical shelters.

Size: Carolina gopher frogs attain a maximum length of slightly more than 3¾ inches.

Coloration/pattern: The Carolina gopher frog has a ground color of grayish white to dark gray. Dark, well-defined, oval to round spots are present dorsally. The dorsal spots may be vaguely outlined with a lighter pigment. The lateral spots are more irregular in shape and more poorly defined. A prominent orange or yellow (males) or yellow to dark (females) dorsolateral ridge is present. A second, similarly colored, but often less prominently delineated ridge runs along the lip, above the forelimbs to about midway on each side. The skin of

77. Carolina Gopher Frog

the back and sides is roughened by many horizontally elongate, round-topped tubercles. The venter is heavily marbled with dark pigment but may be yellow in the limb axillae and groin.

Voice: Males produce a loud, roaring snore.

Similar species: Leopard frogs are often green (but may be brown), are much slenderer and have a smoother skin. Pickerel frogs have squared dorsal spots.

Additional subspecies

78. The Florida Gopher Frog, *Rana capito aesopus*, is an uncommon resident of sandy habitats from southeastern Georgia to southern Florida (not present in the Everglades–Big Cypress wetlands) and westward to the vicinity of Eglin Air Force Base in the Florida panhandle. This frog is quite similar in appearance to the Carolina gopher frog, but not as tuberculate. It is usually of a lighter ground color, and only the anterior of the belly is dark. The ground color may vary from nearly white to dark gray, rarely with purplish overtones. A prominent orange or yellow (males) or yellow to dark (females) dorsolateral ridge is present. A similarly colored ridge runs along the lip, above each forelimb to midway on each side. This frog is adult at 2–4¼ inches long.

78. Florida Gopher Frog, chorusing

79. Dusky Gopher Frog. Photo by James Harding

79. The Dusky Gopher Frog, *Rana capito sevosa*, is a federally protected species. The only known remaining population is in southern Harrison County, Mississippi. The dusky gopher frog is restricted to sandy, longleaf pine habitats. The ground color of this frog is quite dark but changeable. At its darkest the color is a very dark olive that obscures all markings. When the ground color is light the dark dorsal and lateral markings are very evident. Some examples are suffused with a brownish blush on the back and sides. The venter is quite heavily pigmented anteriorly and is sometimes entirely so. An olive to brownish yellow dorsolateral ridge is present. A ridge of similar color runs along the lip, above each forelimb to midway on each side. This frog is adult at 2–3 inches in length.

LEOPARD FROG GROUP
LEOPARD AND PICKEREL FROGS

There are four species (five subspecies) of leopard frogs in eastern North America and one pickerel frog. Its squared dorsal spots easily identify the pickerel frog, but the leopard frogs are confusingly similar and frustratingly variable. Additionally, at present, the exact range delineation of some of the species is not clearly known. In attempting identification, use *all* characteristics as well as range maps, and still be prepared to be stumped occasionally. Because they often wander far from water during the rainy season, leopard frogs are often called "meadow frogs." The males of all have large external bilateral vocal sacs that remain visible as roughened patches at the sides of the throat (or as tiny pouches) when deflated.

80. Rio Grande Leopard Frog

Rana berlandieri

Abundance/Range: This common spotted frog is found throughout western, central, and southern Texas, southern New Mexico, and northern Mexico; it has now also been introduced into some areas of southern California.

Habitat: Permanent and semipermanent waterways of all kinds, and their immediate environs, are utilized by this frog. It often sits or floats amid the emergent grasses.

Size: This leopard frog attains an adult size of 2–3¾ inches.

Identifying features: In keeping with the pallid hues of its aridland habitat, the Rio Grande leopard frog is of tan to pale green ground coloration both dorsally and laterally. The dark oval or rounded dorsal spots are often weakly outlined by a lighter hue. A light stripe is often present on the upper lip. There are usually no spots on the snout and no light central tympanal spot. The thighs bear prominent dark reticulations. The dorsolateral folds are prominent but discontinuous and noticeably inset posteriorly. The belly is white.

Voice: Like other leopard frogs, the vocalizations of the Rio Grande leopard frog are short and rapidly pulsed snores interspersed with squeaky chuckles.

Similar species: Plains leopard frogs have pale posterior thigh reticulations, their dorsal spots do not have light outlines, they have spots on the snout, and they are usually more brightly colored. The ranges of the two are not known to overlap. Southern leopard frogs have more intense ground color and a tympanal spot. The southern crawfish frog is of more robust build and not usually found in ponds except during the breeding period. The pickerel frog has squared dorsal spots.

80. Rio Grande Leopard Frog

81. Plains Leopard Frog

Rana blairi

Abundance/Range: The Plains leopard frog ranges northward from North Texas to southeastern South Dakota and the southern tip of Lake Michigan.

Habitat: This species utilizes all manner of standing water. It may sit on bare banks but often rests or floats amid emergent or water-edge grasses. This frog may wander far from permanent water sources during the rainy season.

Size: This, one of the larger leopard frogs, attains a length of up to 4 inches.

Identifying features: The frog is darkest and most strongly patterned dorsally. The back may be tan, beige, buff, or dark green. The rather rounded or oval dark dorsal spots are usually not encircled by light pigment. The upper sides are usually about the same color as the back but pale rapidly as they near the belly. The upper sides bear spots that are often only about half the size of those on the back. The spots are smaller yet on the lower sides. The dorsolateral ridges are usually interrupted and inset posteriorly. The supralabial (upper lip) stripe is well defined but may not reach the tip of the snout. There are usually one or

81. Plains Leopard Frog. Photo by Scott Cushnir

more dark spots on the snout and a light spot is present in the center of the tympanum. The belly and throat are off-white. There may be a yellowish wash in the groin and dark mottling on the throat. Poorly defined darker reticulations are usually present on the rear of the thigh.

Voice: The vocalizations usually consist of several distinct clucks.

Similar species: Rio Grande leopard frogs are paler and usually lack a tympanal spot. Southern leopard frogs have a more intense dorsal coloration and the dorsolateral ridges are usually not broken and inset posteriorly. Crawfish frogs are stout.

82. Pickerel Frog

Rana palustris

Abundance/Range: This spotted frog is rather generally distributed over the eastern half of the continent from southern Canada to the Gulf Coast. It is common in some regions and rare in others. It is absent from the deep Southeast.

Habitat: This is a frog of the grassy edges of ponds, streams, and most other waterways.

Size: As an adult, this frog is about 3½ inches long.

Identifying features: Against the light brown ground color, the large, brown, paired (rarely there may be rows of three spots) dorsal spots of the pickerel frog are quite diagnostic. Occasionally the dorsal spots may be fragmented. The upper sides are dark and strongly spotted. The dorsolateral ridges are yellowish and not bro-

82. Pickerel Frog

ken. The lower sides are light and may be unspotted. The belly is white (sometimes smudged with dark pigment) but always suffused with bright yellow or orange in the groin and on the concealed surfaces of the hind legs.

Voice: The low-pitched snore of male pickerel frogs may be produced either above or beneath the water surface. The frogs call on cool spring evenings.

Similar species: All leopard frogs and the crawfish frog have randomly scattered rounded or oval spots.

Comments: Pickerel frogs produce toxic skin secretions. Although you should wash your hands after handling any amphibian or reptile, it is a particularly good idea to do so after handling pickerel frogs.

83. Northern Leopard Frog

Rana pipiens

Abundance/Range: Common (but apparently fluctuating in several year cycles), this frog ranges from southeastern Canada to southern West Virginia and from northern Alberta to California, in either natural or introduced populations.

Habitat: It frequents the environs of streams, bogs, pond edges, seepages, stock watering tanks, and other water sources.

Size: The record size for this species is 4⅜ inches.

Identifying features: The ground color on the back and upper sides of this variable frog may be brown, green, or a combination of the two. The rounded to oval dark spots are often proportionately small but may be profuse or sparse. The spots may lack light edging. The spots are fewer and more irregular on the sides. Some spots may join, or most or all may be absent. There is no light center in the tympani. The rear limbs are usually prominently marked with light-edged, elongate dark spots. There are light spots, rather than a reticulum, on the posterior surface of the thigh. The snout is rather gently rounded. There is often a prominent light upper lip stripe, but this may be broken or virtually absent. The prominent dorsolateral ridges are light in color and neither interrupted nor medially inset posteriorly .

Voice: The principal calls are snores but these are interspersed with clucks and

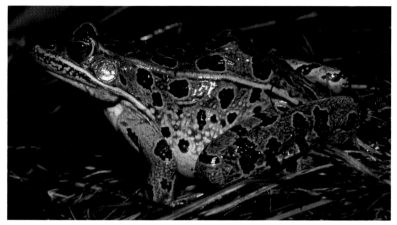

83. Northern Leopard Frog

chuckles. Northern leopard frogs call most frequently late in the winter and early in the spring.

Similar species: Use range as well as appearance when trying to identify this species. Both the Plains and the southern leopard frogs have a light spot in the center of each tympanum. The Plains and the Rio Grande leopard frog have dorsolateral ridges that are interrupted and inset posteriorly. The pickerel frog has squared or rectangular spots and yellow on the belly. The crawfish and gopher frogs are squat and stubby and have randomly scattered spots.

84a. Florida Leopard Frog

Rana sphenocephala sphenocephala

Abundance/Range: This abundant frog is found across the southern three-quarters of the Florida peninsula southward through the Florida Keys.

Habitat: This frog readily colonizes everything from backyard fish pools to brackish estuary edges. Expect to see it near ponds, lakes, ditches, and canals. It is also found along rivers and streams, marshes, and swamps.

Florida
southern

Size: The record size for this frog is 5 inches.

Coloration/pattern: On the mainland the back and upper sides may be brown, green, or a combination of both. The lower sides, belly and throat are white. Very dark (almost black) examples occur on the Florida Keys. Dark spots are

84a. Florida Leopard Frog. Top: green morph; bottom: dark Keys variant

usually large and oval and may be profuse or sparse. They are smaller and more irregularly shaped on the upper sides. A light spot is present in the center of each tympanum. The rear limbs are usually prominently marked with light-edged, elongate dark spots that may look superficially like bars. The snout is sharply pointed and the dorsolateral ridges are light in color, not broken, and are not inset posteriorly.

Voice: Chuckling clucks and squeaks that sound much like those made when rubbing your finger over an inflated, wet balloon are the sounds made by this frog.

Similar species: This is the only slender, profusely spotted frog of southern Florida. The gopher frog is squat, robust, and usually of some shade of gray.

Additional subspecies

84b. The Southern Leopard Frog, *Rana sphenocephala utricularia*, is the more northerly subspecies. Although its range is being frequently updated, the southern leopard frog ranges roughly southward from New Jersey and northern Missouri to eastern Texas and northern Florida. It differs from the Florida leopard frog only in internal anatomy (males of the Florida leopard frog have vestigial oviducts, males of the southern leopard frog do not) and in the fact that the deflated vocal sacs of the southern leopard frog are visible as folds below the angle of the jaws and not visible on the Florida leopard frog.

84b. Southern Leopard Frog

chapter 9

Burrowing Toads

Mexican Burrowing Toad, family Rhinophrynidae

Although it looks like a gigantic narrow-mouthed toad, the Mexican burrowing toad is an anatomically unique anuran.

Among other differences is the tongue structure. Unlike other anurans that flip their tongue forward to secure prey, the tongue of the burrowing toad is secured at the posterior. Its tongue is protruded, just like the tongue of a lizard or mammal.

This is a nocturnal and fossorial toad. Its breeding activities are rather well known but beyond that its natural history is enigmatic. It is not known how often, or even if, the toad emerges from its burrow to feed. It probably preys on termites and non-noxious ants. The toad seems to be able to withstand long periods (months, if not years) of drought and fasting while concealed in its burrow. By way of example, burrowing toads were documented in Texas during a heavy downpour in the mid-1980s, and then not seen at all during ten years of drought. In the late 1990s, extremely heavy rains hit and the barometric pressure dropped and stayed low. Within days, a breeding congregation of the burrowing toads appeared.

In Texas, this toad breeds between February and September. Amplexus is inguinal. The more than 1,000 weakly adhesive eggs separate and sink to the bottom of the flooded ponds and arroyos in which these toads breed. Hatching occurs within a few days. The unique-appearing tadpoles are filter feeders that bear 11 oral disc barbels of short to moderate length. They move in schools to decrease predation.

85. Mexican Burrowing Toad

Rhinophrynus dorsalis

Abundance/Range: Although a common toad in Mexico and northern Central America, the Mexican burrowing toad in southern Texas is both local and rare.
Habitat: In the Lower Rio Grande Valley, the burrowing toad

Desert Rains and Burrowing Toads

We were in South Texas, hoping for rain and hoping for burrowing toads.

Going to South Texas and hoping that it will rain is kind of like the needle in the haystack adage. If rains happen on cue it's almost a miracle. Going to South Texas hoping it will rain *and* hoping that it will rain enough to induce burrowing toads from their burrows—well, that's two miracles! After all, the torrential rains needed to activate Mexican burrowing toads, *Rhinophrynus dorsalis*, seem to happen in South Texas only once every ten to fifteen years.

It had been a long time since the toads had been seen—so long, in fact, it was thought perhaps they had been extirpated. But a strong low pressure system was wheeling its way northward from Mexico, dropping torrential rains; just the kind of rain needed to activate these black-and-strawberry anurans.

We figured the possible payoff enough reason to stay a while. During the day, we drove around and scouted out low spots that looked as if they'd flood if it rained. The sky was a bleached blue tone that echoed the dryness around us, but maybe, just maybe . . .

That noontime, as we ate in a mom-and-pop restaurant, we watched the clouds rolling in from the south. During the meal it got closer and darker, and as desserts arrived, the rains began. By the time we left the restaurant, it was pouring—really pouring.

When darkness arrived and the rains continued we thought that just perhaps we had a chance, so we hopped in the car and began driving. Roadside swales were filled and dips were awash. We found a flooded dirt road that echoed with the calls of Great Plains narrow-mouthed toads, *Gastrophryne olivacea*, and continued through the deluge. We emerged onto another paved road.

Along the shoulder the waters flowed, and a fair-sized pool had formed in a dip. As we neared the pool we heard the unmistakable calls—whoooo-OOOOP, whoooo-OOOOP! There, floating in the still-filling pool, were a half dozen burrowing frogs.

The frogs took turns, it seemed, in singing. As each one began calling, his center of gravity changed. As the vocal sacs filled with air, the head would be elevated well above the surface of the water. As the call waned, the frog's head would sink below the surface and his rump would rise. A minute later he'd redistend his vocal sacs and his rump would sink. He'd call and bob downward again. Although these fat little frogs looked nothing like birds, the action reminded me of the drinking birds you see in souvenir shops, each dipping its bill into a glass of water, rising to a vertical position and beginning again.

We watched for a few minutes, amused by the very serious attitude of the males. They'd waited a long time for this . . .

We took a few photos, climbed back into the car, and left the frogs to the important business of attracting mates.

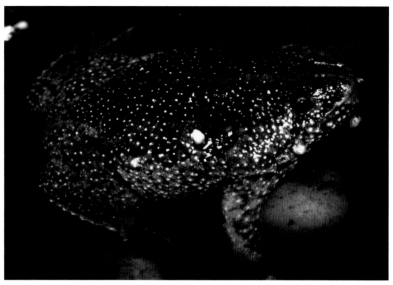

85. Mexican Burrowing Toad

occurs only in the vicinity of a few ephemeral washes, flooded depressions in pastures, and drainage canals.

Size: This anuran is adult at a length 2½–3½ inches.

Identifying features: The back and upper sides of this strange, smooth-skinned anuran are olive black to deep slate black. The dorsal markings, including the broad vertebral stripe, vary from yellowish to strawberry red. The lower sides and belly are slate blue to grayish black. The head is pointed but the nose is blunted at the tip. The eyes are small, protuberant, and have vertical pupils. This is a heavy-bodied frog with short stocky legs. A single, keratinized digging spade is on each heel.

Voice: The calls of this species are of eerie quality, and not at all what most listeners would expect from a frog. Males may call on rainy or humid nights from their burrows, but are most vocal while floating in the breeding pond. The sound made is best likened to a loud, moaning, "whoooooooop" with a rising inflection. The paired vocal sacs are internal. As they call, floating male burrowing toads change their center of gravity until the head and nose are lifted well above the water by the buoyancy of the inflated vocal sacs.

Similar species: None. The black coloration with strawberry highlights is diagnostic.

Comments: This toad inflates itself dramatically when frightened, appearing then like an oversized golf ball with legs and a nose.

chapter 10

Salamanders and Newts

Salamanders and newts are attenuate, secretive creatures than superficially re-semble lizards. As a group, salamanders are referred to as caudates (or cau-datans), meaning "with tail." They are scaleless, moist skinned, and seldom seen.

Variety, both in appearance and in lifestyles, is the name of the salamander game. A few are tiny (2 or 3 inches), most are of moderate size (3½–8 inches) and a few are huge (2–4+ feet). There are those with well-developed legs that stroll at night about woodlands in search of tiny insects. There are those that are permanent larvae. These must spend their whole lives in the water. There are some with legs so small they are useless for walking, and others that have only forelimbs. Some have huge, bushy, external gills; others are lungless. A few are cave dwellers and lack eyes! Many salamanders produce glandular toxins of some consequence to predators. This toxicity is often advertised by bright body colors. Some less toxic species seem to gain protection by mimicking the more toxic species in color.

The salamanders of eastern North America are contained in seven families. These are:

- The mole salamanders, burrowing species of the family Ambystomatidae (11 species)
- The amphiumas (also called mud-eels or ditch-eels), eel-like aquatic sala-manders of the family Amphiumidae (3 species)
- The hellbender, an aquatic salamander, family Cryptobranchidae (1 spe-cies)
- The very variable woodland, brook, and spring salamanders, all lungless, of the family Plethodontidae (89 species)
- The bushy-gilled mudpuppies and waterdogs of the family Proteidae (6 spe-cies)
- The newts, small, poisonous, and with complex life histories, family Sala-mandridae (3 species)
- The sirens, aquatic salamanders having only the two forelimbs, family Sire-nidae (5 species)

10.1. Tiger Salamander (illustration by K. P. Wray III)

Most salamanders of the East have the normal two-staged life. This consists of an aquatic larval stage and a terrestrial adult stage. However, some (including the newts) have three stages in their lives (aquatic, terrestrial, then aquatic again) and others may be always aquatic or entirely terrestrial.

Unlike the frogs, toads, and treefrogs, salamanders are virtually voiceless. Some of the aquatic forms produce clicking sounds while under water and yelping noises when they are restrained above water. But other than these seemingly rather inconsequential vocalizations, caudatans are silent. It is probable that they find each other by following scent (pheromone) trails. Some of these amphibians have a remarkable fidelity to the ponds in which they were spawned, returning to those ponds even when removed a distance away.

Mole Salamanders, family Ambystomatidae

The salamanders of this North American family are all contained in the genus *Ambystoma*. There are about thirty species. The common family name of "mole" comes from the propensity of all terrestrial members of this family to burrow. Where land conditions become untenable, neoteny—the attaining of sexual maturity while still in the aquatic larval stage—is well documented, especially among the tiger salamanders. In fact, some species, the Mexican axolotl among them, are obligate neotenes, never metamorphosing into the adult stage.

The breeding activities and larval-lives of those species in the United States and Canada are well documented. Once those ambystomatids that do metamorphose have left the breeding ponds, much about their lives is cloaked in mystery.

Ambystomatid salamanders are difficult to sex. During the breeding season, reproductively active males develop a conspicuously swollen vent. Only at that time does the external appearance of the adults reveal the sex.

Mole Salamanders, genus *Ambystoma*

Eleven species of mole salamanders occur in eastern North America. Of these only one, the tiger salamander, contains subspecies.

Mole salamanders are pond or stream breeders. The northern species are very cold tolerant and emerge from their subsurface winter lairs with the first sustained warm rains of late winter or spring. Many of the northern species complete their aquatic breeding sequences even before the ice is fully melted from the ephemeral woodland ponds chosen for breeding. Depending on species, eggs may be laid singly or in clusters of a dozen to more than 100. The streamside salamander breeds primarily in streams with limestone bottoms, but may occasionally utilize bordering pools of quiet water. Its eggs are laid singly or in small, single-layered clusters, and are placed on the underside of submerged rocks, twigs, or debris. Other species seek mud-bottomed woodland pools and attach egg clumps to submerged twigs. In the south mole salamanders are winter breeders, accessing their breeding ponds after the weather has cooled, during the passage of a wet frontal system. A very few mole salamanders, among them the marbled, flatwoods, and ringed salamanders, are autumn breeders.

10.2. Ringed Salamander (illustration by K. P. Wray III)

The Search for Spotted Salamanders

To say it was raining would be the understatement of the year, and perhaps of many years. It was pouring so hard I (RDB) could almost see those proverbial cats and dogs dropping earthward. The car had a recalcitrant defroster, and the windows were thoroughly steamed over. The temperature outside was a "warm" 38 degrees. I don't know whether it was colder or warmer inside the car, but I do know that conditions weren't particularly comfortable. Tom Tyning, Patti, and I were "salamandering"—or at least we soon would be. Translated, this could be broken into several facts: (1) it was dark, (2) it was a cold late winter night, (3) it was raining, (4) there was probably still a goodly amount of snow on the ground, and (5) we would soon don hipboots, jackets already weather dampened, and equally damp hats, then grab a flashlight, and voluntarily (*voluntarily*, mind you) leave whatever little protection the car offered to walk around a pond still forming from the run-off in hope of seeing some spotted salamanders, *Ambystoma maculatum*, newly arrived at this breeding site.

I parked and we sat in the car a few minutes longer, hoping the rain would let up just a little.

It didn't.

So out we went, into the cold night, across the busy highway, down a slope still covered with graying snow from storms long past, and onto a tree-clad flat. Old trunks lay helter-skelter tonight, tied together by newly fallen limbs. But as we made our way further away from the road, we could see that the pond was, indeed, forming. In fact, it was already a dozen yards across, and a solitary spring peeper had elected to vocalize in peeps spaced so far apart we knew that (if peepers really consider such things) he was already wondering why he had left hibernation.

It took only about two minutes before we were soaked and shivering, but the cold was forgotten when Tom called "spotted" and pointed to a six-inch salamander trudging across the snow, en route to the puddle.

Within minutes we had seen several more, all males; we knew that later that night or the next they would be joined by females.

A few nights later we again ventured to the pond. It was cold and sparkling clear. The peeper was silent. Ice still rimmed the pond that now held water three feet deep. The salamanders were still there and we could see spermatophores attached to submerged twigs and leaves. A week later the adult salamanders had left, but in their wake were hundreds of egg clumps.

It appeared that it would be another successful year for the little caudatans— and for us, as interested naturalists. The rites of yet another spring had been reenacted.

Two eastern mole salamanders, the flatwoods and the marbled salamanders, differ from the norm in reproductive methodology. These little salamanders lay eggs on land, in soon-to-be flooded situations, in the autumn months. The female marbled salamander often remains in attendance of the eggs until autumn rains actually flood the site. Female flatwoods salamanders do not attend their eggs. In the terrestrial situations, the eggs develop to a point then undergo a diapause until actual flooding of the site occurs. Should the eggs fail to be covered by water, the embryos succumb. Once hatched, the larvae develop aquatically in traditional mole salamander manner.

The diet of the terrestrial adult mole salamanders consists primarily of ground-dwelling or burrowing insects, worms, and other invertebrates. Larger species, such as the tiger salamander, may also eat small vertebrates, including other salamanders. The aquatic larvae feed on small aquatic organisms. Some species, under certain conditions, become cannibalistic. Larvae and newly metamorphosed mole salamanders are usually very unlike the adults in color and pattern.

86. Ringed Salamander

Ambystoma annulatum

Abundance/Range: This is a locally common salamander of the Ouachita-Ozark Mountains of eastern Oklahoma, northwestern Arkansas, and central Missouri.

Habitat: A very secretive salamander, the ringed salamander is most often seen crossing roadways during autumn

86. Ringed Salamander

rains. This creature of dense montane woodlands breeds in ephemeral wood-land pools.

Size: Ringed salamanders may attain an adult size of 9 inches in total length.

Identifying features: For a salamander clad only in subdued colors, this is an attractive species. It is slender, long tailed, and has a small head. The ground color of the back and upper sides is black. The limbs are well developed. Rather than actual "rings," the yellow to white markings are well-spaced bands that cross the back and extend well down onto each side. They may be broken or even absent middorsally. The dark gray lower sides and belly are spotted with white.

Similar species: Only the marbled salamander is similar in pattern and colors to the ringed salamander. However, the marbled salamander is smaller and of robust build, and its belly is plain black. Other black and white salamanders within the range of the ringed salamander are spotted, not cross-banded.

87. Streamside Salamander

Ambystoma barbouri

Abundance/Range: Common but local. The streamside salamander is found in the tristate area of Ohio, Indiana, and Kentucky. Disjunct populations occur in southern Illinois on the Kentucky state line, in western West Virginia, and in central Tennessee.

Habitat: This small-mouthed salamander look-alike is found in hardwood up-lands in the proximity of streams.

87. Streamside Salamander

Size: This robust, small-headed salamander attains a length of 6½ inches.

Identifying features: This salamander is indistinguishable in the field from the small-mouthed salamander. The dorsal coloration is black to brown, with or without blue flecking. The belly is blue gray.

Similar species: The hybrid salamanders once known as Tremblay's and silvery salamanders and the Jefferson's salamander all have proportionately larger, broader heads. Use range maps and habitat to differentiate the streamside salamander and the small-mouthed salamander (95).

88. Flatwoods Salamander

Ambystoma cingulatum

Abundance/Range: This is now a very uncommon, federally protected salamander. It ranges southward on the coastal plain from central South Carolina to North Florida and westward to Mobile Bay, Alabama. As development and natural vegetational succession alter more of the natural pine and wiregrass flatwoods, the flatwoods salamander is becoming increasingly rare.

Habitat: This species burrows in the soils of seasonally flooded pine-wiregrass flatwoods and breeds in shallow ponds and cypress heads. Flatwoods salamanders often reside in crayfish burrows.

Size: The record size for this species is only 5¹/₁₆ inches. Most adults are an inch or so smaller.

88. Flatwoods Salamander

Identifying features: The back, sides, and belly, are blackish brown to black. The pattern of the back and sides is very variable and silvery white to white. The lower sides and belly are peppered with white(ish) flecks or spots.

Similar species: Adult marbled salamanders have a proportionally larger head, and better-defined and broader dorsal crossbars than the flatwoods.

89. Jefferson's Salamander

Ambystoma jeffersonianum

Abundance/Range: Because of extensive hybridization with sympatric and adjacent species, it is difficult to define the range of this salamander. Jefferson's salamanders that seem to display no hybrid characteristics range from southern New York to Kentucky and Indiana. This is a common species.

Habitat: This burrower is a denizen of damp mixed or hardwood woodlands. It breeds in temporary woodland pools and small ponds. It may hide beneath logs, planks, rocks, or similar debris, or in the burrows of small mammals.

Jefferson
intergrade between blue-spotted and Jefferson

Size: A rather slender salamander, Jefferson's salamander commonly measures 5 or 6 inches in overall length. Occasional specimens may attain 8 inches.

Identifying features: This is a rather plain-colored, slender salamander, an im-

89. Jefferson's Salamander

Salamanders and Newts   125

89a. Blue-spotted salamander x Jefferson's Salamander, hybrid

portant consideration when making an identification. The predominant color is bluish gray to bluish brown. There may be a fine flecking of light blue markings dorsally. The light flecks are stronger and larger on the lower sides. The belly is pale. The tail is about as long as the head and body. The head is broad.

Similar species: See also Hybrids in this account. The blue-spotted salamander has much larger and usually profuse blue spots on its sides. The small-mouthed and streamside salamander both have a narrow head with a short snout. Lungless salamanders have a groove from nostril over the contour of the snout to the upper lip.

Hybrids: Hybrids between Jefferson's salamander and two other mole salamander species are well documented. At one time some of these hybrids were even afforded scientific names. The species with which Jefferson's salamander most commonly hybridizes is the blue-spotted salamander, a more northerly form. Two of the more commonly encountered hybrids:

The "silvery" variant, a triploid, all-female hybrid, tends to be less elongate than the Jefferson's salamander in appearance. Its bluish gray ground color is much like that of Jefferson's salamander but the silvery blue flecks are significantly larger and more profuse.

The Tremblay's variant is a triploid, all-female hybrid that is much like the blue-spotted parent in color and pattern, but of elongate form like Jefferson's salamander.

90. Blue-spotted Salamander

Ambystoma laterale

blue-spotted
intergrade between blue-spotted and Jefferson

Abundance/Range: This is a common salamander, but like all mole salamanders it is secretive. It ranges from Labrador and Manitoba to Michigan and Illinois.

Habitat: This boreal species is an inhabitant of hardwood and mixed woodlands. It breeds in ephemeral (sometimes permanent fish-free) ponds and roadside ditches, and springs. Although this mole salamander burrows well, it is more often found beneath ground-surface objects than many other species.

Size: This is a rather small mole salamander, up to 5½ inches, of moderate build.

Identifying features: This is a black or bluish black salamander with a liberal flecking of blue or bluish white on the dorsum. The light flecks are more prominent on the sides than on the back. The belly is almost black.

Similar species: See the accounts for the Jefferson's salamander (including its hybrids) (89) and the small-mouthed salamander (95).

90. Blue-spotted Salamander

91. Mabee's Salamander

Ambystoma mabeei

Abundance/Range: This is a fairly common mole salamander of the Atlantic coastal plain from southeastern Virginia to southeastern South Carolina.

Habitat: This is a mole salamander of sandy pineland areas. Most of its life history, including much of its breeding biology, is poorly documented. However, individuals are often found in the spring of the year beneath surface debris such as logs and trash. It breeds in ephemeral ponds.

Size: This 3–4½-inch salamander is of moderate build.

Identifying features: This is a brownish salamander that may be liberally or sparsely patterned with irregular, purplish blue to whitish spots. Lateral flecking is heavier than dorsal. The belly is grayish with lighter flecks.

Similar species: Juvenile marbled salamanders can be of very similar appearance, but have the heaviest flecking dorsally. Lungless salamanders have a groove from each nostril to the upper lip.

91. Mabee's Salamander

92. Spotted Salamander

Ambystoma maculatum

Abundance/Range: This common to abundant salamander ranges southward from central Quebec and southern Ontario to southern Louisiana.

Habitat: The spotted salamander is associated with both mixed and hardwood forests and woodlands. It breeds in ephemeral ponds and puddles.

Size: This is a heavy-bodied salamander that may occasionally attain 9½ inches in length.

Identifying features: Although variable, this is an easily identified salamander. The tan, yellow, or orange dorsolateral polka-dots are typically present. Rarely, the spots on the body may be lacking, but those on the head are usually at least weakly visible. The head spots may vary from yellow to orange. The sides lack spots and are lighter than the dark dorsum. The belly is gray.

Similar species: Except for very rare variants of Wehrle's salamander, the yellow spotted dorsolateral pattern of the spotted salamander is unique. Wehrle's salamander has a groove from the nostril, over the contour of the snout, to the upper lip.

92. Spotted Salamander

93. Marbled Salamander

Ambystoma opacum

Abundance/Range: This common to abundant salamander is found from central New England to northern Florida and westward to western Missouri and eastern Texas.

Habitat: This is a species of mixed and hardwood woodlands and hammocks. It ranges from log-strewn hillsides in the north to river floodplains in the south. Although this salamander burrows efficiently, individuals are frequently found beneath moisture-retaining trash as well as under, and occasionally in, moldering logs. They require ephemeral ponds for breeding.

Size: Marbled salamanders are adult at 3–4 inches.

Coloration/pattern: This beautiful little salamander is usually sexually dimorphic and both individually and ontogenetically variable. While the dorsal ground color of both sexes is black, the bands of the female are gray or silver and those of the male are normally white. Some or all of the cross bands may occasionally be absent, producing a partially (or fully) striped specimen. Sides and venter are unrelieved black. Marbled salamanders are short tailed, stocky, and broad headed.

Juveniles lack well-defined cross bands, instead having a busy lichenate pattern of gray on black.

Similar species: The flatwoods salamander is less precisely marked, has narrower dorsal banding, a narrow head, and a proportionately longer tail. The ringed salamander is much larger and slenderer and has a less "busy" pattern.

93. Marbled Salamander

94. Mole Salamander

Ambystoma talpoideum

Abundance/Range: This is a rather common but locally distributed salamander. It occurs in many disjunct populations from south central Virginia to northern Florida and southern Illinois to eastern Texas.

Habitat: This persistent burrower is found in pine, mixed, or hardwood woodlands. It requires ephemeral ponds for breeding.

Size: This salamander is adult at 3–4¼ inches in total length.

Identifying features: This short-bodied, short-tailed, large-headed salamander is clad in earthen tones. The back and upper sides are brown to dark grayish black. The belly and lower sides are lighter. Light flecks are present on all surfaces.

Similar species: Although other salamanders are similarly colored, the proportionately immense head and stunted appearance of the mole salamander should be diagnostic.

94. Mole Salamander, adult

95. Small-mouthed Salamander

Ambystoma texanum

Abundance/Range: This species ranges from eastern Ohio and southeastern Nebraska to Mobile Bay, Alabama, and eastern Texas. It is abundant over much of its range.

Habitat: This salamander is a resident of damp mixed or hardwood woodlands. It burrows persistently. Breeding occurs in ephemeral woodland pools, stock watering tanks, and other small bodies of quiet water.

Size: This robust salamander is 5–7 inches long when adult.

Identifying features: Northern examples of this species are often almost uniformly black to brown. Southern examples are typically sparsely to heavily flecked with light blue on the back and sides. The lower sides are usually the most profusely marked. The belly is blue gray with some lighter flecking.

Similar species: Only the streamside salamander (87) has an equally small head. Rely on the range map to separate the two.

Hybrids: All-female hybrid populations between the blue-spotted and the small-mouthed salamander are commonly found in northwestern Ohio and adjacent Michigan. The Kelly Island, Ohio, variation (no picture) is a triploid, all-female hybrid between the small-mouthed, the silvery salamander variant, and the eastern tiger salamander. This latter is a remarkable-appearing, predominantly silvery white salamander.

95. Small-mouthed Salamander

96. Eastern Tiger Salamander

Ambystoma tigrinum tigrinum

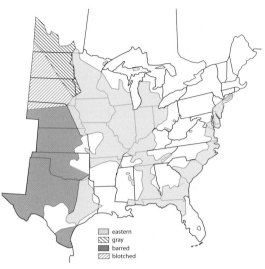

Abundance/Range: This secretive salamander may be common in some areas and rare to absent in others that look equally hospitable. This subspecies ranges southward from Long Island, New York, to northwestern Florida, then westward and northward to eastern Louisiana and southeastern Manitoba.

Habitat: This salamander often breeds in larger pools than many related species. It can be common in woodland habitats. Because of their breeding site fidelity, alteration of a single breeding pond, such as by deepening or by the introduction of predaceous fish, may extirpate an entire population of tiger salamanders. Moderately to heavily vegetated ponds are preferred. Adult tiger salamanders burrow deeply into yielding soils.

Size: This is the largest terrestrial salamander of the East. Larvae often attain a length of 6 or more inches prior to metamorphosing.

Identifying features: This is the most variably patterned of the eastern mole salamanders. The ground color is brown to almost black. The variable markings are olive green to yellow. They may be almost absent, moderately plentiful, or the dominant color. The belly is light olive to yellow with dark markings.

Similar species: The spotted salamander has rounded regularly arranged spots. Also see tiger salamander subspecies (97–99).

96. Eastern Tiger Salamander

Comments: In areas where terrestrial conditions are inhospitable, tiger salamanders may be neotenic: permanent larvae, but yet attain sexual maturity. Among other larval characteristics, these neotenes have large gills and lack eyelids. Many neotenes produce immense clutches of eggs, some having numbered more than 2,000.

The tiger salamanders are the focus of taxonomic disagreement. While some researchers now divide this group of salamanders into an eastern species (*Ambystoma tigrinum*) and a western species (*Ambystoma mavortium*), others do not even recognize subspecific differences.

Additional subspecies

97. The Gray Tiger Salamander, *Ambystoma tigrinum diaboli*, ranges southward from west central Saskatchewan and southern Manitoba to southwestern Minnesota. It is a grayish olive creature with scattered black spots or mottling. The belly is light. This race is often neotenic.

97. Gray Tiger Salamander. Top: adult; bottom: larva

98. The Barred Tiger Salamander, *Ambystoma tigrinum mavortium*, occurs in the Plains states from Nebraska to New Mexico and southern Texas. Although variable, it is a beautiful race, having broad, vertically oriented, yellow bars against a ground color of black to dark brown.

98. Barred Tiger Salamander

99. The Blotched Tiger Salamander, *Ambystoma tigrinum melanostictum*, ranges westward from eastern South Dakota to Washington and British Columbia. It is usually predominantly olive yellow with a thin reticulum of black on the back and sides.

99. Blotched Tiger Salamander

chapter 11

Amphiumas

Amphiumas, family Amphiumidae

Amphiuma is both the generic and common name for these secretive, nocturnal, burrowing, aquatic salamanders. When used in a scientific context, *Amphiuma* is capitalized; when used as a common name it is not. There are three species in the family. They vary in size from the 12-inch one-toed amphiuma to the 3½-foot two-toed amphiuma.

The two-toed and three-toed amphiumas are both common though seldom seen species. The population statistics of the one-toed amphiuma are less well known. It is probably not uncommon, but restricted to areas of soupy mud.

Amphiumas are attenuate with tiny legs. Their alternate name of "mud-eel" rather accurately describes them. They live in mud, they are mud colored, and they are eel-like in shape. These salamanders are able to move overland, but often stay put when their pond dries, burrowing far into the mud and creating a moisture-retaining cocoon in which to await the return of the water.

Fishermen believe these salamanders are poisonous and often kill those caught.

Amphiumas, genus *Amphiuma*

There are only three species contained in this family and they are found in the southeastern and south central United States.

Since female two-toed and three-toed amphiuma often lay their eggs with the advent of warm spring weather, it is assumed that they breed in the autumn or winter. They hollow out a space for their eggs in the mud beneath a log, board, matted vegetation, or other debris in shallow water. (If water levels recede, the nests may be left some distance from the water.) The beadlike string of 150 or so jelly-covered eggs is often folded into a flattened ball. The female amphiuma remains with the eggs during the several-month incubation.

Hatchlings are about 1½ inches long, and for a short time they have barely discernable external gills .

The reproductive strategy of the one-toed amphiuma is not yet known.

These are voracious, nocturnal salamanders with very strong jaws. They eat all manner of aquatic organisms, including mollusks, crustaceans, worms, insects, and small vertebrates such as fish, tadpoles, and frogs. They are very capable of biting the hand that carelessly restrains them. Handle large ones carefully.

100. Two-toed Amphiuma

Amphiuma means

Abundance/Range: This is a common but seldom seen salamander. It ranges southward from southeastern Virginia, through mainland Florida, westward to eastern Louisiana.

Habitat: The weedy shallows of lakes, ponds, streams, ditches, rivers, and canals as well as the root systems of floating plants are favored habitats of this salamander. It burrows readily into pond-bottom mud and detritus.

Size: Most two-toed amphiumas seen are 1–2 feet long but large adults may attain 3½ feet in total length.

Identifying features: The two-toed amphiuma is dark gray dorsally and light gray ventrally. The dorsal and ventral colors blend smoothly. Hatchlings are very dark. There are usually two toes on each of the four legs. The nose is rounded

100. Two-toed Amphiuma

when viewed from above but flattened in profile. The eyes are small and lidless. Vision is probably not acute. A single elliptical gill opening is present on each side of the head.

Similar species: In eastern Louisiana and southwestern Mississippi the ranges of the two-toed and the three-toed amphiumas overlap. The three-toed has three toes on each foot (but this is not always easily determined) and an abrupt change from the dark dorsal to the light ventral color.

The one-toed amphiuma is much smaller, has a more rounded head profile, only one toe on each of the four very tiny legs, and is adapted to a habitat of oozy black mud rather than open water.

All sirens have external gills throughout their lives and lack rear legs. American eels (true fish) have fins and typical gills and gill covers.

101. One-toed Amphiuma

Amphiuma pholeter

Abundance/Range: This tiny amphiuma occurs in several disjunct populations from Mobile Bay, Alabama, to Florida's Gulf Hammock area. The true population statistics of this salamander remain unknown.

Habitat: This species occurs in deep beds of soupy, organic muck. Little is known about the life history of this salamander.

Size: Adults of the one-toed amphiuma are 9–12 inches in length.

Identifying features: This amphiuma is nearly a uniform blackish brown above and only slightly lighter below. Its tiny legs are each tipped with one toe. An oval

101. One-toed Amphiuma

gill opening is present on each side of the head. The snout is rather rounded in profile when viewed from the side. The eyes are lidless.

Similar species: Other amphiumas are larger and have more than one toe on each foot. Sirens have external gills and no hind legs.

102. Three-toed Amphiuma

Amphiuma tridactylum

Abundance/Range: This is a secretive but apparently abundant salamander that ranges westward from southwestern Mississippi to eastern Texas and northward to southeastern Missouri.

Habitat: The three-toed amphiuma occurs in a very wide range of aquatic habitats, but prefers those with muddy bottoms and profuse plant growth such as the bayous and sloughs that freckle its range.

Size: This attenuate salamander may occasionally attain 3½ feet in length. Most are considerably smaller.

Identifying features: The three-toed amphiuma is brown to brownish gray dorsally and light gray below. The colors are clearly separated. The chin and throat are dark. The snout is flattened and the eyes are lidless. There are usually three toes on each of the four tiny legs.

Similar species: Except in southeastern Louisiana and adjacent Mississippi where its range overlaps that of the two-toed amphiuma, there are no similar appearing attenuate salamanders with four legs. See also species accounts 100 and 101.

102. Three-toed Amphiuma

chapter 12

Hellbenders

Giant Salamanders, family Cryptobranchidae

This is a small family of large salamanders. Of the three species, two, both of Asia, attain a heavy-bodied adult length of 4 feet or longer. The third member of the family is the hellbender of America. This 2–2½-foot salamander dwells in nonpolluted eastern and Ozark rivers. Prone to stealing bait from fishermen who think them venomous, the hellbenders are either killed or simply cut free, hook intact, when they are caught.

Hellbenders are flattened creatures that look like a size 8 salamander in a size 10 skin. They have wrinkly lateral folds, tiny lidless eyes, short but fully functional legs, and a flattened oarlike tail. Once common, they are now reduced in numbers and protected in most areas where they are still found. These salamanders eat small fish and their eggs, tadpoles, crayfish, worms, mollusks, and insects. Although active year around, they are most often encountered in the winter and early spring months.

Hellbenders breed in the late summer and autumn. Oviposition may vary depending on latitude and population and may occur from late in the summer until winter. The incubation duration is somewhat longer than two months. Females lay their long strings of eggs (often described as "rosary beads") in a nesting depression created by the male. The nest is excavated beneath a rock or other submerged debris with the opening on the downstream side. Fertilization is external.

103. Eastern Hellbender

Cryptobranchus alleganiensis alleganiensis

Abundance/Range: Hellbenders are historically found from southern central New York to northern Georgia and central eastern Missouri. This big salamander is now quite uncommon or extirpated over much of its range. Populations do seem to remain steady where rivers remain nonchannelized and clean.

eastern
Ozark

103. Eastern Hellbender

Habitat: This huge salamander is a denizen of pools between rapids in fairly large, rocky-bottomed streams and rivers.

Size: Although it occasionally exceeds two feet in length, most hellbenders are 12–18 inches long.

Identifying features: At any size, this is an unmistakable salamander. The head and body are flattened, the tail is vertically compressed and finned. Larvae have external gills, adults do not. The ground color, both above and below, is muddy gray, brown, or buff. There are a variable number of dark spots. There are flanges of loose skin along each side.

Similar species: None.

Additional subspecies

104. The Ozark Hellbender, *Cryptobranchus alleganiensis bishopi*, the smaller race has a record size of 22⅜ inches. It is quite similar to the eastern hellbender in appearance, but has large blotches rather than spots on its back. Its chin is heavily pigmented with black. This subspecies of southeastern Missouri and northeastern Arkansas is now quite rare.

104. Ozark Hellbender. Photo by R. Wayne Van Devender

chapter 13

Lungless Salamanders

Lungless Salamanders, family Plethodontidae

This is a large and diverse family of salamanders that is very well represented in eastern North America, but is also distributed in our West, in tropical America, and in Europe. The family Plethodontidae includes not only the typical wood-land salamanders, but also brook, cave, red, spring, dusky, climbing, and other salamanders.

All members of this family lack lungs. Oxygen and carbon dioxide transfer occurs through the moist skin and mucous membranes. The keyword is, of course, moist. Unless the skin is moist, plethodontids cannot respire and will quickly die.

Reproductive strategies and lifestyles vary tremendously. Some plethodon-tids are fully aquatic while others shun standing water entirely (but are active terrestrially on dewy or rainy nights). Although none are large, some are can-nibalistic predators. Of the aquatic species, many are quite typical in appearance and lifestyles. Others are paedomorphic (permanent larvae with large external gills) and live in the perpetual darkness of caves or subterranean aquifers. Oth-ers, closely related to the cave forms, live beneath shaded stream-edge rocks in otherwise sunny mountain brooks and may sit on stream banks or midstream rocks after darkness has fallen.

A great many of these salamanders are efficient and persistent burrowers, or at least seek shelter by day beneath logs, rocks, or leaf litter. Preferred habitats for the plethodontids as a whole run the gamut from stream to cave to verdant woodlands.

Like other salamanders, plethodontids are primarily nocturnal, but may be surface active on overcast, rainy afternoons. Some climb quite well and on wet nights may be found from one to several feet above the ground on tree trunks or herbaceous plants. All eat insects, worms, and other tiny invertebrates. Some of the larger ones add variety in the form of small vertebrates (including other salamanders) to their diet.

Some plethodontid salamanders produce glandular toxins that repel at least casual predators. Bright colors serve in most cases to advertise the salamander's unpalatability. Some entirely harmless species have evolved colors and patterns that mimic the toxic forms, thus also repelling color-conscious predators.

Plethodontids are characterized by a nasolabial groove that extends downward from the nostril to the lip. In males of some species the grooves extend below the lip on downward projections called nasal cirri.

Their reproductive strategies are variable (and in many species, mostly or entirely unknown). Courtship can be lengthy and complex. The male may stimulate the female by nudging, and/or by emitting secretions from his mental (chin) gland. The male transfers the secretions by rubbing or slapping the snout of the female with his chin or by dragging his chin gland and teeth along her nape and shoulder area. Following stimulation, a female closely trails the male, and straddles his tail with her forelegs. The male responds, at the culmination of the tail-straddling walk, by depositing a spermatophore. The female leaves the male and uses her cloacal labia to pick up the spermcap from the top of the spermatophore. Egg-laying follows.

Plethodontids fall into two subfamilies, the Desmognathinae (hindlimbs about twice the thickness of the forelimbs), and the Plethodontinae (all four limbs of about equal thickness).

Dusky and Related Salamanders, subfamily Desmognathinae

Named for the duskiness of their color, the dusky salamanders are a group of small to moderate-sized salamanders, 2–10 inches long, that are very secretive. Many dwell along brooks, creeks, and small rivers where they hide beneath rocks or in water-edge burrows. Most of these have vertically flattened tails, teardrop shaped in cross-section. Others are woodland dwellers, and may be found beneath logs and rocks or behind the bark on well-shaded, still standing, but long dead trees. These forms usually have tails that are round in cross-section.

Although many of these salamanders are confusingly similar and can be very difficult to identify to species, all are easily placed in this subfamily by comparing the girth of their hindlegs with that of their forelegs. The hindlegs are about twice the thickness of the forelimbs.

Dusky salamanders feed on all types of small invertebrates, but some of these salamanders are large enough to also eat small vertebrates, most notably other salamanders. Duskies, as they are called, are most active on rainy or foggy evenings and especially so during the passage of barometric pressure–dropping frontal systems.

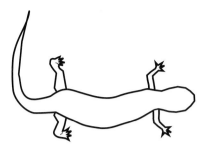 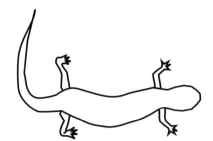

13.1. Chunky hind legs, typical of dusky   13.2. Slender hind legs of woodland
salamanders (illustration by Patricia Bartlett)   salamander (illustration by Patricia Bartlett)

Black-bellied Salamanders, Abundant but Elusive

It was the second week of November and Patti and I were on a little creek in Habersham County, Georgia, looking for the elusive black-bellied salamander, *Desmognathus quadramaculatus.*

"Elusive"? Black-bellies elusive? Actually this big, highly aquatic salamander is not only of wide distribution but abundant as well. Yet, for me at least, finding one had proven to be a real challenge. I had looked for them by both day and night in every clean creek of moderate size in the Blue Ridge and Smoky Mountains but had not been able to find one in a photographable position. I had given up on the thought of *in situ* photography. Now I just wanted to photograph a black-bellied salamander—anywhere!

It had been raining for several hours before we arrived, and the run-off had transformed the creek we sought into a silted mini river, cascading over rocks, logs, and in some areas, its very banks.

It was rapidly turning colder and darkness was closing in. The rain showed no signs of abating as we clambered down into the wooded ravine to the banks of the creek. We were sodden, and well chilled, long before we reached the bottom.

Within minutes we had found slimy salamanders, *Plethodon glutinosus,* Blue Ridge two-lined salamanders, *Eurycea wilderae,* and spotted duskies, *Desmognathus conanti,* in abundance. We even found one dark-phased zigzag salamander, *Plethodon dorsalis,* but no black-bellies.

We moved to the banks of the creek. I turned half a dozen ideal-looking logs. Nothing. Patti walked over to the next log in line, turned it, reached down, and picked up a good-sized black-belly. I still hadn't found one.

Since I'm reluctant to take my electronically metered cameras out into the rain, we put the black-belly in the small bag that already held a gravid two-lined, the zigzag, and a spotted dusky salamander, and I trekked back to the car to take the photos (the salamanders would all be brought back here and released before we left). I was rather thinking that by the time I had reached the car, only the very predaceous black-belly (considerably fatter) would be left in the bag. With this in mind I stuffed the bag full of wet leaves and debris, hoping to better protect the "small fry" from the black-belly, retied it, hooked it over my belt, and set off.

Upon reaching the car, I set up my stage, added a little "furniture," and pulled the bag from beneath my belt. Whoops. The knot had come out.

Since I'd be needing to get into it within moments, I merely folded the top over a couple of times, not bothering to retie it. I unlocked the rest of the car, dug the camera out, and checked it over . . . ready.

About this time Patti, dripping wet, came struggling up the incline to the car, telling me of the "Sumo" black-belly she had seen after I left.

"Did you pick it up?"

"No. Why? You already have one. How many does it take to make a photo?"

Good point. Why, indeed, pick the second one up? I unfolded the bag to find the two-lined sitting right at the top. Good. It was the prettiest so we'd photo it first.

Pose. Snap. Flash. Re-pose. Snap. Flash. Again and again. Done.

Sorting through the debris in the bag, I next found the zigzag. Same sequence.

Next came the slimy (the biggest one I had ever seen, by the way). Pose. Snap. Flash . . .

Then I found the spotted dusky.

Again my strobes flashed . . . once, twice, thrice . . . a half-dozen shots were taken.

Now for the black-belly. That was the one I really wanted.

I rummaged again through the leaves in the bag. Hmmm. More rummaging. Nothing.

I began taking leaves out of the bag . . . carefully, one at a time. I turned each leaf over, just in case I might find a six-inch salamander clinging tightly to the underside of a three-inch maple leaf.

Nothing.

There was no black-bellied salamander in the bag. It must have escaped through the poorly tied knot while I was slogging back to the car.

Now, though, I could answer both of Patti's questions: how many black-bellies it took to make a picture (obviously more than one) and why she should have picked up that second specimen (to cover for my goof).

Well, we'd go back to the creek and try again.

We did. No black-bellies.

We waited until darkness was full upon us and the cold rain falling in torrents and tried again. No black-bellies.

The next spring I was back at that creek and saw so many black-bellied salamanders that I actually tired of finding them. Timing, it seems, is everything.

Dusky Salamanders, genus *Desmognathus*

As a group, the dusky salamanders vary in size from the 2-inch pygmy sala-mander of Appalachian spruce forests to the 8-inch black-bellied salamander of Appalachian streams. Seldom seen by day unless accidentally uncovered, dusky salamanders emerge at night from hiding and forage on the woodland floor or among stream edge rocks. Some species readily climb ferns and other low woodland plants, and seem especially apt to do so on foggy or rainy nights. Courtship is aggressive, with the male biting and abrading the skin of the fe-male. Eggs are usually deposited in the spring. Some species breed terrestrially while others lay their clutches in seepage or at stream edge. Wet mosses and leaf packs are typical deposition sites. The female often attends the clutch. Some species undergo much (if not all) of the development in the egg capsule. The hatchlings may have gill-nubbins for a few days but often do not. The larvae of other dusky salamanders are typically aquatic.

SEEPAGE AND PYGMY SALAMANDERS

105. Seepage Salamander

Desmognathus aeneus

Abundance/Range: This was once a very common sala-mander, and may still be, but it does seem harder to find now in certain portions of its range. It ranges southwest-ward from southwestern North Carolina and adjacent

105. Seepage Salamander

Tennessee to central Alabama. An isolated population is found in western Alabama.

Habitat: This is a salamander of matted leaf litter and other forest debris in the proximity of small streams, of springs and seepages in cool wooded ravines, and of slopes and gorges.

Size: The seepage salamander tops out at a slender 2¼ inches in length.

Identifying features: The back of this small, brownish tan or reddish salamander is lighter than the sides. The delineation between the two colors is in the form of a well-defined and almost straight, narrow dark line. A Y-shaped marking is on the back of the head and the skin of the head is smooth. The venter is off-white, often with darker reticulations. The tail is round in cross-section. There are 13 or 14 costal grooves.

Similar species: Except in southwestern North Carolina, where the ranges of the seepage and the pygmy salamander overlap, all other sympatric dusky salamanders are larger when adult than adult seepage salamanders. The pygmy salamander has roughened skin atop its head and a distinct herringbone pattern on its dorsum. The various mountain dusky salamanders usually have a distinct dorsal pattern.

106. Pygmy Salamander

Desmognathus wrighti

Abundance/Range: This is a common salamander. It is found from extreme southern Virginia to southwestern North Carolina.

Habitat: This tiny salamander avails itself of all manner of hiding materials, from fallen leaves to spruce limbs and loosened

106. Pygmy Salamander

bark on still standing dead trees. It is a terrestrial species found in high elevations.

Size: This, the smallest species of the genus, is adult at 2 inches in length.

Identifying features: The pygmy salamander has a reddish back. There is usually a pronounced herringbone pattern from the shoulders to the tail-base. The upper sides may be of the same reddish color as the back, or may be a darker brown. The lower sides are somewhat lighter. The belly is an unpatterned off-white. The skin on the top of the head is roughened. The tail is round in cross-section. There are 13 or 14 costal grooves.

Similar species: The rather similar seepage salamander has smooth skin on the top of the head and often does not have a distinct dorsal herringbone pattern. The various mountain dusky salamanders usually have a distinct dorsal pattern.

MOUNTAIN DUSKY SALAMANDERS

107. Apalachicola Dusky Salamander

Desmognathus apalachicolae

Abundance/Range: This common dusky salamander occurs in two disjunct ranges. One population is found in Florida on the central panhandle and in adjacent Georgia; the second straddles the state lines in southern Alabama and Georgia.

Habitat: This salamander occurs along ravine-streams and associated seepages and sphagnum bogs.

Size: This rather slender dusky salamander is adult at 4 inches in total length.

Identifying features: Old examples of the Apalachicola dusky salamander are

107. Apalachicola Dusky Salamander

often a nearly unicolored mud brown. Young examples may bear prominent, dark-outlined spots that may coalesce into stripes. The belly is usually white, but may show traces of dark pigment. The tail is round in cross-section except at its tip where it is attenuated and compressed. There are 14 costal grooves.

Similar species: Duskies are among the most difficult of the salamanders to identify to species. Rely on range as your primary identification tool. The various mountain dusky salamanders are more northerly in distribution. The southern dusky salamander may have a row of light spots (often referred to as portholes) along its lower sides and has a dark venter. The belly of the spotted dusky salamander is light but prominently flecked with black. Both the southern and the spotted dusky salamanders have laterally compressed tails.

108a. Allegheny Mountain Dusky Salamander

Desmognathus ochrophaeus

Abundance/Range: This is the most northerly species of this complex. It ranges southward from extreme southern Quebec, Canada, and northeastern Ohio through the West Virginia highlands to south central Tennessee.

Habitat: This is a species of densely wooded montane habitats. It is found beneath rocks and logs on the forest floor, as well as in fissured, damp rock cuts and in the vicinity of springs, roadside seeps, and streams.

Size: The adult size of this salamander (and of others in this group) is 3½–4 inches.

Identifying features: This is a very variable salamander. Variations may be ontogenetic, geographic, and individ-

108a. Allegheny Mountain Dusky Salamander

ual. The snout of newly metamorphosed salamanders is bluntly rounded. That of adults is longer.

Sides are dark, the dorsum is lighter, and the belly is variable (light in young individuals, darkening with age). The dorsal pattern may be tan, orange, gray, olive, or coral and straight edged (usually) or scalloped (more uncommon). This salamander becomes darker with advancing age. Very old examples may be an unrelieved dark gray to grayish black. The tail is rounded in cross-section. All members of this species complex have 14 costal grooves.

Comments: Because the salamanders of this complex are so variable, figures 108a–108f should be considered only a guide and not definitive of the appearance of species in general.

Similar species: This and the following five species of dusky salamanders have broadly overlapping external characteristics. They are best identified by range and cellular (molecular) data. The look-alike species are *Desmognathus abditus, D. carolinensis, D. imitator, D. ochrophaeus, D. ocoee,* and *D. orestes.*

108b. The Cumberland Dusky Salamander, *Desmognathus abditus,* was described in late 2003. It is restricted in distribution to the eastern Cumberland Plateau. It is reminiscent of, but somewhat intermediate in appearance between, the Ocoee and the Allegheny Mountain dusky salamanders. The edges of the dorsal pattern are usually scalloped.

108b. Cumberland Dusky Salamander. Photo by Matthew Niemiller

108c. The Carolina Mountain Dusky Salamander, *Desmognathus carolinensis*, occurs only in central western North Carolina and adjacent Tennessee where it is common. This, too, is a very variable salamander. The dorsum is usually lighter than the sides. The belly darkens with age. The dorsal pattern may brown to orange or olive and usually has scalloped edges.

108c. Carolina Mountain Dusky Salamander

108d. The range of the Imitator Salamander, *Desmognathus imitator*, is virtually identical to the range of the Carolina mountain dusky salamander. In most of its color patterns it is identifiable only by DNA analysis. However one pattern, a red- (or yellow) cheeked mimic of the Smoky Mountain red-cheeked salamander, is peculiar only to *D. imitator*.

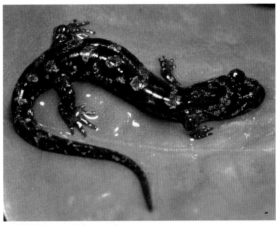

108d. Imitator Salamander

108d. Imitator Salamander

108e. Ocoee Salamander, *Desmognathus ocoee*, occurs in two disjunct populations. One involves southwestern North Carolina and adjacent Tennessee, South Carolina, and Georgia. The second population is found in extreme northeastern Alabama and immediately adjacent Georgia. The dorsal pattern fades with advancing age and often has scalloped edges.

108e. Ocoee Salamander

108f. Blue Ridge Dusky Salamander, *Desmognathus orestes*, is found in southwestern Virginia and adjacent northeastern Tennessee and northwestern North Carolina. This is often a very brightly colored salamander with a straight-sided back stripe of red or orange. Many examples are duller and may have scalloped edges to the dorsal stripe.

108f. Blue Ridge Dusky Salamander

DUSKY SALAMANDER GROUP

109. Southern Dusky Salamander
Desmognathus auriculatus

Abundance/Range: Although unknown phe-
nomena have extirpated this salamander over
large sections of its range, it is now making
reappearances in some areas where it has not
been seen for decades. This salamander ranges southward from southeastern
Virginia to central Florida and then westward to eastern Texas.

Habitat: This salamander occurs in and along quiet standing waters. It utilizes
all manner of moisture-holding ground-surface cover as hiding areas.

Size: The record size for this rather robust dusky salamander is 6⅜ inches.

Coloration/pattern: Two color phases are known. Typically the back and sides
of this salamander are brown to almost black but some may have a light back
and brown to brownish red dorsal area. Both phases have a white-spotted dark
belly. Younger examples usually have 1 or 2 irregular rows of small whitish,
cream, or orangish spots ("portholes") on each lower side. The upper edge of
the tail may be brown, orangish, or buff. The tail is teardrop shaped in cross-
section near the body and more strongly compressed distally. There are usually
14 costal grooves.

Similar species: The tail of the Apalachicola dusky salamander is round in cross
section. The spotted dusky salamander lacks small, light round spots (portholes)
on its sides and tends to be more colorful dorsally. Northern dusky salamanders
have few if any body markings and choose moving rather than standing water
habitats.

109. Southern Dusky Salamander

110a. Northern Dusky Salamander

Desmognathus fuscus

Abundance/Range: The northern dusky salamander can be abundant in some areas. It ranges southward from southern New Brunswick to extreme northern South Carolina.

Habitat: This dusky salamander utilizes a broad spectrum of wet habitats. It occurs along small streams, in seepages, and near springs. It is often found beneath rocks and logs at the base of wet cliffs, along ravines, and in the splash zones of waterfalls.

northern
spotted
Santeetlah

Size: This is a rather robust salamander with an adult length of 5 inches.

Identifying features: This salamander has a ground color of brown to olive tan, with irregular dark dorsal markings. Irregular dark dorsolateral lines may be present. The upper sides are colored like the back. The lower sides are lighter. The belly is white(ish) but may be lightly peppered with dark specks. The tail is teardrop shaped in cross-section. There are 14 costal grooves.

Similar species: The tail of the various sympatric mountain dusky salamanders is round in cross-section. Mountain duskies are also often more brightly col-

110a. Northern Dusky Salamander

ored. The seal salamander often has dark dorsal spots. The black-bellied salamanders have a black belly (when adult).

110b. The Spotted Dusky
Salamander, *Desmognathus
conanti*, is very similar in
appearance to the northern
dusky salamander, but usually more colorful. It has a
ground color of brown to
olive tan, with dark-edged
irregularly paired brighter
buff to dull golden or orangish dorsal spots. The belly
is white(ish) but variably
patterned with light and/

110b. Spotted Dusky Salamander

or dark pepperings. There are 14 costal grooves. It is adult at 4½ inches in
length. A common salamander, this species ranges from southernmost Illinois to Louisiana and the western Florida panhandle. This species is still considered a subspecies of the northern dusky salamander by some authorities.

110c. The Santeetlah Dusky Salamander, *Desmognathus santeetlah*, is a common high-altitude dusky salamander of central western North Carolina and
adjacent Tennessee. It is a very dark-colored dusky salamander. The dorsal color
is often an unrelieved greenish brown. The lower sides and belly are yellowish
with dark mottling or flecking. There is a row of light "portholes" on each lower
side. There are 14 costal grooves. This salamander attains an adult length of 4
inches. It is considered a subspecies of the northern dusky salamander by some
authorities.

110c. Santeetlah Dusky Salamander

111. Ouachita Dusky Salamander

Desmognathus brimleyorum

Abundance/Range: This, the westernmost of the ge-
nus, is a big, relatively common dusky salamander. It
occurs in the Ouachita Mountains of Oklahoma and
Arkansas.
Habitat: This is a very aquatic salamander. It is found
in and along streams and brooks, and beneath rocks and logs.
Size: A large adult may near 7 inches in length.
Coloration/pattern: Ouachita dusky salamanders darken with advancing age.
Many lack contrasting markings both dorsally and ventrally. The belly is light-
er than the back. The dorsum of young adults is often mottled buff and olive
brown. There are 14 costal grooves.
Similar species: None within the range of the Ouachita dusky salamander.
Comments: This is a very aquatic salamander. Adults will readily eat smaller
salamanders.

111. Ouachita Dusky Salamander

112. Black Mountain Dusky Salamander

Desmognathus welteri

Abundance/Range: This is a fairly common dusky salamander of the Cumberland Plateau and Cumberland Mountains of eastern Kentucky, central Tennessee, and extreme western Virginia.

Habitat: Expect to find this dusky salamander at stream edge, in seepages, and near springs.

Size: This is a robust salamander that attains an adult length of 6¾ inches.

Identifying features: This salamander has a ground color of brown to olive tan, with irregular dark dorsal markings. The toetips are dark and horny. The upper sides are colored like the back. The lower sides are lighter. The belly is whitish to pale yellow but may be lightly peppered with dark specks. The tail is oval near the base but strongly compressed distally. There are 14 costal grooves.

Similar species: The northern dusky salamander can be of very similar appearance, but it lacks the darkened, horny toetips. The seal salamander often has dark dorsal spots and a strongly delineated light ventral coloration.

112. Black Mountain Dusky Salamander

113. Shovel-nosed Salamander

Demognathus marmoratus

Abundance/Range: This very aquatic salamander ranges southward from southwestern Virginia to extreme northeastern Georgia. A disjunct population occurs in south central Virginia. This salamander is quite common but of localized distribution.

Habitat: Shovel-nosed salamanders prefer the moving waters of streams and small rivers, seeking shelter beneath rocks and submerged logs and in burrows in the bank.

113. Shovel-nosed Salamander

Size: This salamander attains a length of about 5¾ inches.

Identifying features: The dorsum of adults varies from almost black with no visible pattern to lighter brown with yellow or gray blotches or a double row of light spots. The sides are the same color and pattern as the back. The belly of young salamanders is light; that of mature salamanders remains light in the center and darkens along the outer edges. The tail is teardrop shaped in cross-section, but very narrow and strongly keeled above. There are 14 costal grooves.

Similar species: This is another of the many confusing dusky salamanders that are so difficult to identify. The internal nares (almost impossible to see on live specimens) are narrow and slitlike on this species, but are round openings in other members of the genus. Eliminate species from consideration by checking range maps.

114. Seal Salamander

Desmognathus monticola

Abundance/Range: The seal salamander ranges widely in the Appalachians. Disjunct populations are in southern Alabama and northwest Florida. It is moderately common in some areas and a rarity in others.

Habitat: A salamander of the mountain streams in the north and in the south from cool, ravine streams.

114. Seal Salamander

Size: This salamander is largest in the Appalachians and smallest in the Deep South. The record size is 6 inches.

Identifying features: The back and upper sides of young examples are olive to olive brown with a variable number of discrete darker spots or mottlings. The lower sides are olive gray and may bear lighter flecks. The light gray belly is usually unspotted. Adults are usually darker and more unicolored than young examples. The tail is very sharply keeled above. There are 14 costal grooves.

Similar species: Other species in this genus have flecks on the belly or a black belly.

BLACK-BELLIED SALAMANDERS

115a. Common Black-bellied Salamander

Desmognathus quadramaculatus

Abundance/Range: This is a commonly encountered sala-mander of Appalachia. It is found from southern West Virginia to northern Georgia.

Habitat: This semiaquatic salamander inhabits high-altitude rocky streams.

Size: This, the largest species in the genus, tops out at about 8¼ inches in length.

Identifying features: This salamander is mottled dorsally with shades of brown. The sides are dark and there are two rows of lateral-line "portholes." The belly of adults is black. The belly of young examples is white to gray. Tiny light flecks are present on both the back and sides. The chin is gray. The tail is sharply keeled and there is usually a reddish line on the upper tail surface. There are 14 costal grooves.

115a. Common Black-bellied Salamander

Similar species: The dwarf black-bellied salamander, *D. folkertsi* (115b), is only half as large and much darker, lacks the red stripe on the top of the tail, and is thought to be restricted in distribution to northeastern Georgia.

Comments: This species feeds voraciously on smaller stream-dwelling salamanders, including the dwarf black-bellied salamander.

115b. The Dwarf Black-bellied Salamander, *Desmognathus folkertsi*, was described in 2002. It is common but thought to be restricted in distribution to the Nottely River watershed in Union County in northeastern Georgia. It is adult at 4½ inches or less in length. This very dark salamander displays two dorsal patterns. One is very dark brown with mottlings of black, the other is brown with alternating black blotches. Tiny brass-colored flecks are present on both the back and sides. The belly is black. The chin may be either black or gray. The

115b. Dwarf Black-bellied Salamander

distal third of the tail is gray beneath. Two rows of tiny light spots indicate the lateral lines. The uppermost row converges beneath the chin (this is diagnostic of the species), and the lowermost ends on the chest by the forearms. There is no reddish line on the tail surface. There are 14 costal grooves.

Red Hills Salamander, genus *Phaeognathus*

This monotypic genus contains the most divergent of the desmognathine sala-manders. It is an endangered burrower. At 10 inches, this is the largest species in the subfamily. This attenuate creature eats insects, snails, mites, and sowbugs. Captives eat worms. Eggs, which number only 5–16, are suspended like beads, each from a gelatinous stalk in the burrow of the female.

116. Red Hills Salamander

Phaeognathus hubrichti

Abundance/Range: Although locally distributed within its small range, this federally endangered salamander continues to exist in fair numbers. It is found only in the Red Hills formations of south central Alabama.

Habitat: This salamander requires north-facing wooded ravine slopes having a substrate of claystone overlain with loam. The salamanders burrow persistently.

Size: The record size for this very attenuate, short-legged salamander is $10^{1}/_{16}$ inches long.

116. Red Hills Salamander

Identifying features: This salamander has a ground color of dark brown, both above and below, and no highlighting colors. The soles of the feet and the chin are a somewhat lighter brown. The tail is round in cross-section. There are 14 costal grooves.

Similar species: None.

Comments: This salamander may be seen at night (and sometimes on overcast days) sitting with head and shoulders protruding from its burrow, but it withdraws with alacrity if disturbed. The tail is quite strongly prehensile and probably facilitates movement in the burrow.

Plethdontinae
All other Eastern and Central Lungless Salamanders

Brook Salamanders, genus *Eurycea*

The genus *Eurycea* is restricted in distribution to eastern North America. The twenty-five species range in size from about 3 inches to about 8 inches. Although referred to as brook salamanders, many are cave and grotto dwellers and some wander seasonally far from brooks into woodlands. Among these salamanders are many that lead a normal lifestyle—or at least a lifestyle *we* think of as normal for a salamander: egg, larval, and adult stages. Others, though, lead a diverse lifestyle as aquatic paedomorphs—salamanders that retain larval characteristics throughout their lives. These latter are discussed in accounts 127–140.

Like most salamanders the members of this genus are primarily nocturnal, but may be active during the hours of daylight on overcast or rainy days. Those species living in caves may be active at any time of day or night.

Breeding in those species for which it has been documented occurs from autumn into spring. From a dozen to 100 eggs may be laid. Some species attach their eggs to the underside of stable, submerged debris such as stones or boards. Others deposit the eggs in submerged leafpacks or amid floating plants. Communal nesting has been documented. The female remains in attendance of her clutch and the larvae are aquatic.

Reproductively active males of most species develop nasal cirri.

Nonpaedomorphic Brook Salamanders of the genus *Eurycea*

TWO-LINED SALAMANDERS

117a. Northern Two-lined Salamander

Eurycea bislineata

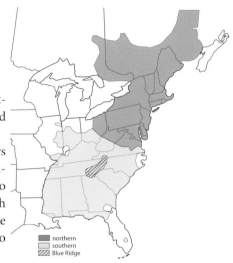

Abundance/Range: This predominantly aquatic salamander is found from Labrador and northeastern Ontario to central Virginia.

Habitat: The two-lined salamander occurs along streams, seepages, and springs throughout its range and is often found well out into damp woodlands. It is often found beneath rocks, logs, and man-made debris. The larvae are common in beds of leaves in shallow to moderately deep streams and in springs.

northern
southern
Blue Ridge

Size: Although this species may attain a length of 4¾ inches, it is often an inch or so smaller and its slenderness makes it look smaller yet.

Identifying features: This is an attractive but variable salamander. The buff to yellow-tan back is separated from the yellow belly by an even-edged brown stripe bordered above by a fine black line. The dark line runs from the eye to the tailtip. There are 5 toes on each hind foot. Males have well-developed nasal cirri. There are 15–16 costal grooves.

Similar species: The southern two-lined salamander is very similar, but has only 14 costal grooves.

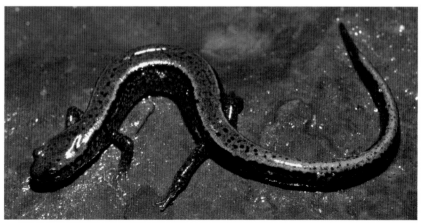

117a. Northern Two-lined Salamander

117b. Southern Two-lined Salamander

117b. The Southern Two-lined Salamander, *Eurycea cirrigera*, ranges south-ward from central Ohio to the Gulf Coast. It is replaced in the Great Smoky Mountains by the Blue Ridge two-lined salamander. The Southern two-lined is variable and can be difficult to differentiate from both the northern and the Blue Ridge two-lined salamanders. The dorsal color may be brown, grayish tan, buff, or a very bright orange. The lateral color may be the same as or paler than the dorsum. A black dorsolateral stripe extending from eye to tailtip is present. Vestiges of a dark vertebral stripe may be present. There are 5 toes on each hind foot. Males have well-developed nasal cirri. There are 14 costal grooves.

The salamander once known as the brown-backed salamander, formerly designated *Eurycea aquatica*, has now been synonymized with the southern two-lined salamander. It is a dark, short-tailed morph.

117c. The Blue Ridge Two-lined Salamander, *Eurycea wilderae*, is found in the mountains from extreme southwestern Virginia, southward along the entire North Carolina–Tennessee border to northeastern Georgia. It is adult at 4¾ inches in length. This is often a very brightly colored salamander. The dorsal color may vary from buff to tan but is often a very bright orange. The lateral color is often

117c. Blue Ridge Two-lined Salamander

the same as that of the dorsum but may be brighter. A black dorsolateral stripe is present on each side. These usually extend from the eye to about two-thirds of the way back on the tail. Dark vertebral spots may be present. There are 5 toes on each hind foot. Males have well-developed nasal cirri. Costal grooves number 14–16.

118. Junaluska Salamander

Eurycea junaluska

Abundance/Range: This is an uncommon to rare salamander that is found at rather low elevations in southwestern North Carolina and adjacent Tennessee.

Habitat: The Junaluska salamander seems to be more firmly associated with stream-edge habitats than the two-lined salamanders. It occurs along rocky streams, but probably disperses into damp woodlands in the summer.

Size: This slender salamander is adult at 4 inches in length.

Identifying features: This species is like a dull and poorly patterned two-lined salamander. It is brownish red to dull orange or greenish dorsally, and there are irregular dorsolateral rows of dark flecks. Nasal cirri are present. There may be vague dorsal and lateral markings. The belly is light. The tail is proportionately short, less than the length of the head and body. There are 5 toes on each hind foot. Males have well-developed nasal cirri. There are 14 costal grooves.

118. Junaluska Salamander

Similar species: Both the two-lined salamanders and the dwarf salamander have long tails (longer than the head and body) and well-defined dorsolateral lines. The dwarf salamander has only 4 toes on each hind foot.

LONG-TAILED SALAMANDERS

119. Three-lined Salamander

Eurycea guttolineata

Abundance/Range: This common salamander ranges southward from northern Virginia to eastern Louisiana and western Tennessee.

Habitat: Associated with water edge or seepage, as well as woodland situations, the three-lined salamander can be particularly common near ravines and grottoes, and in the twilight zone of caves. It is also found in damp areas of many hardwood forests and along streams and river edges.

Size: Adults of this species may grow to a length of about 7 inches.

Identifying features: The three black lines are usually precisely delineated on the trunk. The vertebral stripe terminates just posterior to the hind limbs. The lateral stripes often break into broad vertical bars on the sides of the tail. The dorsal color is yellowish to buff. The venter is cream and bears many dark spots. The legs are spotted and there are 5 toes on each hind foot.

Similar species: The two-lined and dwarf salamanders lack a strongly developed vertebral stripe. Dwarf salamanders have only 4 toes on each hind foot.

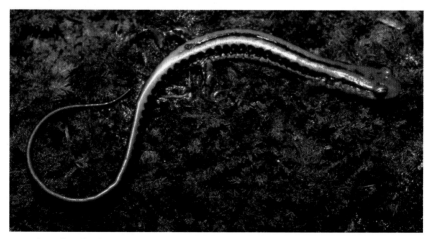

119. Three-lined Salamander

120. Long-tailed Salamander

Eurycea longicauda longicauda

Abundance/Range: This common salamander ranges southward from southern New York to central eastern Illinois and north central Alabama.

Habitat: This is a salamander of stream edges and seepages, damp ravines and caves. It also wanders freely in damp woodlands.

Size: This is a very long-tailed, slender salamander. Adults may grow to a length of about 7¾ inches.

long-tailed
dark-sided

Identifying features: The dorsum (including the sides) is yellowish, buff, or red orange. The back is variably patterned with dark spots. The sides are less profusely spotted. The sides of the tail have a herringbone pattern. The yellowish belly may be immaculate or mottled with darker pigment. The legs are prominently spotted and there are 5 toes on each hind foot. There are 13 or 14 costal grooves.

Similar species: The two-lined and dwarf salamanders lack a herringbone tail pattern. The three-lined salamander has complete rather than broken dorsal stripes. The dark-sided salamander has light-flecked grayish sides.

120. Long-tailed Salamander

Additional subspecies

121. The Dark-sided Salamander, *Eurycea longicauda melanopleura*, is smaller and of duller coloration than the long-tailed salamander. The back is brownish to buff and bears numerous small spots. The gray sides are peppered with tiny light specks. This is the westernmost representative of the long-tailed group. It is found in eastern Oklahoma, Arkansas, Missouri, and western Illinois. It intergrades widely with the long-tailed salamander, producing offspring with intermediate characteristics.

121. Dark-sided Salamander

CAVE SALAMANDER

122. Cave Salamander

Eurycea lucifuga

Abundance/Range: This common salamander ranges westward in a very irregular swath from northwestern Virginia to northeastern Oklahoma.

Habitat: Caves and rock faces are favored habitats, but this salamander can also be found on rocky slopes and near hardwood forest seeps.

Size: This is a very long-tailed, slender salamander. Adults may grow to a length of about 7 inches.

Identifying features: This is a beautiful, attenuate, yellowish red to orange salamander with a prehensile tail. The back, sides, and limbs are heavily flecked with dark pigment, which may form a lineate pattern. Cirri are present on both

122. Cave Salamander

sexes. The belly is off-white to yellowish and usually unspotted. There are 5 toes on each hind foot.

Similar species: The other long-tailed salamanders have well-defined stripes or a pattern of vertical markings on the tail.

FOUR-TOED BROOK SALAMANDERS

123. Chamberlain's Dwarf Salamander

Eurycea chamberlaini

Abundance/Range: Apparently common, this salamander occurs on the piedmont of both Carolinas and the upper coastal plain of North Carolina.

Habitat: This newly described salamander seems to prefer damp seepage areas in the sandhills of the Carolinas.

Size: This salamander attains 3¼ inches in total length, and its tail comprises about three-fifths of that.

Identifying features: This salamander is brownish bronze above and except for the limbs, which are dark, it is tan to yellow below. Dark dorsolateral stripes are usually prominent and a weak vertebral stripe is present. A dark interorbital bar followed by a dark spot is usually apparent. There are only 4 toes on the rear feet. There are 15 or 16 costal grooves.

123. Chamberlain's Dwarf Salamander

Larvae are prominently finned and have 4–6 irregular pairs of spots on the back.

Similar species: The common dwarf salamander is very dark and somewhat larger. The four-toed salamander has a boldly black-spotted enamel-white belly.

Comment: Until formally described in 2003, this salamander was referred to as the "light form" of the dwarf salamander, *Eurycea quadridigitata*.

124. Dwarf Salamander

Eurycea quadridigitata

Abundance/Range: This common salamander ranges southward from eastern North Carolina to eastern Texas. It occurs further southward on Florida's peninsula than any other plethodontid, being found as far south as Miami-Dade County.

Habitat: This salamander is common in pond- and swamp-edge habitats covered with fallen leaves and pine needles, as well as in vegetation floating on quiet waters. On rainy nights adults are often seen crossing roadways that closely parallel canals, drainage ditches, or vegetation-choked streams.

Size: A diminutive species, the dwarf salamander is adult at less than 3½ inches. The tail comprises about three-fifths of the total length.

124. Common Dwarf Salamander

Identifying features: This slender salamander has a brown dorsum (often with an apparent herringbone pattern) and lighter sides that are separated from each other by a broad dark dorsolateral stripe. The dorsal surface of the tail may be reddish. There is often a very thin darker vertebral line. The belly is predominantly dark. There are only 4 toes on each hind foot. There are 17 or 18 costal grooves.

Similar species: The four-toed salamander has an enamel-white belly prominently spotted with black. Chamberlain's dwarf salamander is lighter in color with a yellow belly.

Comments: Biochemical differences among populations suggest that, as now described, the dwarf salamander is a complex of several species.

OUTGROUPS

125. Many-ribbed Salamander

Eurycea multiplicata

Abundance/Range: This relatively common Ozark brook salamander ranges from northeastern Oklahoma to eastern Arkansas and south central Missouri.
Habitat: This tiny salamander occurs along brook edges and in seepages, springs, and other such aquatic habitats. It is often found beneath stones and rocks in muddy situations but even more often found in the shallows of mountain streams.

125. Many-ribbed Salamander

Size: This is a tiny, slender, elongate salamander with a long tail. It is adult at about 3 inches in length, but may occasionally reach 3½ inches overall.

Identifying features: The long-tailed slender build is typical. The overall color is buff to reddish. A herringbone pattern is often visible on the back. There is usually a poorly defined dorsolateral stripe (often no more than some lineate dots) on each side. The sides are often slightly darker than the back and lateral spots may be present. There are 19 or 20 costal grooves.

Similar species: Although the two-lined salamanders are of somewhat similar appearance, their ranges do not overlap that of the many-ribbed salamander. The various woodland salamanders have fewer costal grooves. Larvae of the many-ribbed and the Oklahoma salamanders can be very confusing, but the former usually does not have well-defined lateral "portholes."

Comments: This species is sometimes neotenic, attaining sexual maturity while remaining in larval form. The long-accepted subspecies known as the gray-bellied salamander, *Eurycea multiplicata griseogaster*, has been shown to be genetically identical to the Oklahoma salamander and is discussed under that species (127).

126. Grotto Salamander

Eurycea spelaeus

Abundance/Range: This is an uncommon and very locally distributed salamander of the Ozark Mountains of
Missouri and Arkansas.

Habitat: Adults occur on the ledges and walls of stream-
fed caves and grottoes. Larvae are aquatic.

Size: This salamander has been recorded at lengths of
up to 5¼ inches.

Identifying features: Adults are ghostly pale salamanders. They lack external
gills, the only troglodytic salamander of North America that does. The eyes of
the adult are nonfunctional, but are visible as dark raised spots. The salamanders are slender, have well-developed legs, and lack a tail fin. There are usually
17 costal grooves.

Larvae (outside of caves) are purplish, have relatively small though functional eyes, and a high tail fin. Those inside caves are lighter in color.

Similar species: None as adults. Other aquatic plethodontid larvae in this region have larger eyes and low tail fins.

Comments: Until recently, this species was monotypic and placed in the genus
Typhlotriton. It is the only terrestrial salamander of the East—of North America, for that matter—that is sightless as an adult. Larvae have functional eyes and

126. Grotto Salamander

have been found in gravelly streams both in and out of caves. It is not known whether the larvae return to the cave of their origin or access other caves.

A clutch consists of a small number (perhaps 12) eggs. Near-term eggs have been found during the last part of December and larvae have been found in streams during December and January.

127. Oklahoma Salamander (Gray-bellied Salamander)

Eurycea tynerensis (species complex)

Abundance/Range: This is listed as a federally endangered species. It occurs in eastern Oklahoma and adjacent Arkansas and Missouri.

Habitat: This salamander prefers shallow streams running over small to medium-sized stones and gravel. The larvae find ready refuge in the tiny spaces between the stones. Adults occur under stream-edge rocks.

Size: This very slender, narrow-headed salamander is adult at a length of 2–3 inches.

Identifying features: The dorsum of the aquatic larvae and neotenic adults is tan to gray with very fine darker stippling. The belly is lighter and almost transparent. There are one to three rows of light lateral "portholes." The tail fin is quite low. There are 19 or 20 costal grooves. The metamorphosed adults are very different in appearance from the aquatic form. The adults may be very dark, but some are overwhelmingly similar in appearance to the many-ribbed salamander (125).

Similar species: A great many of the paedomorphic salamanders are confusingly similar in appearance, but this one is more attenuate than most. This is the only paedomorphic salamander in its range. Larval many-ribbed salamanders are also gilled, but

127. Oklahoma/Gray-bellied Salamander, immature

127. Oklahoma/Gray-bellied Salamander, metamorphosed adult

usually have a higher tail fin and tend to have fewer and less well defined lateral portholes as well. However, the two are difficult to differentiate.

Behavior: The larvae of this very aquatic species hide among and beneath stones and gravel by day, but may emerge into open water to forage at night. Adults are shallow water and streamside creatures that are very adept at remaining out of sight.

Comments: As currently described, the Oklahoma salamander is probably a complex of several paedomorphic species. Molecular data show that salamanders long known commonly as gray-bellied salamanders, scientifically as the subspecies *Eurycea multiplicata griseogaster*, are actually metamorphosed Oklahoma salamanders.

PAEDOMORPHIC BROOK SALAMANDERS

These salamanders attain sexual maturity while retaining larval characteristics. Paedomorphic salamanders lack eyelids (several species lack functional eyes), most retain external gills, and they retain epidermal characteristics of the juvenile stage. Many are stream dwellers, but several inhabit caves and aquifers. Many are currently protected. Protection is proposed for others.

Because of the specialized habitats, many species are rarely seen. For example, the Blanco blind salamander, which was found during the drilling of a test well (since capped) in the bed of the then-dry Blanco River, has been found only once. Others, especially the dwellers in surface streams, are seen more frequently.

Several of these interesting salamander species have now been bred in captivity, some for multiple generations. The eggs of these paedomorphic salamanders seem to be placed randomly on pieces of chert, rocks, or gravel substrate.

Paedomorphic salamanders are most diverse on the Balcones Escarpment of central Texas. In fact, of the fifteen currently described species, only two, the Oklahoma salamander, *Eurycea tynerensis*, and the Georgia blind salamander,

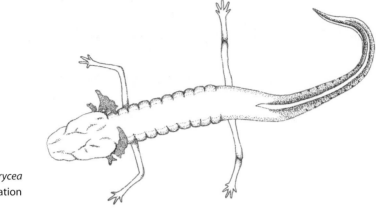

Texas Blind
Salamander, *Eurycea
rathbuni* (illustration
by K. P. Wray III)

Haideotriton wallacei, are not from the Balcones. Several other types, notably a salamander from Comal Springs and another from Pedernales Springs, remain in need of formal identification.

The identification of many of these paedomorphs has been determined through accumulated molecular data. Because of the similarity of appearance, the range—the precise spring, stream, or cave where they were found—will be an important tool in determining the identification of these salamanders.

128. Salado Salamander

Eurycea chisholmensis

Abundance/Range: Population statistics are unknown. Because of habitat vulnerability this is a protected species. It is found in Salado Springs and Robertson Spring, Bell County, Texas. This or a similar salamander has also recently been found at Buttermilk Creek, Texas.

Habitat: So far, this salamander is known with certainty only from the spring system for which it is named. It may be found between and beneath the rocks on the stream bottom.

Size: Adults are a slender 2½ inches in length.

Identifying features: The eyes are of reduced size and not elevated above the

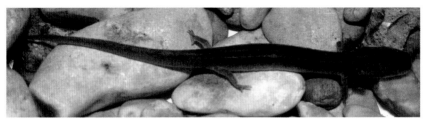

128. Salado Salamander. Photo by K. P. Wray III

lateral contour of the head. There is no dark eye ring. The head is flattened. The dorsal coloration is dark buff to grayish brown with indistinct, fine, light vermiculations. The dorsal tail fin is prominent posteriorly and absent proximally. Ventrally, the tail fin is reduced. The tail fin is edged with yellow along the dorsal musculature. Pigmented cells (iridophores and melanophores) poorly developed on the upper sides. There are 15 or 16 costal grooves.

Similar species: A great many of the paedomorphic salamanders are confusingly similar. Rely on range as your primary identification tool.

129. Cascade Caverns Salamander

Eurycea latitans (species complex)

Abundance/Range: Population statistics are unknown. Known from Bear Creek Spring, Cascades Caverns, Cibolo Creek Spring, Less Ranch Spring, and Kneedeep Cave Spring, Kendall County; Rebecca Creek Spring, Hays County; Cherry Creek, Cloud Hollow Springs, Kerr County; and Honey Creek Cave Spring, Comal County, all in Texas.

Habitat: As currently described this salamander is known only from the springs and creeks of the above locations.

Size: This salamander is adult at 2½–4 inches in length.

Identifying features: This salamander is whitish above and below. The venter is translucent. The head is broad, the nose is flattened, but the forehead slopes steeply upward from the snout to the crown. The nonfunctional eyes are visible through the skin as dark spots. A row

129. Cascade Caverns Salamander. Photo by Paul Chippindale

of translucent dorsolateral spots may be present. There are 14–15 costal grooves.

Similar species: Other neotenic species from near the range of the Cascade Caverns salamander, among them the Comal blind, the Texas blind, and the Valdina Farms salamanders, have very small eyespots.

Comments: The salamanders currently referred to as *Eurycea latitans* actually comprise a complex of several similar appearing species.

130. San Marcos Salamander

Eurycea nana

Abundance/Range: Population statistics are unknown. This salamander occurs in San Marcos, Hays County, Texas.

Habitat: This tiny salamander is found in the mats of algae growing in the source spring of the San Marcos River in Hays County, Texas.

Size: Occasional examples may reach 3¼ inches.

Identifying features: The San Marcos salamander is tan to dark brown. There is a dorsolateral row of yellowish, elongate markings along each side. There are 16–17 costal grooves. The eyes are large and functional. The venter is lighter in color than the dorsum and is translucent.

Similar species: The Texas blind salamander occurs in the same river as the San Marcos salamander. The former is larger and white, with a flattened snout and no functional eyes.

Comments: As is true of many of its congeners, virtually nothing is known of the life history of this salamander in the wild. However, it is currently being studied at the U.S. Fish and Wildlife Service Laboratory in San Marcos, Texas.

130. San Marcos Salamander

131. Georgetown Salamander

Eurycea naufragia

Abundance/Range: Population statistics are unknown. Because of habitat vulnerability this is a protected species. It is found in springs near Georgetown Lake in Williamson County, Texas. Salamanders that are probably of this species occur also in Bat Well and Cowan Creek, Williamson County, Texas.

Habitat: Springs (as above) and possibly caves.

Size: Apparently this salamander is adult at between 1¾ and 2¾ inches in length.

Identifying features: This is a grayish salamander with prominent gills and iridophores on the upper sides. A light rosette surrounds each iridophore. The tail fin has a dark margin along the dorsal musculature. There are 14–16 costal grooves.

Similar species: Many of the paedomorphic salamanders are confusingly similar. Use locale as your identifying criterion.

131. Georgetown Salamander

132. Texas Salamander

Eurycea neotenes

Abundance/Range: Population statistics are unknown. The range of this species is limited to Helotes Creek Spring and Leon Springs, Bexar County, and Meuller's Spring, Kendall County, Texas.

Habitat: This small salamander may be seen in springs, creeks, and seepages, where it seeks refuge beneath submerged rocks.

132. Texas Salamander

Size: Although this species may attain a length of 4 inches, it apparently reaches sexual maturity at a much smaller size.

Coloration/pattern: Texas salamanders are tan to brown above. The sides are patterned with two rows of tiny light portholes. Darker flecking may also be present. The venter is lighter than the back and translucent. The eyes are laterally directed and fully functional. This species has been known to metamorphose occasionally. There are 14–17 costal grooves.

Similar species: This species does not have a steeply sloped forehead and has functional eyes. Rely primarily on range maps for identifications.

133. Fern Bank Salamander

Eurycea pterophila

Abundance/Range: Population statistics are unknown. The Fern Bank salamander is found at Boardhouse Springs, Fern Bank Spring, Grapevine Cave, Peavey's Springs, Zercher Spring, and T Cave, all in Hays County, Texas.

Habitat: Springs and spring runs are the habitat of this salamander.

133. Fern Bank Salamander. Photo by R. Wayne Van Devender

Size: The adult size seems to be about 2½ inches.

Identifying features: This salamander is very similar in appearance to the Texas salamander, *Eurycea neotenes*. However, it differs genetically.

Similar species: A great many of the paedomorphic salamanders are confusingly similar. Use locale as your identifying criterion.

134. Texas Blind Salamander

Eurycea rathbuni

Abundance/Range: This salamander is found in the aquifer beneath the city of San Marcos in Hays County, Texas. Although it does not appear to be uncommon, it is a federally endangered species.

Habitat: The Texas blind salamander has been found in several wells and springs, as well as in pools in Ezell's, Wonder, and Rattlesnake Caves. It is best known, though, from subterranean upwellings in and near Aquarena Springs.

Size: The record size for the Texas blind salamander is 5⅜ inches.

Identifying features: This is a ghostly pale salamander of unforgettable appearance. Adults are an overall translucent white but juveniles bear scattered dark spots on their back and sides. The head is distinctly broadened and the snout is long and flat. The forehead rises steeply. The tiny eyes are nonfunctional. There are 12 costal grooves.

Similar species: Four additional blind salamanders are known to exist in Texas. Use range as the primary identification tool for all.

Comments: If alive when found, these animals are collected (before they become bass food) for federally sanctioned breeding and research programs. The species was formerly placed in the genus *Typhlomolge*.

134. Texas Blind Salamander

135. Blanco Blind Salamander

Eurycea robusta

Abundance/Range: This species is known only from an aquifer beneath the bed of the Blanco River (as it was channeled in 1951) in Hays County, Texas. It is a federally endangered species.

Habitat: It is speculated that the subterranean waters of this robust salamander may be separated from those of the Texas blind salamander

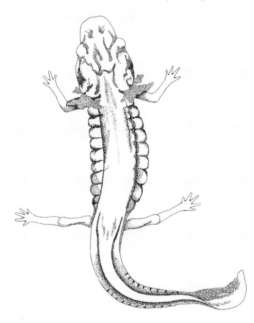

by shelving rocks or other such natural barriers.

Size: The single example known measures 4 inches in total length.

Identifying features: This white, blind salamander is of much more robust build than any of the other blind salamanders of Texas. Similarly, its tiny eyes are buried beneath the skin. The snout is flattened and the forehead slopes strongly upward. Costal grooves number 12.

Similar species: Other blind salamanders are more proportionately slender.

Comments: Only a single preserved specimen of this remarkable salamander now exists. It was long placed in the genus *Typhlomolge*.

135. Blanco Blind Salamander (illustration by K. P. Wray III)

136. Barton Springs Salamander

Eurycea sosorum

Abundance: This salamander occurs only from Barton Springs and hydrologically connected adjacent springs in downtown Austin, Texas. It does not seem to be particularly uncommon but is protected.

Habitat: The algae mats in Barton Springs, the public swimming pool, and spring runoffs are the habitat of this aquatic species.

Size: This salamander is adult at 2¼ inches in length.

136. Barton Springs Salamander

Coloration/pattern: The dorsal coloration of this species is gray to brown. Variably prominent darker markings are present. Some examples bear a row of dorsolateral spots or randomly arranged light mottling on the sides. The venter is translucent. The head is wider than the body and the snout is wedge shaped when viewed from above. The eyes are small but functional. There are 13–16 costal grooves.

Similar species: Use range to differentiate this species from other small stream-dwelling salamanders. The recently described Austin blind salamander (also of Barton Springs) has a more flattened nose, is of a lighter color, and lacks functional eyes.

137. Jollyville Plateau Salamander

Eurycea tonkawae

Abundance/Range: Population statistics are unknown. This salamander occurs in McDonald Well Spring and Spicewood Springs, as well as in Brushy Creek, Bull Creek, Buttercup Creek caves, Kretschmarr Cave, Round Rock Spring, Testudo Tube Cave, and other creeks of Travis and Williamson counties, Texas.

Habitat: This salamander occurs in both surface spring runs and in caves.

Size: Adults attain a length of about 2¾ inches.

137. Jollyville Plateau Salamander. Photo by R. Wayne Van Devender

Identifying features: This is a gray salamander with short but well formed gills. The light edging of the dorsolateral iridophores is squared rather than in rosette form. There are 14–16 costal grooves.

Similar species: Most of the paedomorphic salamanders of Texas are confusingly similar. Use locale as your identifying criterion.

138. Comal Blind Salamander

Eurycea tridentifera

Abundance/Range: Population statistics are unknown. It is found in Honey Creek Cave, Elm Springs Cave, and caves on the Cibolo Creek floodplain in Comal and Bexar counties, Texas.

Habitat: This salamander occurs in pools and creeks in the darkness of caves.

Size: The adult size of this species is about 3 inches.

Identifying features: Juveniles of this species are somewhat darker than the adults. Adults are white with red or pink gills. Dark eyespots are quit visible on juvenile examples but obscure on adults. The snout is flattened and the forehead slopes rather sharply upwards. There are only 11 or 12 costal grooves.

Similar species: The ranges of none of the other white (or grayish) blind salamanders overlap.

138. Comal Blind Salamander. Photo by Paul Chippindale

139. Valdina Farms Salamander

Eurycea troglodytes (species complex)

Abundance/Range: Because of habitat destruction this salamander seems to no longer exist where it was first found in Medina County, Texas. Currently, salamanders assigned to this species complex are found in springs in Edwards, Real, Uvalde, Medina, Bandera, Kerr, and Gillespie counties, Texas, and all are are protected.

139. Valdina Farms Salamander (complex). Photo by R. Wayne Van Devender

Habitat: This salamander may be found in spring runs and cave waters.

Size: This small aquatic salamander is adult at 3 inches in length.

Identifying features: The salamanders of this species complex are gray to brownish in color dorsally and laterally with irregular light flecks. The ventral skin is translucent. The snout is not strongly flattened. The eyes may be fully or only partially covered with skin. There are 13–14 costal grooves.

Similar species: The salamanders of this group can be confusingly similar in appearance to several other species. Use range as the identifying criterion.

Comments: Adult Comal blind salamanders in some populations metamorphose naturally.

140. Austin Blind Salamander

Eurycea waterlooensis

Abundance/Range: Population statistics are unknown. This interesting and distinctive species is known only from Barton Springs in Austin, Texas.

Habitat: This and the Barton Springs salamander coexist in this small spring.

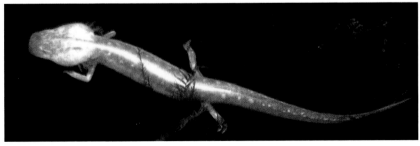

140. Austin Blind Salamander

Size: This flat-nosed salamander is adult at about 3 inches in length.

Identifying features: This is a broad-headed, flat-nosed, aquatic salamander with a whitish lavender body color. Juveniles have darker skin than adults. The eyes are nonfunctional and covered by skin. There are 12 costal grooves.

Similar species: This is the only eyeless salamander in Barton Springs.

Comments: A captive breeding program for reintroduction of the species to the wild is currently in place at the University of Texas, Austin.

141. Georgia Blind Salamander

Haideotriton wallacei

Abundance/Range: This species is protected but not uncommon. Adults are seen less frequently than juveniles. This species is known from Jackson County, Florida, to southwestern Georgia.

Habitat: The Georgia blind salamander occurs in ground water pools in the darkness of caves, and in deep wells and underground solution chambers. It is not found in runoff water.

Size: This salamander is adult at 3 inches in total length.

Identifying features: Because of small patches of dark pigment, juveniles of this species are somewhat darker than the white adults. The external gills are prominent. Eyespots are quite visible on juveniles but obscure with age.

Similar species: None; this is the only eyeless salamander of the southeast.

Comments: Despite its name, this salamander is better known in Florida than in Georgia.

141. Georgia Blind Salamander

Spring and Red Salamander group
Spring Salamanders, genus *Gyrinophilus*

This is a small genus of primarily nocturnal, moderate-sized salamanders that inhabit clean, clear, usually flowing waters and nearby deciduous woodlands. The genus is restricted to eastern North America, primarily Appalachia. There are four species, two cave-dwelling neotenes, one a transforming (metamorphosing) troglobyte, and one a typical stream-dwelling salamander.

Because of the bright colors, the four subspecies of the northern spring salamander were formerly referred to as "purple" salamanders. In fact, they are more often some shade of salmon than purple.

These salamanders eat all manner of small invertebrates, from insects and worms to crustaceans, and if opportunity presents will branch out to eat vertebrates as well. The races of the northern spring salamander are notoriously cannibalistic.

Almost nothing is known about the reproductive biology of the cave-dwelling species. However, the 15–50 eggs of the stream-dwelling spring salamander are laid in submerged cavities and burrows during the summer. Few nests have been found, but among those few, females have been in attendance of most clutches. Incubation seems to take 6–12 weeks depending on water temperature. The larvae are aquatic.

142. Berry Cave Salamander (neotenic species)

Gyrinophilus gulolineatus

Abundance/Range: Uncommon and of very local distribution in eastern Tennessee, this neotenic spring salamander occurs east of the Tennessee River, southward from Roane County to McMinn County, Tennessee.

Habitat: Most common in sinkhole caves.

Size: The largest recorded specimen was 8 15/16 inches long.

Identifying features: This is a big-headed, stocky cave salamander. Unlike many cave creatures, the Berry Cave salamander is quite dark in color. The ground coloration is brown and there are many discrete

142. Berry Cave Salamander

dark spots on the back and upper sides. The lower sides and belly are pinkish. The head is wide and the snout wide and somewhat flattened. There is a well-defined dark marking on the anterior of the throat. There are 17 costal grooves.

Similar species: The pale cave salamander and the Big Mouth cave salamander are very similar. Use location as an identification tool.

Comments: This salamander is still considered a subspecies of *Gyrinophilus palleucus* by some researchers. Although it does not usually metamorphose in nature, this salamander can be induced to do so in the lab.

143. Pale Cave Salamander (neotenic species)

Gyrinophilus palleucus palleucus

Abundance/Range: Reasonably common in caves in south central Tennessee, northern Alabama, and extreme northwestern Georgia.

Habitat: Caves along the south edge of the Cumberland Plateau are the habitat of this salamander.

Size: This is a cave salamander of moderate size. Adults are 4¾–6 inches in length. The largest recorded specimen was 7¼ inches long.

Identifying features: This cave salamander is pale but not white. The body color is flesh pink and usually devoid of darker spots. The lower sides are paler than the dorsum, and the belly is so pale that it is almost translucent. The head is not noticeably large, but may appear so when the large gills are fully extended. The lower sides and belly are pinkish. There are 17 costal grooves.

Similar species: The Berry Cave salamander and the Big Mouth Cave salamander are very similar. Use range as an identification tool.

Comments: Although it only rarely metamorphoses in the wild, this salamander can be induced to do so in the lab.

143. Pale Cave Salamander

Additional subspecies

144. The Big Mouth Cave Salamander, *Gyrinophilus palleucus necturoides*, is found in Big Mouth Cave, Grundy County, Tennessee, and other caves in the Elk River drainage in Rutherford County, Tennessee. This is a dark-colored salamander with a profusion of poorly defined darker spots or blotches. The belly is pinkish. There are 18 costal grooves. Rely on the origin of the salamander for positive identification.

144. Big Mouth Cave Salamander. Photo by R. Wayne Van Devender

145. Northern Spring Salamander

Gyrinophilus porphyriticus porphyriticus

northern
Blue Ridge
Carolina
Kentucky

Abundance/Range: This is a relatively common salamander. The larvae are more easily found and seem more numerous than the adults. It ranges southward from southern Maine and Quebec to northern Georgia and extreme northeastern Mississippi.

Habitat: The northern spring salamander is associated with streamside and spring-run habitats, caves and grottoes. It may wander into surrounding woodlands in rainy or foggy weather. During dry periods spring salamanders seldom stray from a ready source of water. Larvae may be found in gravel beds.

Size: This is a fairly robust salamander that commonly attains 6–7½ inches in total length. The record size is 9⅛ inches.

Identifying features: This race of the spring salamander not only ranges most widely, but is also the dullest in color. Old examples are often purplish brown with a reticulum of darker markings dorsally. The dark markings are usually

145. Northern Spring Salamander

most distinct dorsolaterally but the pattern is still not clearly delineated. The belly is lighter than the back and may or may not be marked with dark pigment. Like all races of this species, the northern spring salamander has a sloping snout, squared off when viewed from above. The dark-edged light stripe running from the eye to the nostril along the canthus, so prominent on Appalachian races of spring salamanders, may be obscure on this race. There are 17–19 costal grooves.

Similar species: The various mud and red salamanders have a rounded snout, lack the canthal stripe, and are generally of brighter color with profuse black flecking.

Comments: During the passage of cool, rainy, low-pressure systems, northern spring salamanders as well as the southern races may often be found crossing rainswept roadways in considerable numbers.

Additional subspecies

146. The Blue Ridge Spring Salamander, *Gyrinophilus porphyriticus danielsi*, is a beautiful and large salamander. The dorsal colors are bright salmon to brownish salmon with a profuse peppering of fine black spots. The canthal stripe (eye to nostril) is prominent and edged beneath by dark pigment. The lips are light with dark spotting. This race is found in a narrow swath along the North Carolina–Tennessee border.

146. Blue Ridge Spring Salamander

147. The Carolina Spring Salamander, *Gyrinophilus porphyriticus dunni*, varies in color from a pale yellowish red to pale reddish brown. The canthal stripe is only moderately delineated. The belly is salmon. This is a salamander of the higher elevations of western South Carolina, northern Georgia, and northeastern Alabama.

147. Carolina Spring Salamander

148. The Kentucky Spring Salamander, *Gyrinophilus porphyriticus duryi*, is a brightly colored form, often reddish salmon above and on the sides. The sides may be liberally speckled with tiny black dots. The canthal stripe is not well delineated. The venter is pinkish white. This salamander is found only in northeastern Kentucky, northwestern West Virginia, and adjacent Ohio.

148. Kentucky Spring Salamander

149. West Virginia Spring Salamander

Gyrinophilus subterraneus

Abundance/Range: Unknown, but probably uncommon and certainly of very restricted distribution. This species occurs only in Greenbrier County, West Virginia.

Habitat: Known only from General Davis Cave.

Size: This is a cave salamander of moderate size. Adults may attain 7 inches in length.

Identifying features: This pale pinkish brown salamander spends its life in the darkness of caves. The larvae are darker than the adults, but both larvae and adults have a weakly defined reticulate pattern. The canthus rostralis (the angle on the sides of the snout) is not sharply angled and the eyes are relatively small. The lower sides are paler than the dorsum, and the belly is pinkish white. There are usually 17 costal grooves.

Similar species: The heads of both the Berry Cave salamander and the Big Mouth Cave salamander are proportionately broader than the head of the West Virginia spring salamander but otherwise quite similar. Use location as an identification tool.

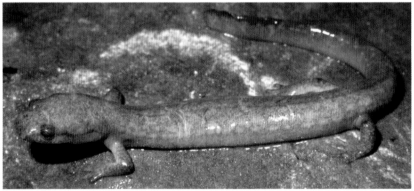

149. West Virginia Spring Salamander. Photo by R. Wayne Van Devender

Mud and Red Salamanders, genus *Pseudotriton*

This genus contains only two species of brightly colored eastern salamanders. The red salamander is associated with clear flowing streams and springs in hardwood forests. The mud salamander inhabits muddy seepages and swamp edges. Varying in size between 4 and 7 inches, these salamanders are moderately robust and spectacularly beautiful. Besides the complement of invertebrates considered typical salamander fare, tadpoles and smaller salamanders are also regularly eaten by the salamanders of this genus.

These salamanders apparently breed in the autumn and oviposit in late autumn or, weather conditions allowing, during the winter months. A clutch may contain more than 175 eggs. The courtship is unknown.

In keeping with their preferred habitat, mud salamanders oviposit in submerged holes and burrows near quiet seeps while the red salamanders deposit their eggs beneath rocks or logs in running water. Females have been found in the proximity of eggs, but it is not known whether they actually attend the clutches. Incubation seems to take 6–12 weeks, depending on water temperature. The larvae are aquatic.

Mud salamanders actively burrow through the soupy mud of seepage areas and wet lowland hammocks. Red salamanders usually use stream edge burrows or sit beneath rocks in shallow running water. Both species are predominantly nocturnal and may occasionally be found crossing rain swept roadways on cool nights.

The red salamanders often (but not invariably) have pale irises while the irises of the mud salamanders are usually dark.

150. Eastern Mud Salamander

Pseudotriton montanus montanus

Abundance/Range: This salamander is secretive and has specific habitat requirements. It ranges southward from southern New Jersey to central Georgia.
Habitat: This is a salamander of muddy seeps, spring edges, brook overflows, swamps, and wet lowland hammocks. Mud salamanders are persistent burrowers.
Size: The record size for this salamander is 8⅛ inches.

eastern
midland
Gulf Coast
rusty

Identifying features: This is a bright to dull orange or red salamander with a pattern of black flecking dorsally and laterally. The belly is the same color as the dorsum and may or may not bear dark spots. The build is stocky and the tail proportionately short. The eyes

150. Eastern Mud Salamander

are (usually) relatively dark. The venter has dark spots. There are 16–17 costal grooves.

All mud salamanders dull in color with advancing age. Some turn a dingy brown with an orangish patina and black spots.

Similar species: The red salamander (see 154–157) is stockier and liberally flecked with dark spots dorsally and laterally. Spring salamanders are of some shade of salmon rather than red and have a distinct angle and light line on each side of the snout.

Additional subspecies

151. The Midland Mud Salamander, *Pseudotriton montanus diastictus*, is the most divergent subspecies. Molecular data show rather conclusively, that this salamander is a species in its own right. Dorsally and laterally this salamander is usually an intense coral red. Old examples may develop a patina or brownish pigment dorsally. Sparse black spotting, often most pronounced laterally, and absent ventrally, is present. The range of this salamander is not contiguous with the ranges of the other races. It occurs from southern Ohio and southern West Virginia to southeastern Tennessee.

151. Midland Mud Salamander

152. The Gulf Coast Mud Salamander, *Pseudotriton montanus flavissimus*, ranges westward from the low country of southeastern South Carolina to eastern Louisiana. Young adults are a rather brilliant, black-flecked orange red to salmon dorsally and laterally and an unmarked pink ventrally.

152. Gulf Coast Mud Salamander

153. Rusty Mud Salamander, *Pseudotriton montanus floridanus*, occurs in northern Florida and southern Georgia. It is the smallest race with the record length being 4⅝ inches. A blotchy patina of dark pigment dulls most of the orange red on the back and much of it on the sides. The venter is lighter with orange-red flecking.

153. Rusty Mud Salamander

154. Northern Red Salamander

Pseudotriton ruber ruber

Abundance/Range: Although not uncommon, this salamander is locally distributed and secretive. It ranges southward from southeastern New York to central Georgia.

Habitat: This salamander is associated with streamside and spring-run habitats. They may burrow into soft streamside soils, but are also found beneath rocks, boards,

northern
Blue Ridge
black-chinned
southern

and other debris both at streamside and in the shallows. During dry periods red salamanders seldom stray from a ready source of water.

Size: This is a fairly robust salamander that commonly attains 4½–5½ inches in total length. The record size is 7⅛ inches.

Identifying features: Young adults of this salamander are resplendent in their black spotted bright red hues. Some light flecking may occur on the snout. Advancing age dulls the coloration, and some old examples (and juveniles) may be a rather dingy reddish brown. Occasional examples are yellowish red. The black flecks go all of the way to the tail tip. The belly is lighter than the back and flecked with black. The iris is often gold or brassy in color, but may be dark. There are 16–17 costal grooves.

154. Northern Red Salamanders

Similar species: The various mud salamanders are more slender, often have darker irises, have a proportionately shorter, more rounded nose, and lack light flecking on the snout. Spring salamanders are some shade of salmon rather than red and have a distinct angle and light line on each side of the snout.

Behavior: By day this is a secretive salamander, remaining in its burrows or beneath a rock, emerging to forage only at night. This is especially true during rainy weather and when barometric pressure is falling. Red salamanders may occasionally be found crossing rainswept roadways at night.

Additional subspecies

155. The Blue Ridge Red Salamander, *Pseudotriton ruber nitidus*, is a small and very brightly colored race. It lacks black spotting on the terminal half of the tail but is otherwise quite like the northern red salamander. This subspecies is adult at about 4½ inches in length and occurs in mountainous southwestern Virginia, western North Carolina, and immediately adjacent Tennessee.

155. Blue Ridge Red Salamander

156. The Black-chinned Red Salamander, *Pseudotriton ruber schencki*, is another brightly colored subspecies of higher elevations. Light flecks may be present on the snout and cheeks. It lacks tail-tip black spotting but has a black rim to the lower jaw. This is a creature of extreme western North Carolina and adjacent South Carolina, Georgia, and Tennessee.

156. Black-chinned Red Salamander

157. The Southern Red Salamander, *Pseudotriton ruber vioscai*, is the least colorful of the subspecies; this is especially true of old adults. The dorsal and lateral coloration is a pale reddish brown to purplish brown. There is a profusion of light flecks anteriorly and dark speckling posteriorly. The venter is lighter than the dorsum and is flecked with black. The iris may be gold or brassy in color, but some are dark. This species ranges from central South Carolina southward to the Florida panhandle and eastern Louisiana. Then, after dipping south of the mountain range, the range extends northward to western Kentucky. The southern red salamander intergrades with the northern red salamander throughout most of its Alabama range.

157. Southern Red Salamander

Woodland Salamanders, genus *Plethodon*

The salamanders of this genus occur in woodlands across North America, ranging northward from New Mexico and the Atlantic Gulf Coast to southern Canada. They are not present in arid regions. These elfin caudatans are surface active at night during moist weather and occasionally on humid overcast or rainy days. They usually remain hidden on breezy nights. The hours of daylight are spent beneath fallen trees or rocks, in escarpment fissures, or in subsurface burrows. Some species seek solace from the summer's heat by retreating underground. Many species are remarkably cold tolerant and active on the cold nights of late autumn and early spring.

The most northerly of the eastern species is the ubiquitous red-backed salamander, *Plethodon cinereus*. Several species of the slimy salamander complex (*Plethodon glutinosus*) are among the most southerly, being found as far south as central Florida and the gulf coast of Louisiana. The greatest diversity of this genus occurs in the southern Appalachian Mountains. The species in the genus *Plethodon* are fully terrestrial.

Costal grooves are prominent and may vary by species from 16 to 22. The toes are not strongly webbed. The tail is round in cross-section. These are very secretive salamanders that may become surface active during the cool, rainy nights of spring and autumn.

There are several pattern classes, and many species have two or more very different color phases. A recurring color scheme among many species in this genus consists of white (or brass) spots against a black ground color. Many species are widespread and abundant, a few are very localized and rare. One (*Plethodon ainsworthi*) may be extinct. When adult the salamanders in this genus range from 3 to about 8½ inches.

Dietary items vary by the size of the salamanders. All species eat insects, other arthropods, and worms. Larger species may be cannibalistic, eating smaller salamanders as well as the normal invertebrate prey.

Although reproductive biology remains unknown in many species, an intricate courtship has been documented for others. The courtship includes trailing by the male of the female; tail undulation by the male beneath the chin of the female; straddling of the male's tail by the female; complex body motions; the rubbing by the male of his mental gland against the female; spermatophore deposition by the male; and sperm cap pickup by the female. Eggs are laid singly and usually suspended from a root, rock, or other overhang by a stalk formed from the gelatinous egg covering. They are laid in rotting logs, underground chambers, or in damp rock fissures. Clutches of small species may contain a dozen or fewer eggs while larger species may lay 25 or more. Incubation usually takes 2–2½ months.

AFFILIATIONS UNKNOWN

158. Catahoula Salamander

Plethodon ainsworthi

Abundance: Rare or possibly extinct (no photographs are available). This salamander is known from only two specimens, collected in 1964 and found in a jar of preservative in 1991. The collection site was two miles south of Bay Springs, Jasper County, Mississippi. No additional living specimens have been found.

Habitat: According to field collection information, the salamanders were collected amid "springhead litter."

Size: 4½ inches is apparently the adult size of this species.

Identifying features: This is a slender salamander with a narrow, somewhat

158. Catahoula Salamander (illustration by Patricia Bartlett)

elongate, head. Because the long-preserved salamanders had been bleached by the preservative, the color in life is unknown with certainty. However, because the collector mistook these for slimy salamanders, it is probable that the ground color was black or dark brown. Unlike slimy salamanders, which are profusely spotted, *Plethodon ainsworthi* may be devoid of a pattern. There are 16 costal grooves.

Similar species: The deteriorated condition of the preserved salamanders renders it impossible to do more than speculate. However, it appears that, of the sympatric salamanders in the region, only the aquatic southern two-lined salamander is as attenuate as the Catahoula salamander.

Comments: The type locality for this salamander is on private land. The habitat has been logged, but tree cover is again present. During the 1990s, several extensive searches for this species failed to divulge additional examples.

OUACHITA MOUNTAIN SALAMANDERS

159. Caddo Mountain Salamander

Plethodon caddoensis

Abundance/Range: Although restricted in distribution to the Caddo Mountains of Polk and Montgomery counties, Arkansas, this can be an abundant salamander.
Habitat: Expect this small salamander on north-facing hillsides amid talus.
Size: This species is adult at 4 inches in length.
Identifying features: This small black salamander is variably patterned with white and brass flecks and rarely may have a very little chestnut pigment on its back. The upper sides are black with light flecks. The lower sides are somewhat lighter. The chin and chest are white shading to gray or black posteriorly. This species has 16 costal grooves.

Similar species: The western slimy salamander in the vicinity of Caddo Mountain has a dark throat and chest, is larger, and is usually less profusely spotted.

Comments: The Caddo Mountain salamander is related to the larger Rich Mountain and Fourche Mountain salamanders, found one mountain range further north.

159. Caddo Mountain Salamander

160. Fourche Mountain Salamander

Plethodon fourchensis

Abundance/Range: This is a relatively common salamander. It is restricted to moderately high elevations in the Iron Fork and Fourche Mountains of Polk and Scott counties, Arkansas.

Habitat: This forest-dwelling salamander may be found beneath fallen limbs, trunks, and surface rocks at elevations of 1,700–2,400 feet.

Size: This species is adult at 6¼ inches in length.

Identifying features: Despite a similarity in appearance to the slimy salamanders, this species is most closely allied to the Rich Mountain salamander, *Plethodon ouachitae*, and considered a subspecies of the latter by some researchers. This is a black-and-white salamander on which the white markings are most prominent and largest dorsally, where they are often in two irregular rows. There may also be tiny white and ochre specks on the back, sides and belly. The lower sides are often white but more blotched than spotted. The belly is predominantly dark and the chin is light. There are usually 16 costal grooves.

Similar species: Slimy salamanders (177–180) usually have the smallest white spots on the dorsum and the largest on the lower sides; those in the Ouachita Mountains also have dark throats. The Rich Mountain salamander usually has at least a little chestnut color on its back and some examples are quite richly colored with chestnut.

Comments: Adult males of this and related salamanders are known to be ag-

160. Fourche Mountain Salamander

gressively territorial. They do not hesitate to attack interloping salamanders of their own or other species. Males bite, and then roll their body on its longitudinal axis to cause the most damage. It is not uncommon that the tail or even the limb of the victim is broken free. It may then be eaten by the attacker.

161. Rich Mountain Salamander

Plethodon ouachitae

Abundance/Range: This is a common salamander. It is found on Rich Mountain and nearby peaks in the Ouachita Mountains of western central Arkansas and eastern central Oklahoma.

Habitat: A denizen of heavily treed, rocky slopes, this salamander is most often found beneath rocks (and occasionally trees) near talus slides.

Size: This salamander attains a length of 6¼ inches.

Identifying features: This is a variably colored salamander. Those from Rich Mountain seem to be brightest, having a variable but often extensive amount of chestnut on the back, beginning on the back of the head and continuing to the base of the tail. White flecks adorn the back. The upper sides are black with white flecking and the lower sides quite heavily spotted with white or almost solid grayish white. The throat is light grayish white and the belly is black. Some examples may lack most or all of the chestnut; these are essentially white-spotted black salamanders.

Similar species: The slimy salamanders from the Ouachita Mountains have dark throats.

161. Rich Mountain Salamander

RED-BACKED, ZIGZAG, AND BIG LEVELS SALAMANDERS

162. Eastern Red-backed Salamander

Plethodon cinereus

Abundance: This is one of the most abundant and frequently seen of the plethodontid salamanders. It ranges eastward to the Atlantic Coast from eastern Minnesota and north from North Carolina to southern Quebec.

Habitat: This is a salamander of moist northern hardwood woodlands. It is tolerant of others of its own species. From one to several individuals may be found beneath a single ground-surface refuge. Rocks, fallen trees, and other surface debris, both natural and human generated, are utilized.

Size: This salamander species is adult at 4 inches in length.

Identifying features: This is a slender salamander with at least three distinctly different phases. Of these, the red-backed phase is very common at all altitudes, but the lead-backed phase seems restricted to lower altitudes. A less common completely orange to red (erythristic) morph is well known in certain areas. The stripe may be red (usual), orange (common), to yellow, is quite straight edged, and usually very well defined. The sides are peppered with light and dark pigments (and some orange flecks) that, in mix, produce a gray color. The belly is flecked with black and white in about equal amounts. The stripe extends to the tip of the tail. The head and limbs have a vaguely peppered appearance, but are usually about the same color as the vertebral stripe.

The lead-backed phase lacks the red pigment but when seen in good light may have a slight olive blush in place of the red. The belly is black and white. The erythristic individuals lack most if not all dark pigment, vary from a rather bright red to orange dorsally, and have a light belly.

There are 17–22 costal grooves, with 19 the norm.

Similar species: Two-lined salamanders are more attenuate, more olive in color, and quite aquatic. Except for the southern red-backed salamander (which can be differentiated by range), other red-backed species of *Plethodon* lack the salt-and-pepper belly or have red pigment mixed in with the peppering.

162. Eastern Red-backed Salamander. Top: red-backed morph; bottom: erythristic morph

162. Eastern Red-backed Salamander, lead-backed morph

163. Southern Red-backed Salamander

Plethodon serratus

Abundance/Range: Common in northwestern Georgia and western North Carolina, this small salamander also occurs in disjunct colonies in Missouri, Louisiana, central western Arkansas, and immediately adjacent Oklahoma.

Habitat: Like the very similar eastern red-backed salamander, the southern red-back conceals itself beneath fallen trees and surface rocks. It may be very common near woodland streams, springs, and seepage areas.

Size: This salamander attains an adult length of 4 inches.

Identifying features: This small salamander has two distinctly different phases. The red-backed phase is the most common in the western part of the range. The sides are peppered with light and dark pigments, which, together, produce a gray color. The broad vertebral stripe is orange red, has vaguely irregular margins, and is wider over each costal groove. The stripe extends nearly to the tip of the tail. The head and limbs have a vaguely peppered appearance, but are usually the same color as or slightly darker than the vertebral stripe. The belly is finely peppered with black and white.

The lead-backed phase lacks the red pigment, but when seen in good light, may have a slight olive blush in place of the red. The costal grooves vary between 18 and 21 in number.

163. Southern Red-backed Salamander

Similar species: Rely on range as your primary identification tool. The dwarf salamander may have a vertebral stripe but has only 4 toes on the hind feet and a laterally compressed tail.

164. Big Levels Salamander

Plethodon sherando

Abundance/Range: This species is relatively common within its small range. As far as is known, it occurs only in the Big Levels region of Augusta County, Virginia.

Habitat: This salamander seems largely restricted to talus (rock slides).

Size: Adult at about 4 inches in length.

Identifying features: This small salamander occurs in a red-striped form, non-striped form, and intermediate broken-striped form. The stripe is smooth edged. The vertebral area of the non-striped form may be vaguely lighter than the upper sides. When the red back is present, it is separated on each side from the gray mottled sides by a dark stripe that extends to the tail tip. The belly is partially pigmented but predominantly light. Proportionately, the head is marginally wider than that of the red-backed salamander and the legs are pro-

portionately longer. There are usually 18 costal grooves.

Similar species: The red-backed salamander and southern red-backed salamanders usually have 19 or more costal grooves. The Shenandoah salamander has 18 costal grooves but a more heavily pigmented belly.

Comments: This red-backed salamander look-alike was described in 2004. It varies in external appearance only

164. Big Levels Salamander. Photo by Scott Highton

slightly from the red-backed, southern red-backed, and Shenandoah salamanders. Exact geographic location will be an important identification tool.

164. Big Levels Salamander. Photo by Scott Highton

165. Ozark Salamander

Plethodon angusticlavius

Abundance/Range: Restricted to the Ozark Mountains of southwestern Missouri, northeastern Oklahoma, and northwestern Arkansas, this is a truly abundant salamander.

Habitat: This is a species of moist, deciduous woodlands, where it utilizes surface rocks, fallen trees, and other woodland moisture-retaining debris for cover. It can be very common low on hillsides in moist seepage areas but it is seldom actually found in standing water. *Plethodon angusticlavius* also utilizes talus and caves, and burrows of their own making or deserted by other small animals.

Size: This salamander is adult at 3¾ inches in length.

Identifying features: This little salamander is very polymorphic. It may have an easily visible but indistinctly edged, narrow, zigzag red to orange dorsal stripe,

165. Ozark Salamander

lack such stripe entirely, or be intermediate between those extremes. The upper sides are reddish brown and the lower sides are gray. The belly is finely flecked with black and white, with smatterings of red pigment interspersed. Costal grooves may vary between 17 and 19 with 18 the norm.

Similar species: The range of the southern red-backed salamander abuts the southern edge of the range of the Ozark zigzag salamander. It has a broader, less wavy-edged dorsal stripe and lacks red pigment on the belly.

Comments: This salamander was long considered a subspecies of the more easterly northern zigzag salamander, *Plethodon dorsalis*. Despite being differentiated from its eastern relative by only minimal biochemical differences, the Ozark salamander has lately been treated as a full species. The ranges of the two are not contiguous.

166a. Northern Zigzag Salamander

Plethodon dorsalis

Abundance/Range: This is a common woodland salamander of the forested east. It ranges southward from central western Indiana (and adjacent Illinois) to southern Tennessee.

northern zigzag
southern zigzag
Webster's

Habitat: A species of moist, deciduous woodlands, the northern zigzag salamander utilizes surface rocks, fallen trees, and other woodland moisture-retaining debris for cover. The salamander can be particularly common near caves and fissured cliff faces and in talus slopes.

166a. Northern Zigzag Salamander

Size: 4¼ inches is the record size for this species.

Identifying features: In coloration, this is a variable little salamander. Striped morphs have a well-defined red to orange stripe that is outlined by a very narrow dark stripe with irregular edges. Plain examples lack striping entirely. Individuals with intermediate characteristics are not uncommon. The upper sides are orange brown to brown (rarely gray) and the lower sides fade gradually to the black-flecked, light belly. Some red pigment is present on the belly. The stripe (when present) *does not* extend to the tail tip. Costal grooves vary between 17 and 19, with 18 being the norm.

Similar species: When striped, the dorsal stripe of the eastern red-backed salamander is quite straight edged. While the edges of the dorsal stripe of the southern red-backed salamander are more serrate, the belly is devoid of red pigment. The stripe of both species extends to the tail tip. The lead-backed phases of both species of redback lack red ventral pigment but have strongly flecked black and off-white bellies.

Molecularly determined species

166b. Southern Zigzag Salamander, *Plethodon ventralis*: The southernmost and easternmost zigzag salamanders differ genetically from the northern form, but are virtually identical in appearance. As with *Plethodon dorsalis* there are two primary color variations (striped and unstriped) as well as intermediates (partially striped) between the two. However the unstriped and partially striped morphs are the more dominant coloration. The unstriped morph often has small random patches of red pigment anterodorsally. The belly of this species is a mixture of black, white, and red pigments. This species occurs in extreme

166b. Southern Zigzag Salamander

western Virginia, eastern Kentucky, eastern Tennessee, western North Carolina, and the northernmost regions of Georgia, Alabama, and Mississippi.

166c. Webster's Salamander, *Plethodon websteri*: This genetically determined species is identical in appearance to the northern zigzag salamander. Identify it by range. The discontinuous range (see range map) includes a small area in South Carolina, tiny pockets in eastern Louisiana, central Mississippi, and southern Alabama, and a large area in central eastern Alabama and adjacent Georgia.

166c. Webster's Salamander

PEAKS OF OTTER, CHEAT MOUNTAIN, AND SHENANDOAH SALAMANDERS

167. Peaks of Otter Salamander

Plethodon hubrichti

Abundance/Range: This woodland species is not uncommon, but of very restricted distribution. It is found only in Bedford, Botetourt, and Rockbridge counties, Virginia. It is most common at elevations above 2,750 feet.

Habitat: Look for this salamander in deciduous woodlands. When at the ground surface, this salamander utilizes fallen trees, rocks, and other surface debris as hiding spots. It is surface active on rainy spring and autumn nights and presumably spends periods of excessive heat and cold in burrows at varying levels beneath the ground.

Size: An adult may be 4¼ inches in length.

Identifying features: This is a small salamander with a rough-edged longitu-

167. Peaks of Otter Salamander

dinal dorsal pattern comprising discrete reddish spots on juveniles but that is gray to brass and quite continuous on adults. Predominantly dark individuals bearing white spots are occasionally seen. The sides are dark with reduced flecking and the belly gray to almost black. Costal grooves number 18–20, with 19 the norm.

Similar species: Other small salamanders from central Virginia with contrastingly colored backs have speckled or flecked bellies.

168. Cheat Mountain Salamander

Plethodon nettingi

Abundance/Range: This is a moderately common woodland salamander with a spotty distribution even within its restricted range. It occurs only in the Cheat Mountains of central eastern West Virginia.

Habitat: Although occasionally found in deciduous forests, the Cheat Mountain salamander is most often associated with spruce-birch forests at elevations of 2,750–4,700 feet.

Size: A length of 4 inches may be attained.

Identifying features: Like many of the montane plethodontids, this salamander is small, dark, and variably flecked with a peppering of lighter pigment. In this case, the lighter flecks are predominantly of brassy color, but occasionally there will be a smattering of white dots as well. The lower sides are very dark and quite sparsely flecked. Both the chin and the belly are gray to almost black. Very young individuals may have some reddish dorsal markings. Eighteen costal grooves are the norm.

168. Cheat Mountain Salamander

Similar species: Other small woodland salamanders found within the restricted range of the Cheat Mountain salamander have red backs or patterned bellies.

169. Shenandoah Salamander

Plethodon shenandoah

Abundance/Range: The entire range of this small and uncommon salamander is contained within the perimeter of Shenandoah National Park, Virginia. This is a protected endangered species.

Habitat: The Shenandoah salamander is a resident of talus slides on wooded, north- or northwest-facing slopes at elevations of 2,600–3,450 feet. Within this precise habitat the salamanders seem most common near the edges of the slides where there is a little soil between the rocks. Population statistics are difficult to assess.

Size: To 4¼ inches.

Identifying features: The Shenandoah salamander looks much like a slender, narrow-striped, dark-bellied, red-backed salamander. Like the redback, the Shenandoah salamander has two color phases, a striped and a non-striped. The striped morph has a yellow to olive-orange stripe with uneven edges. The sides are very dark and blend imperceptibly into the belly color. The non-striped morph lacks a well-defined stripe, but may have scattered patches of orangish pigment along the back. The chin is usually lighter than the belly and bears larger light spots. The belly is brownish to black with scattered, *small*, off-white spots. The number of costal grooves can vary from 17 to 19, but 18 is the normal number.

Similar species: The red-backed salamander is found in some of the same habitats as the Shenandoah. The former has a broader, even-edged stripe and an overall lighter belly with fine salt-and-pepper markings. Hybrids between Shenandoah and red-backed salamanders are documented.

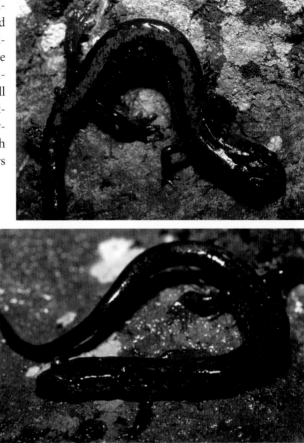

169. Shenandoah Salamander. Top: red-backed morph; bottom: lead-backed morph

MISCELLANEOUS WOODLAND SALAMANDERS

170a. Valley and Ridge Salamander

Plethodon hoffmani

Abundance/Range: This salamander is easily overlooked, even where common. It ranges southward from central Pennsylvania to central western Virginia and adjacent West Virginia.

Habitat: This salamander may be found beneath both natural and human-generated surface debris at medium

valley and ridge
Shenandoah

170a. Valley and Ridge Salamander

to high elevations in the Appalachian Valley and Ridge Province. It also enters caves and fissured cliff faces, including road cuts.

Size: The valley and ridge salamander is adult at 4¼ inches in total length.

Identifying features: This is one of several dark-colored slender salamanders found in the Appalachian region.

This salamander is a very dark brown dorsally and laterally, with a peppering of brassy flecks and occasionally a few white spots. The belly is grayish brown with some white markings. The throat is lighter than the belly. The tail is very long and quite robust. The striped morph is quite similar but with a narrow reddish middorsal stripe.

Similar species: Both of the ravine salamanders have few if any light markings on their belly and occur either further west or further south. The Cheat Mountain salamander has a virtually plain dark belly *and* throat and somewhat larger light flecks on the sides.

Molecularly determined species

170b. The Shenandoah Mountain Salamander, *Plethodon virginia*, has both an unstriped and striped morph. Except for range, the unstriped morph of the Shenandoah Mountain salamander is impossible to differentiate from the valley and ridge salamander in the field. However, the striped morph of the Shenandoah Mountain salamander, found in the mountains of Augusta and Rockingham counties, Virginia, and adjacent West Virginia, can be identified by its dorsal marking. The overall range of the Shenandoah Mountain salamander comprises the Shenandoah Mountains from Rockingham County, Virginia, and Pendleton County, West Virginia, to Hardy and Hampton counties, West Virginia. The range is delineated on the west by the South Fork of the Potomac River and on the east by the Cacapon and Lost Rivers. This species hybridizes in some ar-

170b. Shenandoah Mountain Salamander

eas with the more westerly and southerly valley and ridge salamander. Identify *Plethodon virginia* by range.

171. Pigeon Mountain Salamander

Plethodon petraeus

Abundance/Range: Although found only in two locations on Pigeon Mountain in Walker County, Georgia, this is a fairly common salamander.

Habitat: This salamander inhabits areas of rocky substrate, the twilight zones of caves, and cliff-face fissures.

Size: The record for this salamander is 7⅜ inches.

Identifying features: Adult Pigeon Mountain salamanders are a warm reddish brown to olive brown above (often including the head, face, and upper surface of the tail) with black sides and a black belly. White and gold flecks adorn the brown areas and the sides are liberally speckled with white. There are 16 costal grooves.

Similar species: None on Pigeon Mountain.

171. Pigeon Mountain Salamander

172a. Southern Ravine Salamander

Plethodon richmondi

southern
northern

Abundance/Range: This is a common small woodland salamander. It ranges southward from northern Kentucky and southwestern West Virginia to northwestern North Carolina and adjacent Tennessee.
Habitat: Look for this salamander beneath rocks (a strongly favored habitat) and fallen trees on hillsides and ravine slopes. It often moves from the interior of deciduous woodlands to seek cover under human-generated debris in adjoining backyards.
Size: An adult size of 5½ inches is attained.
Identifying features: This small, dark brown salamander is variably flecked with tiny pepperings of silver and gold. The tail is about half of the total length. The chin is lighter than the belly and mottled with darker pigment. The belly is unmarked and gray to nearly black. Costal grooves vary between 19 and 23.
Similar species: Other lungless salamanders that occur in the range of the ravine salamander have red backs or speckled bellies, or both.

172a. Southern Ravine Salamander

Molecularly determined species

172b. The Northern Ravine Salamander, *Plethodon electromorphus*, is identical in external appearance to its southern relative *Plethodon richmondi*, but differs genetically. This species occurs from northern Ohio, southeastern Indiana, and southwestern Pennsylvania southward to northern Kentucky.

172b. Northern Ravine Salamander

173. Weller's Salamander

Plethodon welleri

Abundance/Range: This high-altitude salamander is quite common but of restricted range. It occurs in several locations in counties along the convergence of the Virginia-North Carolina-Tennessee state lines.

Habitat: The favored habitats are high-elevation spruce-fir forests. However, it occurs sparingly in dense deciduous woodlands at elevations as low as 2,150 feet. This small salamander hides under all manner of surface debris.

Size: This salamander is adult at 3⅛ inches in length.

173. Weller's Salamander

Identifying features: This is a small black salamander with a variable but often profuse spangling of gold flecks on the back and sides. Some examples may be more gold than black. Weller's salamanders on Grandfather Mountain usually have a uniformly dark belly. Elsewhere the dark belly bears tiny white spots. Costal grooves usually number 16.

Similar species: None.

Comments: Two subspecies (*Plethodon welleri welleri*, from Grandfather Mountain, North Carolina, and *Plethodon welleri ventromaculatus*, elsewhere in the range) are occasionally recognized. However, overlapping characteristics indicate that geographic differentiation is not justified.

174. Yonahlossee Salamander

Plethodon yonahlossee

Abundance/Range: Although so secretive that it is seldom seen, the Yonahlossee salamander is actually quite common. It occurs from southwestern Virginia in a southwestward swath along the North Carolina–Tennessee state lines to southern North Carolina.

Habitat: The typical form of this species is found in deciduous forestlands where it spends much of its time below the surface of the ground. It ranges widely through damp woodlands and can be quite common where surface boulders, stones, moss-covered talus, and fallen trees are plentiful.

The Bat Cave variant is often found well away from the ground, in deep clefts in rocky road cuts, cliff faces, outcroppings, or weathered boulders. It is especially partial to rocky habitats and may occur near and in the entrances of caves and fissured escarpments.

Size: At 8$^{11}/_{16}$ inches, this is the largest species in this genus.

Identifying features: This is a remarkably beautiful salamander. The Bat Cave variant is variable both in color and pattern.

The typical Yonahlossee form is a big robust salamander with

174a. Yonahlossee Salamander

174b and c. Yonahlossee Salamander (Crevice Salamander morph)

a solid, uneven-edged, deep red dorsum, light gray to almost white upper sides, and dark head, tail, and upper surfaces of the limbs. The face, sides of the tail, and underside of the limbs are light gray. The belly is dark gray and usually marked with lighter spots. The red of the back may be duller, broken, or almost absent on some examples. The light coloration of the sides may be broken into spots or almost solid.

The Bat Cave variants may have the red of the dorsum prominent, patchy, or even lacking. The sides are dark with light spots.

Similar species: No other salamanders within the range of this species have a red back margined by light pigment. Examples lacking red are quite easily confused with the various slimy (175–178) or Appalachian woodland (180a–180d) salamanders.

Comments: The so-called Bat Cave salamander was once designated as *Plethodon longicrus*. It is found only in Rutherford County in western North Carolina. Bat Cave morphs are shown in photos 174b and 174c. It is still considered a valid species by some researchers.

WHITE-SPOTTED SALAMANDERS

175. Cow Knob Salamander

Plethodon punctatus

Abundance/Range: Although not uncommon, this salamander is of rather restricted distribution. It occurs at high elevations (greater than 2,500 feet) on Shenandoah and North Mountains along the Virginia–West Virginia state line.

Habitat: Look for this salamander on rocky slopes with northern exposure and old-growth mixed woodlands. These salamanders seem to prefer surface rocks rather than fallen trees for retreats.

Size: An adult size of 6¾ inches is attained.

Identifying features: Despite looking very much like a slimy salamander, the Cow Knob salamander is more closely related to Wehrle's salamander.

This is a black salamander with a variable amount of white (or yellowish) flecks. The flecks are smallest dorsally and largest and of most irregular outline laterally. The dark belly may bear sparse or liberal off-white flecking. Either 17 or 18 costal grooves are normal.

Similar species: Slimy salamanders, the group most similar in coloration, have only 16 costal grooves.

Comments: This species was long known by the common name of white-spotted salamander, but with the recent description of the white-spotted slimy salamander, *Plethodon cylindraceus*, the name was changed to avoid confusion. Cow Knob is the type locality of *Plethodon punctatus*, hence its usage as the common name.

175. Cow Knob Salamander

176. Wehrle's Salamander

Plethodon wehrlei

Abundance/Range: This common woodland salamander ranges southward from extreme southwestern New York to extreme northwestern North Carolina. Isolated populations exist in eastern Kentucky.

Habitat: An upland species throughout most of its range, Wehrle's salamander is associated with wooded hillsides and slopes, sometimes quite dry, where it hides by day beneath logs and rocks. In Kentucky it is a rock face and crevice dweller. Some populations inhabit caves.

Size: This salamander is adult at 6½ inches in length.

Identifying features: Northern examples of this salamander tend to have fewer contrasting markings than those from further south.

Typically, the ground color is very dark brown to nearly black and there is a rather profuse pattern of blue to white spots. The spots are smallest dorsally and largest on the sides. The sides may be a shade lighter than the back. The throat is grayish and often patterned with lighter pigment. The belly is usually uniform gray.

Some examples have paired yellowish spots along the back, and on others the spots may be reddish.

One color morph known as the Dixie Caverns variant occurs in Dixie Caverns and Blankenship Cave near Roanoke, Virginia. The ground color tends to be more purplish, both above and below, and the light markings, consisting of both bluish and brassy flecks, are particularly profuse.

176. Wehrle's Salamander

176. Wehrle's Salamander

Juvenile examples of all phases may have reddish spots on the dorsum.

The spots on the sides are larger than the dorsal spots and are bluish white in color. The feet are partially webbed. There are usually 17 costal grooves.
Similar species: Slimy salamanders are often more profusely spotted (especially in the north) and usually have only 16 costal grooves.

SLIMY SALAMANDER COMPLEX

This is a subgroup of the lungless, woodland salamanders. All are of moderate build and adult at 5–6½ inches in total length. All are remarkably similar in appearance; rely on the range maps to determine the identification of these salamanders. The validity of the thirteen molecularly defined species described in accounts 178b–178m has been questioned by some researchers.

Of black ground coloration, the slimy salamanders usually have spots or flecks of white, brass, or pale gold that are most profuse on the sides. Some species have red flecks on their legs. The throat may be light or dark.

In defense, these and the Appalachian woodland salamanders (*Plethodon jordani* complex) coil the body and produce a sticky, cloying, glandular exudate from the tail that is far more adhesive than slimy.

177. Tellico Salamander

Plethodon aureolus

Abundance/Range: Of restricted distribution, this salamander occurs only in Monroe and Polk counties, Tennessee, and in *immediately* adjacent Graham and Cherokee
counties, North Carolina. Most of its range is contained in

177. Tellico Salamander. Photo by R. Wayne Van Devender

the Cherokee National Forest, where it is a relatively common species in suitable habitat.

Habitat: This salamander may be found in moist wooded lowland habitats as well as at high elevations.

Size: A length of 5 inches is attained.

Identifying features: Like other slimy salamanders, the Tellico salamander has a ground color of black. However, its dorsal markings are pale yellow rather than white. The markings on the side of its face and on its sides are white. The chin is white to very light gray and the venter is dark gray to black. Examples from the lower elevations are most profusely spotted. Those from high elevations lack much of the dorsal spotting. There are 16 costal grooves.

Similar species: The other members of the slimy salamander complex from this region tend to have white dorsal spotting and are larger as adults.

178a. Northern Slimy Salamander

Plethodon glutinosus

Abundance/Range: This abundant woodland salamander and its many recently differentiated molecular spin-offs are a familiar sight to anyone who spends time in the woodlands of the northeastern and north central states. It ranges westward from southern New Hampshire to southern Illinois, and from there southward to central Alabama.

Habitat: A secretive woodland dweller, the slimy salamander can be quite abundant beneath moldering logs and surface rocks. Although it does need some ground

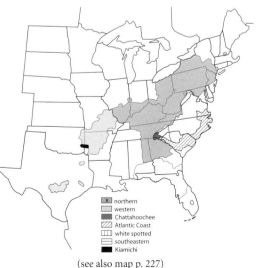

northern
western
Chattahoochee
Atlantic Coast
white spotted
southeastern
Kiamichi

(see also map p. 227)

178a. Northern Slimy Salamander

moisture, this salamander often colonizes surprisingly dry habitats in deciduous and mixed forestland.

Size: This salamander is adult at a length of about 8 inches.

Identifying features: This black salamander has prominent costal grooves. There is a variable amount (often heavy) of white flecking on the back and sides. Some, but not all, specimens have extensive white pigment on the chin and throat. Lateral spots are often larger than dorsal spots. Throat coloration is variable even within a given population. The belly is predominantly dark, but bears tiny light flecks medially and larger areas of reduced pigment ventrolaterally. Newly metamorphosed examples lack most of the light flecking and are an overall gray in color. There are 16 costal grooves.

Similar species: A black ground coloration with flecks or specks of white, brass, or gold is a common theme among the woodland salamanders. In many populations the flecking may be profuse or sparse, but is always heaviest on the sides. Use range maps to assist in the identification of these confusingly similar salamanders. Other look-alike species are documented in accounts 160, 175, 176, 177, 179, 180, and 182.

Comments: As currently understood, the slimy salamander complex consists of at least thirteen molecularly defined species of look-alike salamanders.

The slimy salamanders take their common name from the copiously exuded, cloying skin secretions that are more sticky than slimy.

Molecularly determined species

Species 178b–178m are virtually indistinguishable in appearance from the northern slimy salamander (178a) in the field.

178b. The Western Slimy Salamander, *Plethodon albagula*, has long been known as the white-chinned slimy salamander. It is locally common on rocky, wooded

178b. Western Slimy Salamander

hillsides in three disjunct areas of central and eastern Texas, as well as in Missouri, Arkansas, and adjacent Oklahoma. This salamander may have a white chin, but often does not. The dorsal spotting is of a brassy color. The lateral spotting is white. Ongoing genetic analyses have disclosed that the salamander currently known as *Plethodon albagula* is actually a complex of at least four species.

178c. The Chattahoochee Slimy Salamander, *Plethodon chattahoochee*, occurs in northeastern Georgia and immediately adjacent North Carolina and Tennessee. This is a light-chinned species, often with sparse dorsal flecking, but with profuse white or off-white lateral spotting.

178c. Chattahoochee Slimy Salamander

178d. Atlantic Coast Slimy Salamander. Photo by R. Wayne Van Devender

178d. The Atlantic Coast Slimy Salamander, *Plethodon chlorobryonis*, ranges southward on the coastal plain from southeastern Virginia to central South Carolina, then westward to the western tip of South Carolina. Usually of relatively small size, this species has small, off-white dorsal spots and profuse white or off-white lateral spotting.

178e. The White-spotted Slimy Salamander, *Plethodon cylindraceus*, is a piedmont species that ranges southward from Virginia to north central South Carolina. This species has white spotting both dorsally and laterally.

178e. White-spotted Slimy Salamander

178f. Southeastern Slimy Salamander. Photo by Scott Cushnir

178f. The Southeastern Slimy Salamander, *Plethodon grobmani*, occurs over the northern half of the Florida peninsula, westward to Mobile Bay, and northward to central Georgia. This salamander not only colonizes deciduous and mixed woodlands, but is often found among pines as well. In mixed woodland it is often found beneath fallen pines. Like most of the group, this salamander has brassy to off-white dorsal spotting and white lateral spotting.

178g. The Kiamichi Slimy Salamander, *Plethodon kiamichi*, is the genetic species found in a tiny portion of southeastern Oklahoma and adjacent Arkansas. This is a large slimy salamander with large, brass-colored to off-white dorsal flecks and considerable white to yellowish white lateral spots.

Louisiana
Mississippi
Ocmulgee
Savannah
Sequoyah
South Carolina

(see also map p. 223)

178g. Kiamichi Slimy Salamander

178h. Louisiana Slimy Salamander

178h. The Louisiana Slimy Salamander, *Plethodon kisatchie*, is the representative of the species complex found in central northern Louisiana and south central Arkansas. The populations are disjunct. This slimy salamander is profusely spotted with brassy or off-white flecks above and large white spots on the sides.

178i. The range of the Mississippi Slimy Salamander, *Plethodon mississippi*, extends southward from western Tennessee to the Gulf Coast of Mississippi and eastern Louisiana. This rather small representative of the group has large brassy dorsal flecks and profuse white(ish) lateral spots.

178i. Mississippi Slimy Salamander

178j. Ocmulgee Slimy Salamander

178j. The Ocmulgee Slimy Salamander, *Plethodon ocmulgee*, is the slimy sala-mander of eastern Georgia. This salamander has some white lateral spotting and rather sparsely scattered white to brass-colored dorsal flecks.

178k. The Savannah Slimy Salamander, *Plethodon savannah*, is of restricted distribution. It occurs only in the vicinity of Richmond and Jefferson counties, Georgia. Both dorsal and lateral spotting is white.

178k. Savannah Slimy Salamander

178l. Sequoyah Slimy Salamander

178l. The Sequoyah Slimy Salamander, *Plethodon sequoyah*, is the slimy sala-mander of extreme southeastern Oklahoma and immediately adjacent Arkan-sas. Because of the dryness in that region, this is a locally distributed salaman-der. This large slimy salamander has white to brassy dorsal spots and is heavily marked with white on the sides.

178m. The South Carolina Slimy Salamander, *Plethodon variolatus*, is restricted in distribution to the low country of southeastern South Carolina and adjacent Georgia. This small slimy salamander may have some brassy to off-white dorsal flecking and heavy white to yellow lateral spotting, or it may be basically devoid of markings. Sparsely marked or unicolored examples occur in southeastern South Carolina.

178m. South Carolina Slimy Salamander. Photo by R. Wayne Van Devender

179. Cumberland Plateau Salamander

Plethodon kentucki

Abundance/Range: This, like the other members of this complex, is a common woodland salamander. The range of the Cumberland Plateau salamander includes most of eastern Kentucky, adjacent West Virginia and Virginia and two small regions of Tennessee.

Habitat: This is a species of the moist deciduous woodlands of the Cumberland Plateau where, like other slimy salamanders, it leads a secretive existence.

Size: This white-spotted black salamander attains an adult length of about 6½ inches.

Identifying features: The Cumberland Plateau salamander has a ground color of black. The white spots are smallest dorsally and largest laterally. It is very like a slimy salamander in appearance. The markings on the side of its face and on its sides are white. The chin is white to very light gray, and the venter is dark slate gray. Some individuals are not profusely spotted, especially dorsally. There are 16 costal grooves.

Similar species: The Cumberland Plateau salamander and the sympatric slimy salamander are very similar in appearance. However, the latter is often somewhat larger and almost always has a dark chin.

179. Cumberland Plateau Salamander

180. Southern Appalachian Slimy Salamander

Plethodon teyahalee

Abundance/Range: This fairly common salamander occurs in western North Carolina, adjacent South Carolina, extreme northeastern Georgia, and extreme eastern Tennessee.

Habitat: This is another of the slimy salamanders of mature, moist, hardwood habitats.

Size: The Southern Appalachian slimy salamander is adult at a length of 6½ inches.

Reproduction: Little is known about the breeding biology of this salamander. It readily hybridizes with Appalachian woodland salamanders, producing progeny that are difficult to identify. Breeding probably occurs from late summer to midautumn. Eggs are laid in subsurface chambers, probably in late spring to early summer. Clutch size is unknown.

Identifying features: This is another of the many white-spotted black salamanders of Appalachia. The dorsal markings are small and often sparse. The lateral markings are larger and more profuse. There may be red spots on the legs. The chin is white to very light gray, and the venter is dark gray to black. There are 16 costal grooves.

Similar species: The other members of the slimy salamander complex from this region tend to have more profuse white dorsal spotting, are larger as adults, and have dark throats.

180. Southern Appalachian Slimy Salamander

APPALACHIAN WOODLAND SALAMANDER GROUP

This group of salamanders is fairly closely related to slimy salamanders and inhabits much the same terrain. They are restricted in distribution, however, to the southern Appalachians, and some populations are brightly colored. Like the slimy salamanders, the members of this group exude noxious, cloying secretions from tail glands. These are a deterrent to some predators. In some areas, where the ranges of the Appalachian woodland salamanders and the slimy salamanders abut or overlap, the two interbreed, producing progeny that are difficult to identify.

There is a north to south gradient in overall size, with northern examples of this group being smaller than southern ones.

Once, based on color patterns and sizes, the Appalachian woodland salamanders were divided into seven or more subspecies. Such characteristics as size and the presence or absence of red legs, red cheeks, brassy flecks, or black bellies separated the races. In 1962 these designations were found to be invalid.

As of 2003, on the basis of biochemical findings rather than color patterns, the group has again been split, this time into seven genetically determined species. Some of these are indistinguishable from others in the field, and it will be necessary to rely primarily on range maps to differentiate them.

181. Smoky Mountain Red-cheeked Salamander

Plethodon jordani

Abundance/Range: This common salamander is restricted in distribution to the Great Smoky Mountains of eastern Tennessee.

Habitat: This nocturnal salamander favors moist mountain fastnesses replete with mixed forests, often dominated by conifers. It spends the hours of daylight beneath fallen trunks and mossy stones, but wanders freely at night.

Size: The record size for this salamander is 7¼ inches.

Identifying features: This grayish black or bluish black salamander is easily identified by its tail shape (round in cross-section) and brownish red to bright red cheeks. There are usually 16 costal grooves. The hind limbs are only slightly greater in diameter than the forelimbs, an important feature when comparing this salamander to the red-cheeked color phase of the imitator salamander, *Desmognathus imitator.*

181. Smoky Mountain Red-cheeked Salamander

Similar species: The various species in the slimy salamander complex have white to yellow spots on their back and sides. The look-alike members of the dusky salamander group (the imitator and related salamanders) have hind limbs that are noticeably greater in diameter than the forelimbs.

182a. Southern Gray-cheeked Salamander

Plethodon metcalfi

Abundance/Range: This is a common salamander that ranges widely in western South Carolina, southern and central North Carolina, and the northeasternmost tip of Georgia. Use range maps to differentiate this from the northern, the Blue Ridge, and the South Mountain gray-cheeked salamanders.

southern
Blue Ridge
South Mountain
northern

Habitat: This salamander is found beneath surface debris in deciduous and mixed woodlands.

Size: The record size for this woodland salamander is 7¼ inches.

Identifying features: This is one of the more variable forms of the *jordani* complex. Over most of its range, this is a black or bluish black salamander that may have vaguely lighter cheeks. The tail is round in cross-section. There are no white spots and the limbs are the same color as the body. The belly may be light gray (northern populations) or dark gray (southern populations). In western South Carolina, this salamander species has a variable amount of brassy or gold flecking on the back and sides. The belly of this morph is also dark. There are

182a. Southern Gray-cheeked Salamander. Top: frosted morph

usually 16 costal grooves. The hind limbs are not noticeably greater in diameter than the forelimbs.

Similar species: The various species in the slimy salamander complex have white to yellow spots on their back and sides. The look-alike members of the dusky salamander group have hind limbs noticeably greater in diameter than the forelimbs.

Comments: This salamander interbreeds readily with species in the slimy salamander group. This produces hybrids with the characteristics of both parent species and difficult to identify,.

Molecularly determined species

182b. Blue Ridge Gray-cheeked Salamander, *Plethodon amplus*, is a large, dark salamander lacking flecks and spots of lighter color and having a dark belly and a light chin. This is the member of this species complex from western North Carolina (Buncombe, Henderson, and Rutherford counties).

182b. Blue Ridge Gray-cheeked Salamander

182c. South Mountain Gray-cheeked Salamander, *Plethodon meridianus*, is another large, dark-bellied salamander with a light chin and lacking light dorsal and lateral flecking or spotting. This species is found in the South Mountains (Burke, Cleveland, and Rutherford counties), North Carolina.

182c. South Mountain Gray-cheeked Salamander

182d. Northern Gray-cheeked Salamander

182d. The Northern Gray-cheeked Salamander, *Plethodon montanus*, is very similar to, but often smaller than, the southern gray-cheeked salamander, *Plethodon metcalfi*. The northern gray-cheeked salamander has a light belly and very light chin, and it lacks dorsal and lateral flecking. The northern gray-cheeked salamander occurs in eleven isolated montane populations on Brumley, Buckhorn, Burkes, Clinch, Flat Top, Garden, and Knob peaks in the Appalachian Valley and Ridge region of Virginia, and Bald, Black, Max Patch, Roan, and Sandymush peaks in the Blue Ridges of Virginia, North Carolina, and Tennessee.

183a. Red-legged Salamander

Plethodon shermani

red-legged
Cheoah Bald

Abundance/Range: This salamander is restricted in distribution to medium to high elevations of the Nantahala Mountains of western North Carolina. It is replaced in the vicinity of Cheoah Bald (in the Nantahalas) by the similar-appearing but genetically differentiated *Plethodon cheoah*.

Habitat: Moist forested mountain slopes with an abundance of fallen trees and surface stones are favored by this beautiful salamander. Like all woodland salamanders, the red-legged salamander spends the hours of daylight beneath fallen trunks and mossy stones, but wanders widely at night. It is often seen crossing roadways during nighttime rains.

Size: This salamander attains an adult length of 7¼ inches.

Identifying features: This grayish black or bluish black salamander is easily

183a. Red-legged Salamander

identified by its tail (round in cross-section) and whitish, pink, or bright red legs. There are usually 16 costal grooves. The hind limbs are about the same diameter as the forelimbs.

Similar species: The members of the slimy salamander complex have white to yellow spots on their back and sides. The look-alike dusky salamanders (the imitator and related salamanders) have hind limbs noticeably greater in diameter than the forelimbs.

Behavior: Although you may find a red-legged salamander by turning surface cover by day, it is impossible to accurately judge how common they are until you are in their habitat on a rainy night. Then dozens may be seen foraging on the forest floor and even crossing the roadways that transect their habitat. This species remains surface active to some degree even during the summer months.

Molecularly determined species

183b. The Cheoah Bald Salamander, *Plethodon cheoah*, is very similar in appearance to the red-legged salamander. However, it has less red on the legs and can be molecularly differentiated in the lab. It is from Cheoah Bald, a Nantahala

peak in Graham and Swain counties, North Carolina.

183b. Cheoah Bald Salamander

Plethodontid salamanders without additional (eastern) affiliations

The Green Salamander, an Uncommon Easterner

"Here's one! No, two! No, three! Correction, FOUR!"

I was peering intently into what looked to be a shallow, and what I knew for certain was a narrow, horizontal fissure. Only an inch or so into the fissure my flashlight beam was reflected from four sets of tiny, protuberant black eyes. Further scrutiny divulged that the small, flattened creatures to which those eyes belonged were clad dorsally in a smooth, shiny black skin profusely overlaid with green lichenate markings. The venter was lighter in color and, even as well concealed as the little creatures were, I could see one disproportionately large, splayed hind foot. The toes were long and square tipped.

We had finally found them—green salamanders, *Aneides aeneus*, the only eastern member of an otherwise western genus.

The little plethodontids had set up housekeeping in crevices in perpendicular granitic escarpments that measured four to seven feet in height. The escarpments faced each other across a leaf-littered passageway that measured from narrow to wide.

"Narrow" meant that no matter how I tried, no matter what my position, I could not haul my corpulence between the granitic outcrops. "Wide" equated to enough room, but at times only barely so, to work my way between those cold, unyielding stone shoulders.

From where we stood when we had first located the escarpment, we could see that the passageway, the stem of a T, stretched off for a hundred feet or so. The top of the T then extended out for about a hundred feet on each side of the stem. A few mini fissures ran eastward from the top, but their floors soon ascended to the surrounding woodlands, where their contours were lost.

Sighting along the shoulders of the escarpment, we could see the dampness of intermittent seeps, their outlines delineated by verdant mosses and ferns. Between the seepages were long distances of relatively dry rock clad in dormant liverworts and drought-resistant lichens. Extending back into the rock faces at varying heights, in both the damp and dry areas, were fissures, themselves of variable lengths and widths. Some were created by boulder sitting atop boulder. Others were faults in the rock itself.

And it was here that we had hoped to find and to photograph the green salamanders. (We had earlier found a single inaccessible specimen in a very wet seep, and in an even wetter one had found three pendant egg clusters.)

Once called the green climbing salamander, *A. aeneus* is, by preference, actually more of a rock crevice–dwelling species than an arboreal one. The four in the dry crevice in front of us were living proof of this.

continued

continued

But now we were faced with the problem of inducing an *aeneus* from its crevice that we might photograph the little salamander.

The solution stood just in front of me. There, as if placed by Providence, grew a couple of stalks of a tiny native bamboo. We cut both off near the ground, divested them of leaves and side shoots, and utilizing the sturdy stems like chopsticks (a task to which I am singularly unadapted) worried one of the salamanders into the open, where it posed rather readily for its photographic debut, then slowly retreated again into the darkness of the crevice.

Green Salamander, genus *Aneides*

The green salamander is the only eastern member of this small and otherwise western genus. Because it is usually found on rock faces or in escarpment crevices, this salamander was once referred to as the green climbing salamander. Western species are found in a variety of habitats, including cliff faces, and beneath loosened bark on both fallen and still-standing trees. All have squared toe tips and semi-prehensile tails, adaptations that assist them in their climbing activities.

These salamanders are secretive and, although active by day in the deep recesses of rock fissures or other cover, far more active at night, when they wander freely.

The green salamander breeds during the spring, summer, or autumn. Courtship, involving circling, head bobs by the male, contact of the female by the male's mental gland, tail straddling, and spermatophore depositions, occurs primarily in the spring or autumn. Egg deposition often occurs in June or July. Normally, the eggs are suspended from the ceiling of a damp rock crevice, but occasionally may be placed in a rotting horizontal log. Egg deposition is often biennial, and a female may remain in attendance of her clutch of 6–20+ eggs for the three months of incubation.

The green salamander eats all manner of small invertebrates.

184. Green Salamander

Aneides aeneus

Abundance/Range: Although this small salamander is found over a large region in the east, its habitat is very precise and populations are scattered widely. This species has seemingly been reduced significantly in numbers since the late 1990s.

Habitat: This salamander is normally found in horizontally creviced rock in damp cliff faces, grottoes, and mossy ravines shadowed by a dense overstory of hardwood growth. Occasionally it may be found in decomposing logs.

Size: This salamander attains a length of 5½ inches.

Identifying features: This is a small dark-colored salamander with variable, irregular green markings on its back and upper sides. Its body and head are somewhat flattened. The legs are long and the toes have squared but not dilated tips. The lower sides are gray with tiny lighter dots. The belly is light and usually unmarked. The tail is long and prehensile, an adaptation to help this salamander traverse its corridors of fissured rock.

Similar species: None. This is the only green, smooth-skinned salamander in the region. Adult newts are greenish but aquatic, lack dark blotches, and have rough skins.

184. Green Salamander

Four-toed Salamander, genus *Hemidactylium*

This small salamander of woodlands has four toes on each rear foot and a basal tail constriction. The weakly prehensile tail is fragile and autotomizes (breaks free) easily at the basal constriction.

It is a secretive, locally distributed salamander, with an extensive overall range. Breeding migrations are undertaken, often in the autumn of the year.

Breeding occurs in the autumn. Following breeding, the salamanders migrate to breeding ponds or bogs. Up to three dozen (often fewer) eggs are laid above the water level in sphagnum mats, in moss balls on tree trunks, beneath moss mats on fallen trees, or in other such moisture-retaining locations in acidic areas. Communal nesting is not uncommon. Females remain in attendance of the clutch(es) throughout the incubation period of 1½–2 months. The short-tailed larvae are aquatic.

185. Four-toed Salamander

Hemidactylium scutatum

Abundance/Range: This rather uncommon salamander has the most spotty distribution of any North American caudatan. It occurs in disjunct populations from the Gulf Coast of the United States to southern Ontario and southern Quebec.

Habitat: A good alternate name for this little plethodontid would be bog salamander, for it is almost always associated with sphagnum bogs and nearby woodlands. It seeks refuge beneath logs, fallen limbs and debris, and sphagnum mats.

Size: Most adults are 2¼–3 inches in total length. Occasional specimens attain a length of 4 inches.

Identifying features: This salamander is brownish on the back and upper sides. The brown has a fine but variable peppering of black spots. The belly is enamel white with discrete black spots. The tail is constricted at its base and may be russet dorsally. The nose is short and bluntly rounded.

Similar species: This is the only "pudgy" terrestrial salamander in eastern North America with just four toes on its hind feet. Dwarf and Chamberlain's

185. Four-toed Salamander

salamanders also are four-toed species but are long, slender, striped dorsally, and lack spots on the belly and the basal tail constriction.

Many-lined Salamander, genus *Stereochilus*

This is another monotypic genus. It is slender and narrow headed and very adept at remaining out of sight. The tail is proportionately short. It is a species of quiet seepages and semistagnant waters that often have considerable decomposing plant material along the edges. This small salamander is quite aquatic. When its home pond dries the many-lined salamander seeks seclusion in and beneath rotting logs, sphagnum, and leaf mats.

Clutches of more than 50 eggs (usually fewer) have been found above the waterline in decomposing logs. Females remain in attendance of their eggs during incubation.

186. Many-lined Salamander

Stereochilus marginatus

Abundance/Range: This salamander is found from southeastern Virginia southward along the coastal plain to northern Florida. It is quite uncommon in the latter state, but relatively common elsewhere.

Habitat: The primary habitat of this poorly known salamander is sphagnum mats, decomposing logs, and leaf mats in acidic backwaters and swamps. It may be found in standing water in the mats, or beneath the mats (or other vegetable debris) on the shore.

186. Many-lined Salamander

Size: An adult size of 4 inches may be attained.

Identifying features: This is a slender olive brown to almost black salamander on which the namesake striping can be very difficult to discern. The most visible markings include a dark stripe from the eye to the back of the head and broken, dark lines on the lower sides. The dark-speckled belly is usually somewhat lighter than the back.

Similar species: The various dusky salamanders are more robust and have hind legs that are stouter than the front legs.

chapter 14

Mudpuppies and Waterdogs

Mudpuppies and Waterdogs, family Proteidae

Although several of the species in this interesting family are taxonomically sound, the small, stream-dwelling form from the eastern Gulf Coastal Plain remains scientifically undescribed.

Whether they are known as waterdogs or mudpuppies, these salamanders are fully aquatic throughout their lives.

Waterdogs have only four toes on each foot and, as permanent (obligate) neotenes, retain three pairs of external gills, lack eyelids, and have a flattened, paddlelike tail. During active oxygen gathering the gills are extended away from the sides of the head and the filaments are bright red.

All, save a single species, are found in streams and rivers in the southeastern and south central United States. The single exception, the northern mudpuppy, occurs in rivers and lakes from northern Georgia to extreme southeastern Canada.

Small numbers of rather large eggs are deposited during cool weather (in the winter in the south, in the spring further north) in protected areas such as hollows or burrows in banks, under snags, or beneath rocks. One parent, often the female, usually remains with the clutch during incubation.

The waterdogs and mudpuppies eat all manner of small aquatic animal life. Among the dietary items are insects, crustaceans, tiny mollusks, isopods, worms, minnows, tadpoles, and occasionally other salamanders.

In the south these salamanders are often quite inactive during the summer when water temperatures are warmest.

Traditionally, the belly patterns were thought to be important in determining species and subspecies of mudpuppies. Studies have now shown considerable variation in belly pattern, even among examples from short stretches of the same stream. Use range and overall appearance when attempting identification.

187. Black Warrior Waterdog

Necturus alabamensis

Abundance/Range: This is an apparently uncommon waterdog of Appalachian portions of the Black Warrior River system of northern Alabama.

Habitat: This waterdog prefers cool streams of moderate size having a fair current. Waterdogs are found beneath submerged rocks and where cover in the form of snags and beds of leaves occur.

Size: This waterdog attains an overall length of about 10 inches.

Identifying features: The Black Warrior waterdog undergoes considerable ontogenetic change. Adults have a muddy ground color with large discrete spots on the back and sides. The midbelly is light colored and devoid of markings. The body is quite flattened, and in this the Black Warrior waterdog closely resembles the common mudpuppy. Juveniles bear a prominent light dorsolateral stripe on each side, another characteristic shared with the mudpuppy.

Similar species: This and the more busily spotted Eastern Gulf Coast waterdog (193) are found sympatrically in some streams. The latter is more rounded (in cross-section) and has a finely speckled belly.

187. Black Warrior Waterdog

~~~~~~

The Search for a Waterdog

It was November, and the call of a roadtrip was too strong to resist. We needed photographs of the black warrior waterdog, *Necturus alabamensis*, a species found in northern Alabama. We didn't know how successful we'd be but the trip would be a welcome break in routine.

There are, in a way, two black warrior waterdogs. There's a northern type, our quarry, that's found north of the fall line in clear rivers with rapid water flow. They grow to 8¼ inches in length, and are distinct from a smaller waterdog found south of the fall line. For years these were all grouped as the black warrior waterdog but recent studies have proved the groups to be distinct from each other. The southern group is as yet unnamed.

We spent the night in the little village of Wren, Alabama, and headed out on the photographic sojourn the next morning. Dick had been to the area about ten years previously and seemed to remember where river access was possible.

We visited several sites. The first pool was just a stone's throw from the paved roadway. We crossed a low bridge and pulled off in the verge to park. Just upstream from the bridge was a deep bend in the river. The bottom was dotted with piles of submerged leaves, a favored cold-weather hiding spot for the waterdogs. We used dip nets to scoop up a few leaf piles, dump them on the edge of the bank, and paw through them to find the waterdogs. This was November, and the water was cold. The rubber gloves I brought proved useful in sorting the wet, cold leaf piles. We found dragonfly larvae, tiny crawdads, and snails but no waterdogs.

The second site was down a side road, past a half-dozen "posted" areas, and at the bottom of a deeply rutted, steep roadway leading to a boat ramp. The boat-ramp area was large enough for a couple of cars with trailers but that cold morning we were alone. We pulled out the nets and the buckets and clomped to the river in our rubber boots.

The cliff on the far side of the river bore sedimentary stripes of white, brown, and gray and hung over the river. The river was fast moving and so clear the water was pale green in the deeper portions. Piles of leaves marked the bottom, some tumbling in the water's flow.

We picked a patch of leaves within a net's-reach of the shoreline, scooped, and dumped. Crawdads. Snails. A couple of very small fish. But wait—atop a mud-soaked leaf a tiny wriggle revealed a creature with a squared nose and brown, black, and white stripes on the body. It was a larval black warrior waterdog, about an inch-and-a-half long. A few scoops later we found a five-incher.

In turn, we placed each atop submerged leaves in a shallow water-filled dish and photographed them. Within minutes of being found, both of the little waterdogs had been released to continue life amid the river-bottom leaves.

~~~~~~

188. Gulf Coast Waterdog

Necturus beyeri

Abundance/Range: Juveniles and subadults are commonly found. There are two disjunct populations, one in eastern Texas and west central Louisiana and the other in the Pearl River drainage of eastern Louisiana and southern and central Mississippi.

Habitat: This is a waterdog of sandy, spring-fed streams of small to moderate size with a fair current. These waterdogs can be common where snags and beds of leaves are adequate.

Size: This is a small waterdog. Adults may attain a length of 8½ inches but are usually smaller.

Identifying features: The dark-spotted back and sides of this waterdog are muddy brown. The belly is peppered with tiny dark spots. Immature waterdogs of this species are similar in color and pattern to the adults.

Similar species: This is the only large aquatic salamander in Texas and central western Louisiana with four toes on all four of its feet. In central western Louisiana the range of this species abuts that of the Red River mudpuppy, a more flattened species that is striped when a juvenile. The easternmost edge of the eastern range of the Gulf Coast waterdog abuts that of a very similar appearing waterdog that differs genetically, the Eastern Gulf Coast waterdog (193). Depend on range maps to differentiate the two.

188. Gulf Coast Waterdog

189. Neuse River Waterdog

Necturus lewisi

Abundance/Range: This waterdog seems to be moderately uncommon. It is the smaller sizes that are seen most often. It inhabits streams and rivers (Neuse, Tar-Pamlico drainages) of moderate size in central eastern North Carolina.

Habitat: This is one of the more extensively studied of the southern waterdogs. It has been found to prefer streams greater than 15 feet wide and with moderate to fast flow rate. The Neuse River waterdog occurs on various substrates, varying from bedrock to muck, but seems most common on hard substrates where cover in the form of rocks, snags, and leafbeds is plentiful.

Size: Adults of this waterdog may occasionally reach 10½ inches long.

Identifying features: This waterdog is clad in a ground color of rusty brown dorsally and laterally. The belly is duller brown to gray. Discrete bluish black spots of variable size are present on all body surfaces but somewhat larger dorsally than ventrally. Adults become increasingly darker with advancing age. Juvenile Neuse River waterdogs are prominently spotted.

Similar species: This is the only *large*, four-toed, externally gilled salamander in eastern North Carolina. The sympatric dwarf waterdog may be speckled but lacks large spots.

189. Neuse River Waterdog

190. Common Mudpuppy

Necturus maculosus maculosus

common
Red River

Abundance/Range: This mudpuppy ranges southward from southern Quebec and southeastern Manitoba to northern Georgia and northern Mississippi. It is common to abundant through much of this range.

Habitat: This huge salamander may be found in streams, rivers, and their associated impoundment lakes, ponds, and oxbows, as well as in both shallow and deep isolated lakes.

Size: This is the largest species of the genus. Adults are commonly 9–14 inches long. The record is 19⅛ inches.

Identifying features: The common mudpuppy has a reddish yellow to mud gray or reddish brown back and sides. There is a vague light and dark longitudinal pattern on each side, and large (sometimes obscure) dark spots on the back and sides. The grayish belly is also prominently spotted but the spots are smaller than those on the dorsum. A dark eye stripe is present. Juveniles are prominently patterned with light and dark stripes.

Similar species: None. This is the only mudpuppy/waterdog within its range.

Comments: Often the only way this nocturnal salamander is known to be in a given body of water is when one is caught on hook and line by a startled angler.

190. Common Mudpuppy. Top: adult; bottom: juvenile

Additional subspecies

191. The Red River Mudpuppy, *Necturus maculosus louisianensis*, is the southwestern representative of this species. It ranges from Oklahoma and southern Missouri to central Louisiana.

It is very similar in appearance to the common mudpuppy, but tends to be a little yellower in ground color. It retains vestiges of the juvenile striped pattern until well into adulthood and usually has a pure white, unspotted belly.

191. Red River Mudpuppy

192. Dwarf Waterdog

Necturus punctatus

Abundance: This waterdog is common over much of its range, which extends southward from southeastern Virginia to central Georgia.
Habitat: This is the smallest of our waterdogs. It occurs in both large and medium-sized slow-flowing streams. It prefers areas with an accumulation of detritus on the bottom.
Size: The adult's length is 7½ inches or less.
Identifying features: This small waterdog may lack flecking or be liberally peppered with tiny spots. The dorsal and lateral color of mud tones affords wonderful camouflage. The belly is usually a little lighter than the back. Immatures are similar to the adults.
Similar species: The Neuse River waterdog is the only species sympatric with the dwarf wa-

192. Dwarf Waterdog

terdog. The Neuse River waterdog is prominently spotted. Dusky salamanders have five toes on their hind feet and adults lack gills.

193. Eastern Gulf Coast Waterdog

Necturus species cf *beyeri*

Abundance/Range: This is an abundant waterdog. Juveniles are especially easily found. They occur in streams of the Gulf Coastal Plain from Florida's central panhandle to the Pearl River drainage of Mississippi.

Habitat: These salamanders prefer leafbeds in streams of small to moderate size with a fair current.

Size: Adults measure 5–8 inches in total length.

Identifying features: This is a very dark-colored waterdog. Some examples are so dark that it is difficult to determine the busy pattern of dark spots scattered profusely on the back and sides. The venter is light and unspotted. Immatures are similar to the adults.

Similar species: This is the only large, aquatic salamander in Florida and the Gulf Coast streams of Alabama and Mississippi with four toes on all four of its feet. It does ascend some streams well into the uplands. It is sympatric with the Black Warrior waterdog in some stretches of the Black Warrior River drainage in Alabama. The Black Warrior waterdog has much larger and many fewer spots and a more flattened body and is striped as a juvenile.

Comments: The systematics of this undescribed waterdog are under study.

chapter 15

Newts

Newts, family Salamandridae

Just as all toads are frogs, but not vice versa, all newts are salamanders, but not all salamanders are newts. There are only three species of newts in eastern and central North America, but one of these has four subspecies. The various races of the red-spotted newt still seem to be common to abundant whereas the black-spotted newt of Texas and the striped newt of the deep Southeast are now uncommon.

Under ideal conditions, the life of the newts found in the east can be divided into four stages: the aquatic egg stage, the aquatic larval stage, the terrestrial eft stage (this may be skipped if terrestrial conditions are hostile), and the adult stage. The adult stage is preferentially aquatic, but may be terrestrial if the home pond dries. Populations of newts are known occasionally to be neotenic, retaining larval characteristics yet attaining sexual maturity.

Adult newts have rough skin. The skin of the larvae is smooth and slimy. During the breeding season (spring in the North and throughout the year in the South) males develop heightened tail fins and black, roughened excrescences on the inner sides of the hind legs and on the toetips. These serve the male in his breeding embrace. The female is grasped around her neck or shoulders by the "nonskid" hind legs of the male. Tail undulations by the male apparently waft stimulatory pheromones to the female. After adequate stimulation she will pick up a sperm packet from the tip of a spermatophore with her cloacal labia. Following this the eggs are laid singly and often loosely wrapped in the leaf of an aquatic plant.

Newts eat tiny insects, worms, and other invertebrates.

194. Texas Black-spotted Newt

Notophthalmus meridionalis meridionalis

Abundance/Range: Once quite common along the Gulf Coast of South Texas, this is now a rare and protected species. It is also found in northeastern Mexico.

Habitat: This is a locally distributed newt that may be fairly common in a given pond for one or two years, then seems to disappear for a variable duration. Look for the black-spotted newt in and near permanent to semipermanent bodies of still water from Point Lavaca southward.

Size: This newt attains an adult size of 4¼ inches.

Identifying features: Both the adult and the eft of the black-spotted newts are grayish green to dark olive green dorsally. Wavy light lateral lines and a light vertebral line are usually visible. The venter is peach to orange. They bear a profusion of black spots on all body surfaces.

Similar species: None. No other newt or salamander in Texas exhibits the colors of the black-spotted newt.

194. Texas Black-spotted Newt

195. Striped Newt

Notophthalmus perstriatus

Abundance/Range: Historically this newt ranged northward from Florida's north central peninsula and eastern panhandle to easternmost Georgia. It is now absent in many areas where formerly found and uncommon in others. It is a protected species.

195. Striped Newt. Bottom: neotenic adult

Habitat: The striped newt has a curiously spotty distribution. It may be present in one location, but absent from nearby areas that look virtually identical. Look for it in and near temporary ponds and cypress heads in pine flatwoods and pine sandhills.

Size: This species is adult at 3½ inches in length.

Identifying features: Adults and efts are yellowish green, olive, or nearly brown dorsally. The red dorsolateral stripes begin on the head and continue to about one-third of the tail. A series of red spots may be present on the terminal two-thirds of the tail. There may be a line of red ovals or rounded spots on the trunk below the red stripe. The belly is yellow and bears a sparse peppering of black spots.

Similar species: None. Within the range of the striped newt, no other newt or salamander has a continuous red stripe along each side.

Comments: This newt is able to withstand sustained droughts (apparently up to several years) by burrowing.

196. Red-spotted Newt

*Notophthalmus viridescens
viridescens*

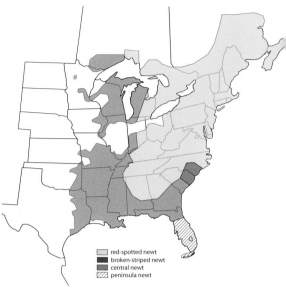

red-spotted newt
broken-striped newt
central newt
peninsula newt

Abundance/Range: This rough-skinned salamander is a common species from Nova Scotia and southern Ontario southward to central Georgia.

Habitat: This newt prefers heavily vegetated, permanent waters, and may inhabit canals, lakes, ponds, oxbows, slow streams, and drainage ditches. There is usually a terrestrial eft stage.

Size: This newt is adult at 5½ inches in length.

Identifying features: Dorsally and on the upper sides the red-spotted newt is olive or khaki green. A dorsolateral series of tiny, black-outlined red spots is present on each side. The lower sides and belly are yellow and heavily peppered with tiny black spots. The larvae are a rather nondescript olive. Efts are coral red to orange (olive orange to almost black just before reentering the ponds as adults) with black-edged, brighter red dorsolateral spots. The eft lacks a fin on the tail.

Similar species: None, but see accounts 197 and 198 for descriptions of the broken-striped and central subspecies of this newt.

196. Red-spotted Newt, amplexing pair

196. Red-spotted Newt, eft stage

Additional subspecies

197. The Broken-striped Newt, *Notophthalmus viridescens dorsalis*, occurs in southeastern North Carolina and adjacent South Carolina. It is very similar to the red-spotted newt in appearance but somewhat smaller, seldom exceeding 4 inches in length. This subspecies has broken, black-outlined, red dorsolateral stripes rather than spots. The eft phase, if assumed, is darker than the adult, and the red markings are not strongly outlined.

197. Broken-striped Newt

198. Central Newt

198. Central Newt, *Notophthalmus viridescens louisianensis*, ranges southward from southwestern Ontario to the Gulf Coast and from eastern Texas to southeastern South Carolina. It attains a 5-inch adult length. The central newt has a yellowish green to olive dorsum and may or may not have a dorsolateral row of tiny red spots on each side. The red spots, if present, are not edged with black. The eft stage is often omitted.

199. Peninsula Newt, *Notophthalmus viridescens piaropicola*, is the most nondescript of the eastern newts. It may attain 4 inches in total length. The dorsum is dark olive, olive brown, or nearly black. Small black spots, heaviest laterally, may be present. There are no red spots. The venter is dark olive yellow heavily peppered with fine black dots.

199. Peninsula Newt

chapter 16

Sirens

Sirens, family Sirenidae

The fact that sirens have only forelimbs makes them unlike any other salamander.

The five species in this family of southeastern and south central salamanders are aquatic and bear three pairs of bushy external gills throughout their lives. Dwarf sirens have only a single gill slit while the greater and lesser sirens have three. The eyes of all species lack lids.

Although fully functional, the forelimbs are small. The greater and lesser sirens have four toes on each foot but the dwarf sirens have only three toes. The forelimbs are folded along the side while the siren is swimming, brought forward as the siren comes to rest, and moved as typical legs when it crawls.

Differentiating the species and subspecies of sirens can be very confusing. Patterns may overlap widely and are not, in themselves, reliable differentiating features. The counting of costal grooves (very difficult on a moving salamander) and range must also be factored in.

These eel-like creatures are primarily nocturnal in their activity patterns. During periods of drought that deplete or dry their ponds and sloughs, the salamanders burrow into the bottom muck and form slime cocoons to conserve body moisture.

Dwarf Sirens, genus *Pseudobranchus*

This genus consists of two species of confusingly similar, tiny, slender, eel-like salamanders, each with subspecies. The narrow-striped and Everglades dwarf sirens have a rounded snout and are often found amid the root systems of floating plants or burrowed into mats of floating vegetation.

The remaining three forms, all subspecies of the broad-striped dwarf siren, have a more pointed nose and are persistent burrowers in pond bottom detritus.

Dwarf sirens eat tiny aquatic organisms.

Despite the fact that these species scatter their eggs, it is thought that egg fertilization is external.

200. Narrow-striped Dwarf Siren

Pseudobranchus axanthus axanthus

narrow-striped
Everglades

Abundance/Range: This is a common species. It is restricted to Florida, from Jacksonville and Gulf Hammock to the vicinity of Tampa Bay and Vero Beach.

Habitat: This salamander may often be found in the root systems of aquatic plants. It is a pond, lake, and marsh dweller.

Size: Adults of this diminutive siren may attain a length of 9 inches.

Identifying features: The light lateral striping of this dark-colored siren tends to be suffused (at least in areas) by dark pigment and to have irregular edges. The back and sides are olive gray to nearly black. There are 4 thin, dark dorsal stripes that may be difficult to see on examples having a dark ground color. The gray venter has light spots. The head is rather broad and the snout rather rounded. Juveniles are similar to the adults in coloration.

Similar species: The greater and lesser sirens have 4 toes on each hand. The various races of the broad-striped dwarf siren are very similar (202, 203, 204), but do have a sharper nose and differ in habitat preference.

200. Narrow-striped Dwarf Siren

Additional subspecies

201. The Everglades Dwarf Siren, *Pseudobranchus axanthus belli*, is smaller and more precisely patterned. Adult at 4–6 inches, it ranges southward from the latitude of northern Lake Okeechobee to the southern tip of the peninsula. Its venter is a nearly unicolored gray; the lateral stripe is buff, bordered both top and bottom by a light stripe; the dorsum is dark (olive black) and contains three lighter stripes.

201. Everglades Dwarf Siren

202. Broad-striped Dwarf Siren

Pseudobranchus striatus striatus

202. Broad-striped Dwarf Siren

broad-striped
Gulf Hammock
slender

Abundance/Range: This dwarf siren ranges southward from southeastern South Carolina to extreme northeastern Florida.

Habitat: Acidic cypress pools and swamps having a soft substrate are favored. These may be in rather open areas or located in pine and mixed flatwoods. The subspecies of this siren are all persistent burrowers in pond bottom muck and detritus.

Size: This species is adult at 8 inches.

Identifying features: The broad-striped dwarf siren has a narrow, somewhat pointed head. The dark back is edged by a rather broad tan line on each side. A narrow light vertebral line is present.

The cream to tan lateral line is broad, usually straight edged, and bordered above and beneath by a narrower dark line. The gray belly is rather strongly marked with dark reticulations.

Similar species: The two races of the narrow-striped dwarf siren have rather rounded heads and prefer life amid floating vegetation (200, 201). The lesser and greater sirens both have four toes on each forefoot.

Additional subspecies

203. The Gulf Hammock Dwarf Siren, *Pseudobranchus striatus lustricolus*, continues to evade searchers. It was found in the 1950 in floodwaters following a hurricane. It is known only from the immediate vicinity of Florida's Gulf Hammock area in Citrus and Levy counties. This 8-inch dwarf siren is the most distinctively patterned of the dwarf sirens. Three precisely defined yellowish stripes trisect the broad black dorsal area. An orange-buff dorsolateral and a silvery gray ventrolateral stripe are on each side. The belly is dark.

203. Gulf Hammock Dwarf Siren (illustration by Dale Johnson)

204. The Slender Dwarf Siren, *Pseudobranchus striatus spheniscus*, is the palest of the three subspecies. The colors tend to shade into each other rather than being precisely delineated. The dark middorsal field contains three poorly de-

204. Slender Dwarf Siren

fined buff stripes and shades to olive brown at the edges. The pale lateral stripes contain a variable amount of dark pigment. The lower sides are gray and flecked with the same color as the light lateral stripe. The venter is gray(ish) with irregularly placed obscure light spots. Despite its common name, it is of the same body proportions as its relatives. It is found in southern Georgia and the Florida panhandle.

Greater and Lesser Sirens, genus *Siren*

The species in this genus measure 8–38 inches in length as adults. Collectively they range southward along the coastal plains from southern mainland Maryland to extreme northeastern Mexico. They are powerful predators, eating all manner of small aquatic organisms including fish, frogs, and other salamanders. Although very little is known about the reproductive biology of these salamanders, female lesser sirens have been found attending eggs in mats of floating vegetation. The largest known nest contained 381 eggs.

205. Eastern Lesser Siren

Siren intermedia intermedia

Abundance/Range: This is a common salamander of vegetation-choked waterways from southeastern Virginia to central Florida, then west to central Alabama.
Habitat: A ubiquitous salamander, this species inhabits river edges, ditches, canals, and cypress ponds. It may occasionally be found amid tangles of floating vegetation but seems to prefer rooting through the bottom muck and detritus.
Size: The record size for this subspecies is 15½ inches.
Identifying features: The back and sides are olive black to olive gray. Throughout most of its range, this salamander develops a pattern of dark spots anteriorly. In Florida's Big Bend and southern panhandle, the entire body may bear small black spots. The ventral color is usually somewhat lighter than the back and sides. Some develop bulbous heads. The tail tip is rather narrowly pointed. Juveniles are often darker than the adults. Juveniles and subadults may have a red(dish) to white band along the jawline. There are 35 or fewer costal grooves.
Similar species: The greater siren may have light or dark dorsal and lateral markings. It is of more robust build and has a more bluntly rounded tail tip and

205. Eastern Lesser Siren

more than 36 costal grooves. Juvenile greater sirens can be very difficult to differentiate from lesser sirens. Dwarf sirens retain stripes throughout their lives and have only three toes on their forefeet.

Additional subspecies

206. The Western Lesser Siren, *Siren intermedia nettingi*, is a common salamander from Mississippi to eastern Texas and northward up the Mississippi River valley to central Illinois. Molecular interpretations have led some researchers to consider this form a full species. It is a large race, with record lengths up to 19¾ inches. The ground color is olive to greenish. It has light facial stripes. It is liberally marked dorsally with dark spots. This race has light spots on its belly. Hatchling western lesser sirens may have indications of light vertebral and ventrolateral stripes as well as dark spots. Old adults may be an almost unicolor olive black.

206. Western Lesser Siren

207. Greater Siren

Siren lacertina

Abundance/Range: This is a common but seldom seen salamander. It is found northward from southern mainland Florida to Alabama's Mobile Bay and eastern Maryland.

Habitat: It is abundant in shallow, soft-bottomed swamps, marshes, canals, ponds, and lakes, but may also be found amid vegetation in sandy-bottomed creeks. Hatchlings and juveniles are commonly found in mats of floating vegetation.

Size: The record size for this salamander is a robust 38½ inches.

Identifying features: The ground color of the greater siren can vary from brown to olive green both dorsally and ventrally. The lower sides may be somewhat lighter than the dorsum. The back and sides are mottled or reticulated with spots or bars of darker and/or lighter pigment. The sides are flecked with black, blue, green, or gold. Examples from the Florida panhandle often bear liberal black spots. Large examples may be an almost unicolored brown to olive black. The venter is usually lighter than the back and sides.

Hatchlings and juveniles have indications of longitudinal striping and light chin, cheeks, and belly.

When not truncated by injury, the compressed tail tip of the greater siren is rather bluntly rounded in profile.

There are 36 or more costal grooves.

Similar species: The lesser siren may have a bluish cast to its brown body and has dark spots on the head, back, and sides, a much more sharply pointed tail tip, and 35 or fewer costal grooves.

207. Greater Siren

208. Texas Siren

Siren texana

Abundance/Range: This is an uncommon and protected salamander of southern Texas and extreme northeastern Mexico.
Habitat: The Texas siren can be found in a variety of habitats,
but prefers resacas (oxbows) and drainage canals choked with
aquatic vegetation. Hatchlings and juveniles may occasionally be found in mats
of floating vegetation. These salamanders burrow deeply when their water
sources temporarily dry.
Size: This large siren occasionally attains a length of 27 inches.
Identifying features: This large, robust siren seldom has a distinct pattern, instead having its olive-tan to olive-green dorsum vaguely peppered with tiny
black flecks. The belly is lighter than the back. Juveniles may be darker overall
than the adults and hatchlings may have a red(dish) band on the sides of the
head and (often) across the top of the head. This siren normally has 36–38 costal
grooves.
Similar species: The western lesser siren, with which this species interbreeds
where the ranges abut, normally has 34–36 costal grooves and has not yet been
documented at a length of more than 17 inches.
Comments: This siren was long considered a subspecies of the lesser siren,
Siren intermedia.

208. Texas Siren

Glossary

Adpress—Extend a foreleg directly rearward and a rear leg directly forward to count the number of body (costal) grooves between them or to ascertain the length of the hind limb.

Aestivation—A period of warm-weather inactivity, often triggered by excessive heat or drought.

Ambient temperature—The temperature of the surrounding environment.

Ambystomatid—A mole salamander.

Amplexus—The breeding embrace of amphibians or toads.

Anterior—Toward the front.

Anuran—A tailless amphibian.

Anus—The external opening of the cloaca; the vent.

Arboreal—Tree dwelling.

Bilateral—On both sides equally.

Bufonid—A toad.

Canthus-rostralis—An angle on the sides of the snout.

Caudal—Pertaining to the tail.

Caudata—The taxonomic order containing all salamanders. The word Caudata is occasionally replaced with Urodela.

Caudate, caudatan—As used here, a salamander.

Chert—Flintlike rock pieces.

Cirri—Downward projecting appendages associated with the nostrils of some male plethodontid salamanders.

Cloaca—The common chamber into which digestive, urinary, and reproductive systems empty and which itself opens exteriorly through the vent or anus.

Congeneric—Grouped in the same genus.

Cornified—Horny, roughened, hardened.

Costal grooves—Vertical grooves on the sides of some salamanders.

Cranial crests—The raised ridges on the top of the head of toads.

Crepuscular—Active at dusk and/or dawn.

Deposition—As used here, the laying of eggs or birthing of young.

Deposition site—The nesting site.

Diapause—A naturally occurring, temporary cessation in the development of an egg.

Dichromatic—Exhibiting two color phases, often sex linked.

Dimorphic—A difference in form, build, or coloration involving the same species, often sex linked.

Direct development—As used with amphibia, complete development within the egg capsule; no free-swimming larval stage.

Disjunct—Separated.

Diurnal—Active in the daytime.

Dorsal—Pertaining to the back or upper surface.

Dorsolateral—Pertaining to the upper side.

Dorsolateral ridge—A glandular longitudinal ridge on the upper sides of some frogs.

Dorsum—The upper surface.

Ecological niche—The precise habitat utilized by a species.

Ectothermic—"Cold-blooded," pertaining to an organism that absorbs its body heat from the environment.

Endemic—Confined to a specific region.

Endothermic—"Warm-blooded," pertaining to an organism that produces its own body heat.

Erythristic—Displaying an inordinate amount of red coloration.

Femur—The part of the leg between the hip and the knee.

Form—An identifiable species or subspecies.

Genus (*pl.* **genera**)—A taxonomic classification of a group of species having similar characteristics. The genus falls between the next higher designation of family and the next lower designation of species. The generic name is always capitalized when written and the name is always written in italics.

Gravid—The amphibian equivalent of mammalian pregnancy; carrying unborn young.

Gular—Pertaining to the throat.

Herpetologist—One who indulges in herpetology.

Herpetology—The study (often scientifically oriented) of reptiles and amphibians, conducted by a **herpetologist**.

Hybrid—Offspring resulting from the breeding of two species or noncontiguous subspecies.

Hylid—A treefrog family member.

Intergrade—Offspring resulting from the breeding of two adjacent subspecies.

Interorbital—Between the eyes.

Interrupted—As used here, a break in the dorsolateral ridge followed by an inset of the ridge that follows.

Intertympanic—Between (or connecting) the **tympani**, the external eardrums of anurans.

Iridophore—Cells that contain reflective platelets.

Juvenile—A young or immature specimen.

Lappet—As used here, a flap of skin on the throat of some male toads that covers the deflated vocal sac.

Larval—Pertaining to **larvae**, the aquatic immature stage of amphibians.

Lateral—Pertaining to the side.

Mandibular—Pertaining to the jaws.

Melanism—A profusion of **melanin**, a black pigment.

Melanophore—A cell that synthesizes melanin.

Mental gland—An often large pheromone-secreting gland on the chin of some salamanders.

Metamorph—A baby amphibian newly transformed from the larval to the adult stage.

Metamorphosis—The transformation from one stage of an amphibian's life to another.

Middorsal—Pertaining to the middle of the back.

Midventral—Pertaining to the middle of the belly.

Monotypic—Containing only one genus or species.

Montane—Associated with mountains.

Nasal cirri—*See* **cirri**.

Nektonic—Free swimming.

Neotenic (or **paedomorphic**)—Pertaining to a salamander that permanently retains larval characteristics.

Nocturnal—Active at night.

Nominate—The first named subspecies within a species.

Ocelli—Dark- or light-edged circular spots.

Ontogenetic—Age-related (color) changes.

Oviparous—Reproducing by means of eggs that hatch after laying.

Oviposition—The laying of eggs.

Paedomorphic—*See* **neotenic**.

Papillae—Small, fleshy, nipplelike protuberances.

Parotoid glands—The toxin-producing shoulder glands of toads.

Parthenogenesis—Reproduction without fertilization.

Phalanges—The bones of the toes.

Photoperiod—The daily/seasonally variable length of the hours of daylight.

Plethodontid—A lungless salamander.

Pollywog—A tadpole.

Postorbital—To the rear of the eye.

Preocular—Anterior to the eye.

Race—A subspecies.

Ranid—A typical frog.

Reticulum—Netlike markings; a network.

Rugose—Wrinkled, warty, or rough.

Saxicolous—Adapted for life on or among rocks.

Scansorial—Adapted for climbing.

Sibling species—Two or more similar appearing species supposedly derived from the same parental stock. Sibling species are often unidentifiable in the field.

Spade—As used here, the darkened, keratinized, digging tubercles on the heels of some anurans.

Species (*abbr*. **sp.**, *pl*. **spp.**)—A group of related creatures that produce viable young when breeding. The taxonomic designation that falls beneath genus and above subspecies.

Spermatophore—The stalked reproductive body, tipped with a sperm cap, by which many salamanders accomplish internal fertilization of the eggs.

Subcaudal—Beneath the tail.

Subdigital—Beneath the toes.

Subgular—Beneath the throat.

Subocular—Below the eye.

Subspecies (*abbr*. **ssp.**)—The subdivision of a species. A race that may differ slightly in color, size, scalation, or other criteria.

Subsurface—Beneath the surface.

Supraocular—Above the eye.

Supratympanal—Above the tympanum.

Sympatric—Pertaining to closely related species that occur in the same geographic area but usually do not interbreed.

Taxonomy—The science of classification of plants and animals.

Terrestrial—Land dwelling.

Thermoregulate—To control body temperature. *See* **ectothermic** and **endothermic**.

Tibia—Lower hind limb.

Tibial tubercles (or **glands**)—Enlarged toxin-secreting warts on the tibia of some toads.

Troglodytic, troglobytic—Dwelling in caves.

Tubercles—Wartlike projections on the skin of toads and other anurans.

Vent—The external opening of the cloaca; the anus.

Venter—The underside of a creature; the belly.

Ventral—Pertaining to the undersurface or belly.

Ventral disc—The U-shaped disc on the belly of tropical frogs.

Ventrolateral—Pertaining to the sides of the belly.

Vertically elliptical—The vertically oriented slitlike pupil in the eye of some amphibians.

Vocal sac—The distensible, resonating pouch of skin on the throats of male anurans.

Warts—The tubercles on the body of a toad or other amphibian.

Additional Reading

There is a never-ending succession of Web sites that pertain to amphibians. By entering one or more keywords (such as tadpole or marbled salamander) in search engines such as Teoma or Google you will find many specific references.

Books and Articles on Amphibian Biology, Identification, and Systematics

Altig, Ronald. 1970. A Key to the Tadpoles of the Continental United States and Canada. *Herpetologica* 26(2): 180–207.

Anderson, Jennifer A., and Stephen G. Tilley. 2003. *Systematics of the* Desmognathus ocrophaeus *complex in the Cumberland Plateau of Tennessee.* Herpetologica Monographs no. 17, 75–110. Emporia, Kans.: Herpetologists' League.

Ashton, R. E., Jr., S. R. Edwards, and G. R. Pisani. 1976. *Endangered and Threatened Amphibians and Reptiles of the United States.* Herpetology Circular no. 5. Lawrence, Kans.: Society for the Study of Amphibians and Reptiles.

Ashton, R. E., Jr., and P. S. Ashton. 1988. *Handbook of Reptiles and Amphibians of Florida. Part III, The Amphibians.* Miami: Windward Publishing.

Bart, Henry L., Jr., Mark A. Bailey, Ray E. Ashton, Jr., and Paul E. Moler. 1997. Taxonomic and nomenclatural status of the Upper Black Warrior River waterdog. *Journal of Herpetology* 31(2): 192–201.

Behler, John L., and F. Wayne King. 1979. *The Audubon Society Field Guide to North American Reptiles and Amphibians.* New York: Alfred Knopf.

Bishop, Sherman C. 1943. *Handbook of Salamanders.* Ithaca, N.Y.: Comstock.

Blair, W. Frank. 1972. *Evolution in the Genus* Bufo. Austin: University of Texas Press.

Bragg, Arthur N. 1965. *Gnomes of the Night.* Philadelphia: University of Pennsylvania Press.

Camp, Carlos D., Stephen G. Tilley, Richard M. Austin, and Jeremy L. Austin. 2002. A new species of black-bellied salamander (genus *Desmognathus*) from the Appalachian Mountains of northern Georgia. *Herpetologica* 58(4): 471–84.

Chippendale, Paul T., Andrew H. Price, and David M. Hillis. 1993. A new species of perennibranchiate salamander (Eurycea; Plethodontidae) from Austin, Texas. *Herpetologica* 49: 248–59.

Chippendale, Paul T., Andrew H. Price, John J. Wiens, and David M. Hillis. 2000. Phylogenetic relationships and systematic revision of central Texas hemidactyliine plethodontid salamanders. *Herpetological Monographs* 14: 1–80.

Cochran, Doris M. 1961. *Living Amphibians of the World.* Garden City, N.Y.: Doubleday.

Collins, Joseph T. 1974. *Amphibians and Reptiles in Kansas.* Lawrence: University of Kansas.

Conant, Roger, and Joseph T. Collins. 1991. *A Field Guide to The Reptiles and Amphibians of Eastern and Central North America*, 3rd ed. Boston: Houghton Mifflin.

Cope, E. D. 1889. The *Batrachia* of North America. Washington, D.C.: U.S. National Museum.

Crother, Brian I. (Chair). 2000. *Scientific and Standard English Names of Amphibians and Reptiles of North America North of Mexico, with Comments Regarding Confidence in our Understanding.* Herpetology Circular no. 29. Lawrence, Kans.: Society for the Study of Amphibians and Reptiles.

Degenhardt, William G., Charles W. Painter, and Andrew H. Price. 1996. *Amphibians and Reptiles of New Mexico.* Albuquerque: University of New Mexico Press.

DeGraff, Richard M., and Deborah D. Rudis. 1983. *Amphibians and Reptiles of New England.* Amherst: University of Massachusetts Press.

Dixon, James R. 1987. *Amphibians and Reptiles of Texas.* College Station: Texas A&M University Press.

Duellman, William E., and Albert Schwartz. 1958. Amphibians and Reptiles of Southern Florida. Gainesville: Bulletin of the Florida State Museum 3.

Dundee, Harold A., and Douglas A. Rossman. 1989. *The Amphibians and Reptiles of Louisiana.* Baton Rouge: Louisiana State University Press.

Dunn, Emmett Reid. 1926. *The Salamanders of the Family Plethodontidae.* Northampton, Mass.: Smith College.

Elliott, Lang. 1992. The Calls of Frogs and Toads, Eastern and Central North America (audio tape). Ithaca, N.Y.: Lang Elliott Nature Sound Studio.

Faccio, Stephen D. 2003. Postbreeding emigration and habitat use by Jefferson and spotted salamanders in Vermont. *Journal of Herpetology* 37: 479–89.

Garrett, Judith M., and David G. Barker. 1987. *A Field Guide to Reptiles and Amphibians of Texas.* Austin: Texas Monthly Press.

Godley, J. Steve. 1983. Observations on the Courtship, Nests and Young of *Siren intermedia* in Southern Florida. *American Midland Naturalist* 110: 215–19.

Green, N. Bayard, and Thomas K. Pauley. 1987. *Amphibians and Reptiles in West Virginia.* Pittsburgh, Pa.: University of Pittsburgh Press.

Halliday, Tim, and Kraig Adler (Eds.). 1986. *The Encyclopedia of Reptiles and Amphibians.* New York: Facts on File.

Harding, James H. 1997. *Amphibians and Reptiles of the Great Lakes Region.* Ann Arbor: University of Michigan Press.

Harrison, Julian R. III, and Sheldon I. Guttman. 2003. A new species of *Eurycea* (Caudata: Pletodontidae) from North and South Carolina. *Southeastern Naturalist* 2(2): 159–78.

Huheey, James E., and Arthur Stupka. 1979. *Amphibians and Reptiles of Great Smoky Mountains National Park.* Knoxville: University of Tennessee Press.

Hunter, Malcolm L., Jr., Aram J. K. Calhoun, and Mark McCollough. 1999. *Maine Amphibians and Reptiles.* Orono: University of Maine Press.

Johnson, Tom R. 1977. *The Amphibians of Missouri.* Lawrence: University of Kansas.

Klemens, Michael W. 1993. *Amphibians and Reptiles of Connecticut and Adjacent Regions.*

Hartford: Connecticut Department of Environmental Protection.

Lazell, James. 1998. New Salamander of the genus *Plethodon* from Mississippi. *Copeia* 1998: 967–70.

Levell, John P. 1995. *A Field Guide to Reptiles and the Law*. Excelsior, Minn.: Serpent's Tale Natural History Books.

McCoy, Krista A., and Reid M. Harris. 2003. Integrating developmental stability analysis and current amphibian monitoring techniques: an experimental evaluation with the salamander *Ambystoma maculatum*. *Herpetologica* 59: 22–36.

Minton, Sherman C. 2001. *Amphibians and Reptiles of Indiana*. Indianapolis: Indiana Academy of Science.

Moler, Paul E. 1990. A Checklist of Florida's Amphibians and Reptiles (Revised). Tallahassee: Florida Game and Fresh Water Fish Commission.

Moler, Paul E. (Ed.). 1992. *Rare and Endangered Biota of Florida*. Vol. 3, *Amphibians and Reptiles*. Gainesville: University Press of Florida.

Mount, Robert H. 1987. *The Reptiles and Amphibians of Alabama*. Auburn, Ala.: Auburn Printing.

Neill, Wilfred T. 1951. A New Subspecies of Salamander, Genus *Pseudobranchus*, from the Gulf Hammock Region of Florida. Silver Springs, Fla.: Ross Allen's Reptile Institute.

Noble, G. Kingsley. 1954. *The Biology of the Amphibia* (reprint). New York: Dover.

Oldfield, Barney, and John J. Moriarty. 1994. *Amphibians and Reptiles Native to Minnesota*. Minneapolis: University of Minnesota Press.

Pfingston, Ralph A., and Floyd L. Downs (Eds.). 1989. Salamanders of Ohio. Columbus: Bulletin of the Ohio Biological Survey.

Phillips, Kathryn. 1995. *Tracking the Vanishing Frogs: An Ecological Mystery*. New York: Penguin.

Potter, Floyd E., and Samuel S. Sweet. 1981. Generic boundaries in Texas cave salamanders, and a redescription of *Typhlomolge robusta* (Amphibia: Plethodontidae). *Copeia* 1981: 64–75.

Reno, Harley W., Frederick R. Gehlbach, and R. A. Turner. 1972. Skin and aestivational cocoon of the aquatic amphibian, *Siren intermedia*. Copeia 1972(4): 625–31.

Richter, Stephen C., and Richard A. Seigel. 2002. Annual variation in the population ecology of the endangered gopher frog, *Rana sevosa* Goin and Netting. Copeia 2002 (4): 962–72.

Schwartz, Albert, and Robert W. Henderson. 1991. *Amphibians and Reptiles of the West Indies*. Gainesville: University of Florida Press.

Smith, Hobart M. 1946. *Handbook of Lizards*. Ithaca, N.Y.: Comstock.

Vogt, Richard Carl. 1981. *Natural History of Amphibians and Reptiles in Wisconsin*. Milwaukee, Wis.: Milwaukee Public Museum.

Wilson, Larry David, and Louis Porras. 1983. *The Ecological Impact of Man on the South Florida Herpetofauna*. Lawrence: University of Kansas.

Wright, Albert Hazen. 1932. *Life Histories of the Frogs of the Okefinokee Swamp, Georgia*. New York: Macmillan.

Wright, Albert Hazen, and A. A. Wright. 1949. *Handbook of Frogs and Toads of the United States and Canada*, 3rd ed. Ithaca, N.Y.: Comstock.

Zug, George R., Laurie J. Vitt, and Janalee P. Caldwell. 2001. *Herpetology, An Introductory Biology of Amphibians and Reptiles*, 2nd ed. San Diego, Calif.: Academic Press.

More references on Amphibian Adventure and Husbandry

Bartlett, R. D. 1988. *In Search of Reptiles and Amphibians*. New York: E. J. Brill.

Bartlett, R. D., and Patricia P. Bartlett. 1996. *Frogs, Toads and Treefrogs: Everything about Selection, Care, Nutrition, Breeding, and Behavior*. Hauppauge, N.Y.: Barron's Educational Series.

———. 1999. Terrarium and Cage Construction and Care. Hauppauge, N.Y.: Barron's Educational Series.

Indiviglio, Frank. 1997. *Newts and Salamanders: Everything about Selection, Care, Nutrition, Disesases, Breeding, and Behavior*. Hauppauge, N.Y.: Barron's Educational Series.

Index

Richard D. and Patricia Bartlett have coauthored numerous books, including *A Field Guide to Florida Reptiles, Reptiles and Amphibians of the Amazon*, and *Florida Snakes: A Guide to Their Identification and Habits*. Together they lead interactive tours to many areas of the Amazon Basin. Richard has published more than 500 articles about herpetology in *Tropical Fish Hobbyist, Reptiles, Reptile and Amphibian*, and others. Patricia is former director of the Fort Myers Historical Museum.

Related-interest titles from University Press of Florida

30 EcoTrips in Florida: The Best Nature Excursions (and How to Leave Only Your Footprints)
Holly Ambrose

A Field Guide and Identification Manual for Florida and Eastern U.S. Tiger Beetles
Paul M. Choate, Jr.

Florida's Snakes: A Guide to Their Identification and Habitats
R. D. Bartlett and Patricia Bartlett

Guide and Reference to the Crocodilians, Turtles, and Lizards of Eastern and Central North America, North of Mexico
R. D. Bartlett and Patricia Bartlett

Guide and Reference to the Snakes of Eastern and Central North America, North of Mexico
R. D. Bartlett and Patricia Bartlett

A Guide to the Birds of the Southeastern States: Florida, Georgia, Alabama, and Mississippi
John H. Rappole

Hiker's Guide to the Sunshine State
Sandra Friend

Reptiles and Amphibians of the Amazon: An Ecotourist's Guide
R. D. Bartlett and Patricia Bartlett

Wild Orchids of the Canadian Maritimes and Northern Great Lakes Region
Paul Martin Brown with drawings by Stan Folsom

Wild Orchids of North America, North of Mexico
Paul Martin Brown with drawings by Stan Folsom

Wild Orchids of the Southeastern United States, North of Peninsular Florida
Paul Martin Brown with drawings by Stan Folsom

The Windward Road: Adventures of a Naturalist on Remote Caribbean Shores
Archie Carr

For more information on these and other books, visit our website at www.upf.com.